A CHILL
IN THE
HOUSE

A CHILL IN THE HOUSE

Actor Perspectives on
Change and Continuity
in the Pursuit of
Legislative Success

LEWIS G. IRWIN

State University
of New York
Press

Published by
State University of New York Press, Albany

For information, address State University of New York Press,
90 State Street, Suite 700, Albany, NY 12207

Production by Susan Geraghty
Marketing by Anne M. Valentine

Chapters 1, 3, and 4 contain excerpts from "Dancing the Foreign Aid
Appropriations Dance" by Lewis G. Irwin, which appeared originally in *Public
Budgeting & Finance* (Summer 2000). The excerpts are reprinted by permission
of the publishers.

Library of Congress Cataloging-in-Publication Data

Irwin, Lewis G.
  A chill in the House : actor perspectives on change and continuity in the pursuit of
legislative success / Lewis G. Irwin.
     p. cm.
  Includes bibliographical references and index.
  ISBN 0-7914-5173-9 (alk. paper) — ISBN 0-7914-5174-7 (pbk. : alk. paper)
    1. Legislation—Political aspects—United States. 2. Legislation—Social aspects—United
States. 3. Legislation—United States—Case studies. I. Title.

KF4945 .I79 2001
328.73'077—dc21
                                                                    2001020668

10 9 8 7 6 5 4 3 2 1

CONTENTS

For Marcia

ACKNOWLEDGMENTS

The completion of this project would not have been possible without the generous and valuable assistance of many talented and likewise busy people. I would first like to thank the numerous legislators, staffers, and other key participants in the legislative process who were willing to make their time and insights available in interviews and other less formal discussions. As I promised them, their comments are not attributed to them by name in the book but rather by job title, but a list of these great Americans is included in the interview methods appendix. Further heartfelt thanks go David Mayhew, Alan Gerber, Stephen Skowronek, and Chris Gibson for their keen insights and wise counsel throughout the process of turning abstract idea into empirical analysis. My thanks also go to the Everett McKinley Dirksen Congressional Research Center and the United States Military Academy's Academic Research Division for their financial support of the project. Most of all, though, I thank my wife, Marcia, who not only served (as always) as my confidant, advisor, and best friend throughout the completion of this project but whose innumerable sacrifices, hard work, and sense of humor made the book possible in the first place.

CHAPTER 1

Legislative Success in the U.S. House of Representatives

"Legislative success," eh? It's hard to come up with a list, because every issue has its particular constituencies. But I'll tell you this much, the spadework takes time—and most of it outside of committees. There's a whole lot more to it than just putting on the ribbons and getting the words right.

—House member with service in the 1960s and 1990s

EMPHASIS AND CHANGE

Several years ago, I began to wonder whether the body of scholarship comprising the study of the American Congress might be underemphasizing important features of the legislative process.[1] In particular, I suspected that the congressional literature, with its modern primary emphasis on quantifiable formal procedures and other easily qualifiable features of the legislative process, might be unfairly accentuating those more accessible aspects of legislating while discounting other less accessible features. Similarly, I wondered whether the average legislative actor's perspectives on the policymaking process would match up well with the conventional wisdom shared among contemporary political scientists. How would the average lawmaker, pursuing policy goals on a daily basis, characterize the legislative process? What concerns would that average actor identify as crucial in seeking to advance a legislative initiative? Might some other features of the legislative proceedings, features less readily accessible to the average political scientist, be just as or more important to the legislative actors themselves in achieving policy success?

Furthermore, I had grown a bit suspicious of the congressional scholarship's ubiquitous emphasis on "change" in describing legislating in the modern era. A glance at the congressional literature shows that in recent years, most congressional scholars have asserted or assumed that the major constant of the national legislature over the last several decades has been change, emphasizing change of both featuristic and broader institutional varieties. In one sense, this emphasis is not all that surprising, given the natural incentives of the publishing process. But while there was no question that a whole host of well-documented variables had shifted in Congress over recent decades, I again wondered how the legislators themselves might view those changes.

To be more precise, I decided to subject the legislative scholars' assertions and assumptions of wholesale and consequential changes in Congress since the early 1960s to an empirical scrutiny from the legislators' point of view. If representative cases of legislative success and the perspectives of key legislative actors in the early 1960s were compared to representative cases from the 1990s, would the literature's claims of consequential change hold up? In recounting their successful efforts to convert an idea into law, would legislators of the earlier decades describe essential legislative requirements all that different from their counterparts of the 1990s? Would the legislative actors themselves describe key actors, chamber procedures, actor strategies, or legislative products all that different from those of the earlier period? What would the actors emphasize as most important to understanding the legislative process? Would the legislative actors themselves underline the process or people as most important in explaining policy outcomes?

This book provides an empirical answer to these questions, as it assesses the incidence and consequence of changes in the U.S. House of Representatives and legislating since the 1960s, viewed from the perspective of participants involved in the process. I use a comparison of key congressional characteristics, six carefully selected and constructed legislative histories, and the insights of numerous legislative participants and observers from the 1960s and 1990s to paint portraits of the legislative process in those two periods. Then, through a comparison of these portraits of legislating, taken in conjunction with other interview data and relevant chamber characteristics, I assess the consequences and relative significance of documented changes in Congress and the policy-making process since the 1960s as they relate to that process viewed as a whole. At the same time, I identify important underlying continuities deemed by the participants themselves to be critical to the realization of legislative success and comment on the implications of the story that emerges from the comparison.

The three types of evidence I employ here are intended to proceed sequentially from a broader to a finer resolution in drawing complete pictures of the legislative process in the 1960s and the 1990s. I begin with a simple comparison of the congressional environment, or policy-making context, and then proceed to offer three carefully constructed accounts of legislative success in both periods by weaving together first-person accounts, public records, and media descriptions of the passage of the carefully selected laws. The third step then is to deconstruct each of the components of the legislative process for all six of those cases in order to compare and contrast the significance of the actors, procedures, strategies, and legislative products that pertain to each of those episodes. Viewed collectively, these three types of evidence allow us to address each of the questions posed above in a systematic and empirical fashion.

In large part, this research was motivated by my sense that while many legislative actor behaviors and other characteristics lend themselves forthrightly to quantification or qualification, it is more difficult to assess the relative significance of those behaviors or features as they relate to the legislative process altogether. For instance, we can note that floor attendance at House debates has declined during the last several decades, but can we easily and objectively assess the impact of this behavioral change as it relates to the average legislator's pursuit of his or her policy goals? Could it be the case that the concurrent rise of C-Span and its presence in nearly every congressional office has offset that decline in attendance at floor debates, in ways that matter? Given the complexity of the policymaking process in general, we can theorize that identified changes have had an impact on the legislative proceedings, but a valid empirical test of that change's influence within the process comes only through the eyes of the legislative actors themselves. Essentially, I aimed to employ that perspective here, viewing the policymaking process from the bottom up instead of taking the usual view from the top down.

A few definitions are in order up front. *Change,* as used here, simply refers to a variation in some congressional phenomenon, such as a change in the average number of amendments per bill considered on the House floor or a change in the number of lawyers serving in Congress. There is no question that consistent with the literature, a variety of well-documented changes have occurred in the Congress over the last several decades. However, it is also obviously the case that not all of these changes have been *consequential* ones. I use the term *consequential change* to indicate changes in congressional phenomena that have in turn contributed to fundamental shifts in the way that legislative business is done on a day-to-day basis. The word consequential is therefore used here in its sense as an indicator of causality, indicating changes noteworthy for their significant and associated repercussions. Similarly, the term *essential continuity* refers to elements or aspects of the legislative process that have not only remained constant over the decades but were indicated by the respondents and case evidence to have been of fundamental significance to the process viewed generally. That is, essential continuities are those continuities that were deemed by the actors them-selves to have been vitally important to the construction of the support-ive voting majorities necessary to the realization of legislative success.

Viewed theoretically, there are four categories of change that could have plausibly brought about consequential changes in the Congress and its processes since the 1960s, and I assess each possibility in this book. Change in the legislative *actors* refers to any changes in the qual-ifications, activities, motives, average tenure, likely voting behaviors, or other personal and professional characteristics of the legislative actors themselves. This category includes an examination of shifts in the attributes and activities of the legislators, their staffs, the chamber lead-ers, interest groups, presidential and administrative actors, the media, constituents, and other actors. Change in the legislative *procedures* refers to the various formal "rules of the game" and standard operating procedures that define the House's day-to-day operations. These proce-dures include sponsorship, committee jurisdiction and referral, the selec-tion and use of policy vehicles, committee and subcommittee proce-dures, the Rules Committee practices, floor activities, floor management, and the consideration of the legislation in conference committee. The characteristics of the average congressional workday, the legislators' average workload, and the average legislative timeline were also consid-ered as part of this procedural category of change.

A third category of potential change is that of change in the legisla-tive *strategies* employed by the various actors in seeking to realize legisla-tive success. I assessed the nature and impact of changes in the "informal rules of the game," or norms, innovations, and other strategic considera-tions that shape actor strategies in the pursuit of policy goals. This analy-sis involves an assessment of key changes and continuities in coalition-building strategies, including an appraisal of the methods of persuasion, legislative packaging techniques, and procedural innovations used by the various actors to pursue success. The evaluation of this category of change also included an examination of congressional norms and their strategic value to the legislative actors. The fourth and final type of potentially meaningful change is that of legislative *product* change. This category of change includes an analysis of the various congressional products, among them the hearings, committee and conference committee reports, the *Con-gressional Record*, and the statutes themselves. Each of these legislative products was examined for changes in length, complexity, relevance, number, and nature, as well as for the implications of those changes.

All four of these categories of plausible change are investigated in the book. Using comparative case analysis, interview respondent con-sensus, and the analysis of relevant chamber and member characteristics since the early 1960s, we will look at each sequential step in the legislative process to determine how the various components influence the construction of supportive voting majorities, the necessary precondition to legislative success. I then use those findings to construct a model of legislative success, combining the consequential changes and essential continuities in creating a checklist for practical policy success in the modern era. Given the book's effort to stretch across the whole of the legislative process, I have made the strategic decision to react to research primarily concerned with broader institutional assessments of the Congress, rather than the more specialized accounts that address one or a few particular features of the process.

Likewise, in terms of depth and breadth, the six cases are carefully constructed accounts of the enactment of the six laws, explanations that identify the events and interactions deemed by the respondents and observers to have been most important in explaining the legislative outcomes. However, they are not intended to provide the level of detail such as is found in Richard Cohen's (1992) description of the passage of the Clean Air Act amendments or other such exhaustive case studies.[2] Instead, these legislative histories are intended to describe the key events, most important actors, crucial features, and basic chronologies that led to the passage of the six laws, as identified by participants and observers and supported by background research. The book strives to provide systematic descriptions of the most important aspects of the legislative process as determined by the House actors involved in the laws' passage, thus enabling us to place the significance of these components of the process into their larger context.

With all of this in mind, several audiences should find the book to be useful. First, academics concerned with the ways of Congress and policymaking can use the book as a tool with which to calibrate our field's important quantitative perspectives on the nature of contemporary legislating. Scholars applying quantitative methodologies seeking to reckon where their particular interests fit into the larger whole also should find the book to be useful. Other students of American politics will find the actors' various correctives to commonly held maxims in the field to be of interest. Practitioners of the legislative arts will also find the book to be useful, as it not only offers an assessment of the ingredients of success but also offers perspectives on successful strategies and opportunities for process reform. Additionally, these findings offer myriad suggestions for future research. Finally, political historians will find the comparisons between the two periods and the case histories to be of interest, particularly for those scholars interested in the fields of education policy, the appropriations cycle, and foreign aid programs. I believe many readers will find the six case histories to be interesting as individual stories in their own right.

THE ARGUMENTS THAT EMERGE

A mix of consequential changes and essential continuities emerges from this comparison of legislative success in the early 1960s and 1990s, but participants in the policymaking process repeatedly cited the underlying continuities as being most important to the understanding of that success. The basic argument of this book is that a large net increase in contextual impediments to coalition building have made the realization of policy success far more difficult in the U.S. House of Representatives since the 1960s, even as the essential elements of that success have remained constant over the years. As indicated by the respondents and the case evidence, the key defining characteristic of the American government was, and is, its system of shared, separated, and fragmented powers, a characteristic that predicates policy success upon the construction of ad hoc issue coalitions. Legislative actors nearly unanimously translate this defining principle into the simple operating premise that the pursuit of legislative success is a gradual and incremental whipping operation. That is, the realization of legislative success is determined by the construction of a supportive voting majority at each step in a lengthy sequence.

Simply put, a willful agent seeking to realize legislative success must align just enough of the fragmented legislative authority at each gate to enact an idea into law, a proposition harder to carry out in recent years than it was in the 1960s. At its final stage, this supportive majority might consist of a simple majority in Congress with the concurrent support of the president, or it might be a less likely super majority within Congress able to overcome presidential opposition. At the outset, this effort might merely consist of getting the bill referred to the committee of choice for further consideration. With the nature of the system being this directly sequential and majoritarian, any one step in the legislative process can rise up to become a significant impediment to success. I assessed each step and component of the legislative process against this simple standard to identify those steps in the process deemed to be crucial ones by the participants. The case evidence and the respondents' accounts combine to portray a contemporary legislative system in which members have fewer opportunities and fewer natural advantages in seeking to overcome these basic challenges in the modern era.

Specifically, I make six principal arguments and suggest one practical model of legislative success in this book. First, I argue that the contextual impediments to the realization of legislative success in Congress have clearly increased over the period from the early 1960s to the early 1990s. These impediments to success are both procedural and personal in nature, but without exception the respondents emphasized the personal aspects of the heightened difficulties as being most significant. This net increase in the obstacles to policy success is indicated both by the case analysis and by the respondent accounts, and this finding is consistent with many, though not all, changes documented in the congressional literature. Second, however, in spite of these contextual changes, the underlying and essential elements of legislative success have remained constant over the period, viewed from the individual legislative actors' perspective. Furthermore, as a third key assertion, the legislative participants view the identified essential continuities, rather than the consequential changes, as the most critical features of the process. This operating assumption commonly influences many would-be legislative champions in their strategic decision making.

Furthermore, I argue that the congressional scholarship's emphasis on formal institutional procedures and the actions of macroactors, while explaining a great deal of the broader institutional characteristics, misses a significant portion of the relevant story at the individual outcome level. That is, the evidence shows that key individuals, each treated as a unit of analysis with corresponding personal motives and agendas, explain an unexpectedly crucial portion of each legislative outcome that is missed by the lenses of aggregated interests, parties, and other macro explanations we commonly employ. Put another way, when applied to explain "average member" behaviors, the legislator motives of reelection, "good" public policy, and D.C. influence identified by Fenno, Mayhew, and Kingdon are powerful explanatory assumptions. However, when seeking to explain individual legislative outcomes, the cases show that key individual legislative actors routinely have a disproportionate influence over these outcomes, and purely personal (and arbitrary) motives can intrude upon the process, even if they conflict with the Fenno, Mayhew, and Kingdon motives. It is important that participants in the process view these key individual actors and their motives, rather than institutional procedures, aggregated interests, or parties, as the most useful unit of analysis in the explanation and prediction of legislative outcomes. In the eyes of the participants, people trump procedure in importance in making public policy.

Finally, the interpersonal "glue" that held 1960s-era legislators together has weakened considerably over the decades, with serious consequences for the nature of the legislative process viewed in the aggregate. This trend represents the loss of a valuable resource once readily available and frequently utilized to aid in the construction of ad hoc policy majorities. As a result, at a time in which legislators perceive a wholesale increase in strident partisanship, compared to the congressional climate of the 1960s, the powers of personality and personal motive have become largely negative forces. It is not surprising then that legislative actors have taken logical steps toward strategies such as omnibus packaging and appropriation riding, among others described in this book, to pursue policy success. These techniques require much less in the way of consensus-building and personal politicking while offering solid probabilities of success. Taken in concert, these findings and other evidence from the respondents and cases enable us to construct a working model of legislative success. To summarize, there is a definite "chill" in the House that has made the realization of legislative success much more difficult in recent years, even as the recipe for that policy success has remained fundamentally constant over the decades.

DESIGN AND METHODS

I employ a mixture of comparative case analysis, interview respondent consensus, and aggregated chamber and member characteristics as evidence in identifying key changes and continuities in the legislative process since the early 1960s. As such, this project is probably best described as a mixture of history and political science, or rather as a mix of statistical and historical comparative analysis, a strategy I believe to be appropriate to the research objectives. The goal was to weave the three types of evidence together to create a complete and accurate representation of both the aggregated nature and the disaggregated features of the legislative process in both the early 1960s and 1990s. These carefully constructed portraits of policy success and the supporting contextual evidence allow for a focused and structured comparison of the process over the period of interest. Subsequently, a primary goal of the research design process was to control for several theorized extraneous variables and to minimize the random and nonrandom errors that would prevent a valid analysis of change and continuity in the pursuit of legislative success over the period since the early 1960s. The main strategies for accomplishing this goal were careful case selection, the use of appropriate interview structures and techniques, and the application of the standard of triangulation, among other design considerations.

Given the questions at hand, the examination of the period from the early 1960s to the 1990s for changes in the Congress is particularly appropriate for several reasons. First, the period since 1960 encompasses the generally accepted increase in the media's influence in politics as well as the increase in their importance in the eyes of the members of Congress. It is during this period that members are argued to have begun the move toward media-centered electoral and legislative activities in contrast to the party-centered activities chronicled earlier by Schattschneider (1960) and others. Second, the period is significant because it frames the decentralizing reforms of the early 1970s, thus allowing us to examine legislative cases before and after the reforms, as these reforms are some of the "usual suspects" often blamed for wholesale changes in Congress since 1960. This period also encompasses the explosive growth in the congressional staff often blamed for a variety of consequential changes in the legislative process. Finally, it is in the period since 1960 that interest groups, including the political action committees created by the reforms of the 1970s, are often argued to have posted significant gains in money, membership, organization, sophistication, and influence. These characteristics define our time as the modern congressional era, and the period examined frames the time in which these and other phenomena usually blamed for having caused significant change in the legislative process came about.

The case selection process had crucial implications for the validity of the inferences I make; thus it deserves a brief accounting at the outset. It was desirable to examine a minimum of three laws enacted near both endpoints of the period of interest in order to achieve a sufficiently diverse sample while allowing for the depth of analysis and description desired. The overarching goal of case selection was to minimize the effects of extraneous and random variation by controlling for the unwanted variation, while simultaneously selecting representative cases of lawmaking in the two periods. I identified three categories of extraneous variables and controlled for these using precondition, pairing, and issue variance criteria. A full accounting of these selection criteria is included in the case selection methods appendix.

As a quick overview, however, I first controlled for differing conditions of party control of Congress and the executive branch. While Mayhew's careful analysis of the effects of divided party control of the branches of government indicates that the consequences of divided control are far less than one might expect, I still chose to compare laws passed under the condition of unified party control by the Democrats, as it was the most common condition near the endpoints of the period of interest to this study.[3] As table 1.1 indicates, Democrats most commonly controlled the Congress over these decades, while control of the executive has routinely passed back and forth between the parties. Consistent with this move, respondents almost uniformly indicated that while differing circumstances of party control over the chambers and branches substantially influenced the policy agenda, the conditions of party control did not have much impact on the policymaking process itself.

I also aimed to avoid the unwanted variation that would likely result from differing levels of media scrutiny relative to the period in which the laws were passed, imposing two measures of media scrutiny on the case selection that are detailed in the case selection appendix. Similarly, I imposed a criterion that controlled for varying levels of legislative sig-

TABLE 1.1
Party Control of Government 1961–2000

Congress	Presidency	Senate Control	House Control
87th (1961–63)	D	D	D
88th (1963–65)	D	D	D
89th (1965–67)	D	D	D
90th (1967–69)	D	D	D
91st (1969–71)	R	D	D
92nd (1971–73)	R	D	D
93rd (1973–75)	R	D	D
94th (1975–77)	R	D	D
95th (1977–79)	D	D	D
96th (1979–81)	D	D	D
97th (1981–83)	R	R	D
98th (1983–85)	R	R	D
99th (1985–87)	R	R	D
100th (1987–89)	R	D	D
101st (1989–91)	R	D	D
102nd (1991–93)	R	D	D
103rd (1993–95)	D	D	D
104th (1995–97)	D	R	R
105th (1997–99)	D	R	R
106th (1999–2001)	D	R	R
Totals	10 D–10 R	14 D–6 R	17 D–3 R

nificance, and it was also desirable to eliminate the likely random changes in the actors, procedures, strategies, or product that probably would result from committee-to-committee idiosyncrasies. The research design had to control for these and other likely sources of unwanted variance in the dependent variables, and the specific measures that I used to accomplish these controls and other details of the selection process are included in the first methods appendix. The laws that emerged from the selection algorithm include PL87–872: The Foreign Aid Appropriation for FY1963; PL88–204: The Higher Education Facilities Act of 1963; PL88–365: The Urban Mass Transportation Act of 1964; PL103–87: The Foreign Operations Appropriation for FY 1994; PL103–204: Thrift Depositor Protection Act of 1993; and PL103–227: "Goals 2000" Educate America Act of 1994. As one would expect, I paired the cases for comparison in accordance with their respective committees of origin. The mass transit law and the thrift bailout law both originated in the House Banking Committee.

In constructing the detailed case histories, I relied heavily upon interviews with individuals directly involved in the passage of the laws in question, interviews conducted after a thorough background research into newspapers, government records, and other secondary sources that described the events in question. The respondents were a rich source of insight into the process, and the study benefited tremendously from the in-depth interviews with former and current participants in the legislative process. I conducted thirty-two formal interviews ranging from the shortest of twenty-five minutes (one congressman about to give a speech) to the longest of one hundred minutes (a retired member and thoughtful observer of the contemporary House), with most lasting about fifty minutes. Of the thirty-two formal interviews, seventeen of the respondents had served in or closely observed the House and had participated in or watched the passage of the case laws of the early 1960s, and twenty-one served in or observed the House's legislative process and the cases in the early 1990s. Six respondents participated in or observed the process in both periods. *Service in the House*, when used as a descriptor of the respondents, refers to both staff members and the legislators themselves.

Respondents included House members and staffers, executive branch personnel with significant House responsibilities, and other key legislative actors. Among them were one former president, Democratic and Republican House leaders, a long-time and well-respected observer of American politics, and key administration personnel charged with congressional liaison responsibilities. Additionally, this research benefited greatly from a lengthy series of less formal discussions with thirty-one other participants in the policymaking process. Complete lists of the respondents and discussants by name and position held during the periods of interest are contained in the second methods appendix.

A few notes on the interview techniques and structures are appropriate up front as well. In terms of the interview methodology, after careful consideration, I borrowed from the approaches used by Kingdon and Fenno in various works, seeking like them to maximize validity of information gathered at the minor cost of precision of quotation. With this in mind, like them, I used only pen and paper in recording the interviews and have paraphrased the responses carefully, having promised the respondents anonymity. Thus, if a quotation is a direct quote, then it is attributed in the text by name and will have been taken from a published document or the public record. In the cases where I paraphrase, the paraphrase appears in quotation marks but is attributed to "a member of the subcommittee," "subcommittee staff member," or some other job title. The analysis and interpretation of the data took place as the interviews proceeded, with the goal being to incorporate information gained previously into the interviews to further decrease measurement error without biasing the subsequent interviews.

Essentially, this approach meant following the original interview format for all interviews while focusing the probing portions of the interview on an elaboration of information gleaned earlier. Given that I also wanted to troll for unanticipated types of changes or continuities, the interview format allowed room for the respondent to move the interview in unexpected directions. Nonetheless, my primary task as interviewer was to ensure that all of the formatted questions were addressed before completion. I conducted both personal and telephonic interviews, as Frankfort and Frankfort-Nachmias (1996) show no loss of validity in using telephone interviews in lieu of personal interviews.[4] Further details are included in the interview methods appendix.

The standard of triangulation served as the litmus test for inclusion of evidence throughout the study. Triangulation refers to the approach that no observations on the variables were accepted as "fact" until confirming accounts were attained, either through multiple independent interviews or through background research and a confirming interview. The goal in data collection was to weave observer accounts, the public record, and respondent consensus into a comprehensive analysis of the legislative process in both periods of interest to the study. Despite the seemingly limited degrees of freedom available in a study of three pairs of episodes of legislative success, the fact that these episodes were observed at multiple levels of analysis by numerous interview respondents makes the observations on the variables of interest much greater than the n would imply.

A few other notes regarding the methods, scope, and objectives are appropriate here at the start. As the case histories tie together all of the significant events in the years that led to the passage of the case laws, it is important to read the case histories in order to place all of the disaggregated features of their passage into context. This reading also helps to make the case for the relative weighting of the various components from the perspectives of the legislative actors themselves. Essentially, the case legislative stories tell the history from start to finish. The subsequent "component" chapters then inspect these outcomes feature-by-feature to explore the impact and significance of that aspect of the process as it relates to the whole. The goal was to weave all of the evidence together to provide the reader with a comprehensive picture of the legislative process in both the early 1960s and 1990s, while systematically assessing the changes and continuities in the components as well as each component's place in the "big picture."

It should be noted that the comparative case study approach offers both distinct advantages and corresponding challenges in this effort to assess the importance of change and continuity in the pursuit of legislative success in the modern era. I selected this approach primarily to benefit from an important and relevant advantage that the method offers over quantitative methodologies. As King and others (1994) note, valid quantitative measures of "what we want to know" are always desirable, but these quantitative measures do not always offer the depth of explanation that is directly relevant to the research task at hand.[5] In this study, I aimed to explain how and why these legislative outcomes came about, and as such, these research questions required a thicker descriptive detail and greater confidence in the response validity than would be available through traditional quantitative methods. The case structure, interview methods, and other background research activities I employed were aimed at achieving the structured, focused comparison gained through disciplined data collection that King, Keohane, and Verba describe. I used the comparative case method as well as the data collection methods that I did because they afforded the best chance of correctly identifying the actor motives and perspectives that were crucial to the assessment of consequential change and essential continuities over the decades.

However, Lieberson (1991), Collier (1991), King and colleagues (1994), and others express important concerns about the methodological appropriateness of causal inferences based on only a few cases, and I had to consider these potential problems in constructing the research design.[6] Lieberson has misgivings about the implicit assumptions he imputes to small-n comparative case analyses. Specifically, he sees an inappropriate assumption of determinism (versus probabilistic estimates), an assumed disregard for potential measurement errors, an assumed absence of interaction effects, and inappropriate claims of single causes.[7] While Lieberson's methodological misgivings are certainly valid, I believe his concerns are more correctly applicable to all social science research designs, rather than being pitfalls singularly associated with small-n studies. That is, regardless of the number of observations incorporated into a project's research design, the researcher must consider the potential for measurement errors and potential interaction effects while avoiding overly optimistic claims of single-variable (or deterministic) causal models. Collier echoes some of Lieberson's concerns, though his larger purpose is to address the relative advantages and disadvantages, and appropriateness, of small-n and large-n studies for alternative applications. Regardless of the range of applicability, however, the authors' concerns are significant ones. I have applied a number of King, Keohane, and Verba's (1994) correctives to these potential pitfalls in the design, and these steps are described in the methods appendices.

Last, legislative success is defined here as the enactment of a major policy initiative into law. While actors identified three kinds of policy initiatives—major national initiatives, recurring district or regional initiatives, and "one-time" district or regional initiatives—this study focuses on the legislative success in the form of major national policy outcomes. While there is no intuitive reason to believe that there would be any significant differences in the pursuit of these different objectives, this study deals with the initiatives of a national legislative variety alone. Similarly, while the Senate's actions are inextricably mixed up in any accounts of the pursuit of legislative success in the House, my data collection and case construction efforts focus on the House of Representatives. I focused on change and continuity in the legislative process in the House for the simple reason that the House and Senate are clearly two distinct problems, a fact described well by longtime congressional participant and observer Charles Tiefer (1989) and others.[8] While I have used the House of Representatives as my main congressional vehicle, due primarily to the resource constraints imposed by the approach I applied, many of the findings will likely apply well to both chambers. Conversations and interviews with senators and their staffs bear out this contention. However, astute readers will be able to differentiate between the likely general lessons and the House-specific ones. The usual political scientist's conventions apply, and when I refer to the Congress, I am referring to both chambers.

THE PLAN OF THE BOOK

This book can generally be described as proceeding from chamber and member statistical profiles to the historical case accounts, to the component analyses, and then to the broader conclusions. Chapter 2 provides a focused comparison of the key actors and chamber characteristics of the 87th, 88th, and 103rd Congresses, as well as a description of the political environment in which the case laws were passed, to provide the context for the comparisons of legislative success that follow. Chapters 3 and 4 furnish detailed histories of the enactment of the laws in the early 1960s and early 1990s respectively. As noted, these histories focus on the key events leading to passage of each law, and they represent a weaving of respondent accounts, public records, and observer analyses into a chronological history from the actor perspectives. This treatment allows a sufficiently detailed understanding of the internal and external events and actors that dictated the terms and timing of the eventual legislative success, at the same time identifying the key features of the process as identified by the participants and observers.

In chapters 5 through 9, I deconstruct the legislative process and then compare and contrast the various components of the process as they shaped the pursuit of policy success in the early 1960s and early 1990s. Each of these component chapters probes one broad category of elements of the process in the search for evidence of change and continuity between the 1960 cases and the 1990 cases, including the actors, procedures, strategies, and products that define the legislative process. These chapters begin with a brief theorization of potential changes and a brief accounting of relevant literature. After summarizing the statistical measures, event descriptions, and respondent perspectives that measure any changes in the component examined, I comment on the significance of each element as it related to the passage of the laws. Chapter 5 takes a focused look at the internal House actors, including an analysis of trends in the average House legislator, the chamber and committee leaders, and the various House staffs. This chapter also examines the phenomenon of the legislative champion, or "willful agents," instrumental to the realization of legislative success in the six cases. Chapter 6 analyzes change and continuity in the actors external to Congress who influence the pursuit of legislative success in the House of Representatives, among them the president, executive agencies, senators, interest groups, the media, and others. Chapter 7 examines the formal procedures of the House, identifying evidence of continuity and change in the advantages and constraints available to "willful agents" seeking to realize or deny some policy outcome. Chapter 8 identifies and analyzes trends in the informal legislator strategies employed by the key actors over time, as noted by the respondents and identified in the cases, while chapter 9 subjects the various legislative products to the same treatment.

The concluding chapter, chapter 10, summarizes the meaningful changes and continuities that define the legislative process in general, synthesizing the consequential changes and essential continuities discovered in the research into a model of legislative success. In chapter 10, I also comment on the implications of the findings. Following that is a short epilogue capturing some of the often-disturbing concerns for the future expressed by respondents looking at some relevant trends in the 104th Congress and later. The epilogue is followed by the supporting methodological appendices, which describe the case selection criteria and selection process, as well as the interview methods and respondents.

In sum, while observers of American politics have commonly assumed that lawmaking has changed in the modern era to make our place in the history of legislating a unique one, there are important commonalities deemed by participants in the process to be most important in understanding and realizing legislative success. Over the course of these chapters, we will paint a portrait of an American legislative process that has become a tougher game than it was in the 1960s. At the same time, players from the earlier period would recognize the same fundamental rules that shaped their own legislative experiences. What follows then is an explanation of the challenges and opportunities facing actors seeking to realize legislative success in the American Congress.

CHAPTER 2

The Congresses

In the 1960s, we could make a model for it, get organizational
support, and fund it. You don't shop ideas or programs now . . .
times make quite a difference.

—House staffer with service in the 1960s and 1990s

The logical place to begin our analysis of consequential changes and
essential continuities in the legislative process is with an examination of
the characteristics of the congressional bodies of the 1960s and 1990s.
The 87th, 88th, and 103rd Congresses enacted the six laws that serve as
the vehicle for our analysis, and those Congresses provide a particularly
apt basis for controlled comparison across the decades. The 87th and
88th Congresses (1961–64) were remarkably similar to the 103rd
Congress (1993–94) in their political circumstances and makeup, as well
as the eventual legislative results produced by each of these Congresses.
At the same time, a comparison of these Congresses offers our first evidence of the increasing obstacles to legislative success over these decades
that have altered the tempo and temper of the modern policymaking
game.

THE HOUSE OF REPRESENTATIVES
IN THE 87th AND 88th CONGRESSES

The 87th Congress (1961–62), like the 103rd Congress decades later,
was a transitional Congress, in that the House Democratic majority
enjoyed concurrent Democratic control of the legislative and executive
branches for the first time in nearly a decade. While a loose coalition of
conservative southern Democrats and Republicans effectively stymied
the budding liberal Democratic agenda during this Congress, President
Kennedy still managed to achieve success on 48.4 percent of his 355 legislative proposals in 1961 and success on 44.6 percent of his 298 proposals in 1962.[1] On those measures that the Kennedy and Johnson
administrations were able to get to a floor vote, the success rate aver-

aged a fairly constant 85 percent during the four years from 1961 to
1964. While higher-profile legislative failures and the various conservative legislative roadblocks received much of the public and media attention, the 87th Congress had many significant legislative accomplishments. These included emergency feed grain legislation, a minimum
wage increase, the depressed areas aid bill, foreign development and
United Nations loan authorizations, a massive federal housing aid law,
the initial funding of the Peace Corps, a major welfare revision, and the
Trade Expansion Act of 1962, among numerous others. The 88th
Congress (1963–64) similarly engendered a variety of major legislative
initiatives. Among these were the urban mass transportation law, the
first major college aid law, funding for the space program, numerous
agricultural subsidies, a large tax cut, and civil rights and antipoverty
initiatives, in addition to the usual spate of cyclical authorizations and
appropriations.

The Democrats of the 87th Congress held a nominal 262–175 seat
majority in the House, but of those 262 Democratic seats, southern
Democrats held 98. Most of those legislators lined up more closely ideologically with their generally conservative Republican colleagues.[2]
While the majority party agenda-setting powers and the numerical committee advantages devolved to the Democratic Party leadership and the
nominally Democratic caucus, the more important mix of ideological
preferences favored the conservatives, making "the 'majority' of
Democrats . . . more apparent than real."[3] This mix did not change in
the 88th Congress, as the Democratic majority stood at 258–176 with
one vacancy immediately after the election.[4]

The House of Representatives in the 87th Congress was led at the
outset by Sam Rayburn (D-TX), the dynamic and forceful Speaker
described by each respondent from that period as the House's legislative
and political center of gravity. He was, in the words of one respondent
and senior colleague, "A kindly tyrant. He controlled himself the legislative agenda of the House." At the same time, respondents remembered Rayburn as being an accessible Speaker and a "great listener,
regardless of the member's length of service." John McCormack (D-
MA) served as the House majority leader, with Carl Albert (D-OK) as
the majority whip. Charles Halleck (R-IN) was the minority leader, and
Leslie Arends (R-IL) served as minority whip.

By all respondent accounts, these party leaders worked together
closely and often exclusively in setting the House agenda. McCormack
succeeded Rayburn as Speaker upon his death in November of 1961,
and his ascension to the Speakership loosened that office's hold over the
day-to-day affairs of the House and its floor proceedings, in the view of
most respondents from that era. Additionally, Presidents Kennedy and

Johnson, despite their sharply contrasting personal styles and strengths, both exercised great influence in the House's legislative affairs in the view of those same respondents, taking full advantage of the numerous personal relationships they had each developed during their service in Congress. While the House agenda was set centrally by these party leaders, respondents from this period described the chamber as a legislatively decentralized one, with committee chairmen retaining great autonomy in determining the substance and pace of the legislative process.

Committee work occupied much of the average member's time, and this committee work proceeded at a fairly methodical pace. From the 84th Congress to the 90th, the number of subcommittees of the standing House committees increased from 83 to 133, just as the number of subcommittees of joint committees increased from 11 to 15. This expansion translated to an increase in assignments from 1.2 committee, 1.6 subcommittee, and 0.2 other committee assignments in 1956 to 1.5 committee, 3.2 subcommittee, and 0.4 other committee assignments by 1971, an increase in total committee load from 3.0 to 5.1.[5] Expressed another way, the workload in the House of the 87th and 88th Congresses included the introduction of 14,328 bills in the 87th and 14,022 in the 88th, for an average of 32.9 and 32.2 per member respectively. There were 4.0 and 3.7 hours per session day in the 87th and 88th Congresses, and 3,402 and 3,596 committee and subcommittee meetings, respectively.[6] These and other features of the House of the 87th and 88th Congresses are summarized and compared to the same features of the House of the 103rd Congress in tables 2.1 and 2.2.

Demographically, the House members of the early 1960s were most often lawyers by occupation, with 250 lawyers among the 435 representatives of the 88th Congress.[7] The next most common profession was banking and business, represented by 134 members in that Congress followed next by 45 members working in agriculture, 36 as educators, and 33 as journalists.[8] Two hundred ninety-one members of the House in 1963 were military veterans. Three African Americans served in the House of the 87th Congress (the number rose to 4 in the 88th), and 18 of the representatives of the 87th were women. The 88th Congress seated 66 freshman, and the mean term of service for the membership was 5.7 terms, while the median term was the fifth term.[9] Only 26 members of the House retired in 1960 (eleven of them Democrats), and a similarly small 24 (ten Democrats) retired in 1962.[10] While accurate campaign finance records are not available for this period, the anecdotal numbers cited by respondents as campaign budgets for their House races in this period ranged from "a couple of thousand," to "five thousand," to Lee Hamilton's high-water mark of $30,000 in 1965.[11] While these ballpark numbers are likely biased downward, none of the respondents

TABLE 2.1

Characteristics of the House in the 87th, 88th, and 103rd Congresses, Part I

Feature[12]	87th/88th Congresses	103rd Congress
Democratic majority	262–175/258–176 (1 vacant)	258–176 (1 independent)
Southern contingent	98D–6R (after '60 election)	77D–48R
First-term members by number/%	66/15% (after '62 election)	110/25%
Ten or more terms, number/%	74/17% (after '62 election)	67/15%
Mean term	5.7 (after '62 election)	5.3
Median term	5 (after '62 election)	4
Incumbent retirements[13]	11D–15R/10D–14R	41D–24R
Incumbency reelection rate[14]	92.6%/91.5%	88.3%
Percent safe seats[15]	58.9%/63.6%	65.6%
Split ticket districts	114 (26.1%)[16]	100 (23.0%)
Party line voters House vote	80%/83%	77%
Party unity scores in the House	48%/53%	63.5%
Standing committees	19/20[17]	22
Subcommittees/standing committees	83/133	115
Select and special committees	2/1	1
Joint committees	10/10	4
Subcommittees to joint committees	11/15	0
Committee/subcommittee meetings	3,402/3,596	4,304
Closed committee/subc. meetings	2,100/2,226	0[18]

TABLE 2.2

Characteristics of the House in the 87th, 88th, and 103rd Congresses, Part II

Feature	87th/88th Congresses	103rd Congress
Bills introduced (all types)	14,328/14,022	6,647
Average number per member	32.9/32.2	15.3
Bills passed	1,927/1,267	749
Public bills enacted	885/666	465
Pages of statutes	2,078/1,975	7,542
Average number of pages per statute	2.3/3.0	16.2
Private bills enacted	684/360	8
D.C. House staff members	2,441/4,055[19]	7,400
District staff members	1,035[20]	3,130[21]
Days in session	304/334	265
Hours per session day	4.0/3.7	7.1
Recorded votes	240/232	1122
Average campaign expenditures	$30,000[22]	$408,240
Presidential vetoes	20/9	0
Vetoes overridden	0/0	N/A
Congressional mailings[23]	85.1 million /94.7 million	200.7 million
President's legislative vote victory %	83.1–85.0%/83.1–88.5%	87.2%–87.2%

from the 1960s viewed fund-raising as a particularly significant aspect of his or her electoral or reelectoral efforts. In 1978, the first year that fairly accurate records became available, the mean expenditure for all House candidates was $109,440.[24]

THE HOUSE OF REPRESENTATIVES
IN THE 103rd CONGRESS

The 103rd Congress (1993–94), like the 87th, was a transitional Congress in that the Democrats again controlled both the executive and the legislative branches for the first time after a lengthy period of Republican control of the White House. While the nominally Democratic southern delegation of the early 1960s had not yet completed the regional conversion to the Republican Party that would culminate in 1994, the southern states were represented by 48 Republicans out of 125 members. The overall party mix of the 103rd Congress was identical to that of the 88th at 258 Democrats and 176 Republicans. President Clinton, much like Presidents Kennedy and Johnson of the early 1960s, was able to win legislative victories on 87.2 percent of his initiatives that came to a vote in the House in both 1993 and 1994.[25] Key legislative accomplishments enacted by the 103rd Congress included the national service initiative; "don't ask, don't tell, don't pursue" (as part of the defense authorization); the family and medical leave law; deficit reduction; the crime bill and related Brady bill; NAFTA; the "Goals 2000" initiative; and GATT, among others.

The party leadership in the House of the 103rd Congress included Speaker Thomas Foley (D-WA), Majority Leader Richard Gephardt (D-MO), and Majority Whip David Bonior (D-MI), on the Democratic side, with Minority Leader Robert Michel (R-IL) and Minority Whip Newt Gingrich (R-GA) on the Republican side of the aisle. Most respondents described this leadership group as far less cohesive than the party leadership of the early 1960s, and most cited ideological and stylistic differences as the chief reasons for this characteristic. One longtime observer of the House described Speaker Foley as "a recognized intellectual heavyweight among his House colleagues. Speaker Foley was trained for the job by 'Scoop' Jackson (Senator Henry Jackson, D-WA) and tried to be a traditional, decentralized Speaker. He was an issue guy." A member of the party leadership at that time described this characteristic as an "old school respect for seniority and the process." While Michel and Foley sought to apply this traditional model of party leadership in the House, other respondents recollected different objectives on the part of Gingrich and Gephardt, with each seeking to further centralize their parties and direct the legislative efforts from their offices. The party leadership of the 103rd can be characterized, then, as leadership marked by clashes in personal styles, objectives, and techniques, a theme we return to in later chapters.

Table 2.1 shows clear evidence of an increased workload for the rank-and-file members of the House of the early 1990s over that of their counterparts from the early 1960s. In addition to the increased demand for the legislators' time for meetings and hearings, respondents with service in the House in both periods most frequently cited the increased time dedicated to fund raising and other campaign activities as the single most significant change in House workload over those decades. While some House leaders increasingly looked to gain party electoral benefits through centralized information campaigns, a trend several respondents believed began with Speaker Wright, the House of the 103rd Congress still remained essentially legislatively decentralized in the view of most respondents. The crafting of policy and the negotiation and adjudication between interested actors still took place primarily within the committees and subcommittees.

Demographically, the House of Representatives in the 103rd Congress, like the 87th and 88th Congresses before it, was well represented by the legal profession, with 181 lawyers among the membership. Businesspersons and bankers accounted for 131 members, and there were also 66 educators, 24 journalists, 19 farmers, 10 law enforcement officials, and 87 members listed as "public service" or "political" professionals. One hundred fifty-five members listed some form of military service in their official biographies.[26] The House of the 103rd Congress had within its membership 39 African Americans (38 Democrats) and 48 women (36 Democrats).

Comparing these institutional characteristics from the early 1960s to the early 1990s, then, in the House of the 103rd Congress we see a chamber with a Democratic House majority, at least nominally very similar to the House of the early 1960s. Electorally, however, we already see evidence of flux within the membership in that the chamber had forty-four more first termers and seven fewer senior members with ten or more terms of service. Even as the percentage of safe seats rose by a small margin, incumbent reelection rates for those seeking reelection fell several percentage points, and retirements had increased. Most notably, the congressional workload had increased in response to increased campaigning demands and increased committee meetings, hearings, and other legislative activities. Members had far more legislation to sort through, as the number of statute pages enacted increased almost fourfold over the period, even as the chamber passed a little over half as many laws. Party unity scores were up over 10 percent from the 1960s' levels, though President Clinton had chosen to veto no laws passed by the 103rd Congress, in contrast to the twenty-nine presidential vetoes between 1961 and 1964. The district and D.C. staffs increased greatly in size over the decades, which helped the members as they prepared to cast almost five times as many recorded votes packed into approximately seventy fewer legislative days, days that averaged three more work hours than comparable session-days in the early 1960s. The legislative decentralization begun by Speaker McCormack and maintained several Speakers later by Speaker Foley left most legislative initiatives to the individual members and the committees.

Sifting through this evidence, then, we find that in spite of the comparable political circumstances and the other defining characteristics common to the 87th, 88th, and 103rd Congresses, already a pattern of increasing obstacles to would-be policymakers emerges from the comparison. Facing a far greater workload than their counterparts from the 1960s, House members of the 1990s juggled increasing electoral demands against a backdrop of the increased number of meetings, greater time spent raising funds, increased committee assignments, and a large increase in statute pages enacted, among other indicators. It is interesting that at the same time the number of statute pages enacted by those members increased dramatically, only about 60 percent as many laws were passed in the latter period, a point we will revisit. But reduced incumbent reelection rates, increased retirements, heightened "party unity," and great increases in the number of recorded votes, campaign costs, and hours per session day all combine to portray a House that had become a far more frenetic and less enjoyable place to be in the modern era.

In sum, this context of an increased workload for the members, coupled with a less homogenous membership and a leadership less willing to work together toward policy goals, have all adversely influenced the average member's opportunities to realize legislative success in the modern House. Not surprisingly, the cases and respondents reinforce this impression that the modern congressional context has had seriously detrimental effects on member interaction, oversight responsibilities, legislative deliberation, and other social and professional activities that offer hard-to-qualify but crucial advantages to the performance of the policymaking process.

CHAPTER 3

Legislative Histories: The 1960s

There's no doubt that some of my best friends were Republicans. We'd sit down and work problems out without getting mean about it. Members gravitated to those with similar interests and floor voting records, regardless of party. And you got what you worked for.

—House member from the 1960s

Laws are assigned individual public law numbers upon passage, but each law represents a temporary convergence of past streams of ideology and interests, as well as prior public and private debates. Each new law in turn contributes to future public discourse in relevant policy areas. Correspondingly, none of the six laws that are described in the next two chapters was created in a vacuum. Instead, each law was passed only after the political planets finally lined up, and they must be considered within the context of the Congresses and general political climates in which they came into being. To paraphrase Kindgon's (1995) words, "Their time had finally come." Each of the chronologies that follow begins at least as far back as the presidential administration preceding the one in which passage took place. However, it is nearly always the case that the roots of any legislative success run much deeper. As such, it is not uncommon for the origins of a legislative initiative to have predated the careers of the legislative champions who eventually achieved the policy success. Nonetheless, respondents in all six cases identified a small core of key agents they deemed to be primarily responsible for the realization of success, and the stories of these legislative champions and their efforts offer a variety of noteworthy insights into the essence of the American legislative process.

To elaborate on the method of case construction a bit, I first assembled the outlines of the cases through an examination of media accounts and government records to establish a basic chronology for each law. I then used respondent accounts to fill in the details of the passage of the laws, asking each respondent to emphasize those events or aspects that were directly relevant to the realization of that legislative success. Respondent assertions were only accepted as "fact" when the public record or other respondents corroborated them. Given this standard of triangulation, each of the six stories that follow identifies the key events, most important actors, and crucial features of the policymaking process as distinguished by the respondents who participated in the events that led to the passage of the laws.

PL87–872: THE FOREIGN AID APPROPRIATION FOR FY 1963

The foreign aid appropriation for fiscal year 1963 was signed into law on October 23, 1962 (HR13175). In its seven pages, the law appropriated $3.93 billion for economic and military aid and more than $2.35 billion for other related projects, setting the total foreign operations budget at just under $6.3 billion. This sum was nearly $1 billion less than the amount requested by the Kennedy administration.[1] The major public debate on the legislation centered around two provisions, one of which dealt with the general presidential authority to provide aid to Communist nations, and the other, barring aid to any countries furnishing economic or military aid to Cuba. The House version of the law denied any military or economic aid to Communist nations or to other nations providing such assistance to Cuba. However, the House eventually compromised with the Senate and the administration by modifying those provisions to allow aid in the event that the president waived the prohibition based upon his assessment of risk to American national interests.

As signed by the president, the law appropriated just over $2.6 billion for economic aid, including aid in the form of development grants, investment guarantees, funds earmarked for international relief organizations, administrative expenses for state and AID, contingency funds, and other specifically targeted assistance projects.[2] Military aid provisions in the law accounted for $1.325 billion of the package. The law also appropriated just over $2.35 billion in funds for other foreign operations, such as the Peace Corps, the Inter-American Bank, the International Monetary Fund, the Ryukyu Islands administration, Cuban refugee relief, the Philippine war damage claims administration, State Department relief initiatives, and the U.S. Information Agency. The 1962 law, with a final funding level almost 21 percent less than the Kennedy request, was only $14.3 million (or less than 1 percent) more than the 1961 foreign aid level, which itself had been 19 percent less than the administration's requested level of funding.[3]

Like all cyclical appropriating legislation, the impetus for the foreign aid appropriation for fiscal year 1963 came from the funded agencies, stated presidential and administration policy objectives, the relevant congressional overseers and implementers, contextual international events, and various other interested proponents and opponents of federal spending in this policy area. Foreign aid funding, like the yearly legislative branch appropriation, has a long history of eliciting broad congressional opposition, given its few natural constituents and the ease with which members can appear fiscally responsible by publicly opposing any foreign expenditures "when we still have so many needs back here at home." Despite the seemingly natural fit between foreign aid and the foreign policy objectives of cold war–era politics, foreign aid was as unpopular and as likely to draw vocal and publicly stated congressional opposition in the early 1960s as at any other time, as table 3.1 shows.

The foreign operation appropriation for fiscal year 1961, as a precursor to the passage of the FY1963 law, would be no different. Despite President Eisenhower's tremendous foreign policy credentials, his fiscal 1961 foreign aid proposal drew immediate and vocal opposition from House and Senate leaders on both sides of the aisle after he submitted it to Congress in February of 1960. This opposition came from the rank-and-file members, the two parties' leaders, and the chambers' foreign aid authorizers and appropriators. In the Senate, Assistant Majority Leader Mansfield (D-MT) attacked the president's proposal as "too much money" (with) "too little change in administration," while the Senate Foreign Relations Committee chairman, J. W. Fulbright (D-AR), denounced the president's "inability to respond (to Soviet space and foreign aid initiatives) with a carefully thought-out and firm program extended beyond one year."[4] Members of the president's own party joined in the criticism, as did the longtime opponent of foreign aid and strategically placed House Appropriations Foreign Aid Subcommittee chairman, Otto E. Passman (D-LA). Describing the president's proposal as "unrealistic and excessive," he predicted a $1 billion cut in the package, as did the *Wall Street Journal*.[5] The executive-legislative foreign aid dance had begun.

After testimony and lobbying from a variety of administration, military, and interest group leaders, the House and Senate authorizers agreed on a modest $88.68 million cut in the authorizing legislation, signed on May 17, 1960.[6] Handed the administration's Mutual Security Program virtually intact, however, Chairman Passman said the program was "riddled with corruption, scandal, and blackmail," predicting this time that his subcommittee would cut up to $1.5 billion from the Eisen-

TABLE 3.1

Foreign Aid Appropriations in the 1960s and 1990s

Fiscal Year	Total Foreign Aid Approp. in Billions of Dollars[7]	Original Presidential Request in Billions of Dollars	Total Budget in Billions of Dollars	Foreign Aid as Percent of the Total Budget	Total Foreign Aid Approp. in Billions of FY1992 Dollars	Percent Reduction from Presidential Request
'60	3.23	3.93	92.19	3.5	16.20	17.8
'61	4.43	4.87	97.72	4.5	21.65	9.0
'62	3.66	4.76	106.82	3.4	17.62	23.1
'63	3.93	4.78	111.32	3.5	18.25	17.8
'64	3.00	4.53	118.53	2.5	13.69	33.8
'65	3.25	3.52	118.23	2.7	14.61	7.7
'66	3.22	3.46	134.53	2.4	14.04	6.9
'67	3.49	3.95	157.46	2.2	14.76	11.6
'68	2.30	3.13	178.13	1.3	9.33	26.5
'69	1.62	2.92	183.64	0.9	6.24	44.5
'70	1.87	2.71	195.65	1.0	6.80	31.0
'90	14.44	15.16	1253.16	1.2	15.60	4.7
'91	15.39	15.52	1324.40	1.2	15.87	0.8
'92	14.60[8]	28.03	1381.68	1.1	14.60	47.9
'93	26.26	27.43	1409.41	1.9	25.61	4.3
'94	12.98	14.43	1461.73	0.9	12.37	10.0
'95	13.83	14.08	1551.73	0.9	12.84	1.8
'96	12.10	14.80	1560.51	0.8	10.95	18.2
'97	12.24	12.90	1601.23	0.8	10.80	5.1
'98	13.00	16.90	1667.82	0.8	11.23	23.1
'99	12.80[9]	13.55	1733.22	0.7	10.83	5.5

hower program.[10] In spite of Eisenhower's special message to Congress, his foreign policy credentials, his own personal and public notes to the congressional leaders, and intense lobbying by Vice President Nixon and other administration officials, foreign aid for fiscal 1961 was still cut to just over $3.716 billion. This sum was nearly $500 million below the president's request.[11] The vote to slash the funds (agreeing to the conference report) came moments after Minority Leader Charles Halleck (R-IN) read a personal plea from the president to the assembled members asking them to restore the funds on the House floor, in which he expressed his "grave concern" over the cuts.[12] The plea was to no avail. President Eisenhower signed the measure into law, acting on forty-one other measures as well on the afternoon of September 3, 1960.[13]

This legislative outcome eventually had a direct impact on the passage of the foreign operations law for fiscal year 1963, as foreign aid became one of several defining differences between Nixon and Kennedy in the presidential election year politics unfolding concurrently with the passage of the 1960 law. Like most policy initiatives, the terms of the policy debate had been defined prior to the current consideration of the issue, something true in all six cases examined in this study. While Nixon had lobbied hard for support of the Eisenhower program through member contacts, letters, and public appearances, he had also carefully positioned himself in favor of "self-help" and private-sector administration of any aid to be distributed. Kennedy, however, supported a broader governmental role during the campaign, in terms of both the magnitude of aid and the administration of foreign assistance.

Upon his election, Kennedy quickly called for a broad program of foreign aid in his first State of the Union address, describing his proposal as a "towering and unprecedented" plan intended to build a strong and expanding economy for the non-Communist world.[14] Subsequently, in May, the Kennedy administration sent to Congress a proposed bill authorizing $1.7 billion in economic assistance for fiscal year 1962, as well as a larger package of $8.8 billion in lending authority over the next five years, with a concurrent overhaul of the foreign aid administering agencies.[15] The administration began to press its case to the public and the Congress then, as Kennedy gave numerous addresses to business and civic groups and Secretary of State Rusk spent hours before the Senate and House foreign affairs committees expounding upon the administration's case in closed session. Senator Fulbright expressed optimism that the Kennedy bill (which in total would increase the year's foreign operations appropriation to more than $5 billion) could be passed relatively intact, and both Rusk and Treasury Secretary Dillon sent letters to each member of the House and Senate asking for their support. Kennedy exhorted the Congress to comply with his request, noting in a speech that "I consider this bill to be probably the most vital piece of legislation in the national interest that may be before the Congress this year."[16]

Despite a comfortable 13–4 vote for the Kennedy plan coming out of the Senate Foreign Relations Committee and a comparably comfortable 19–10 vote in the House Foreign Affairs Committee, opposition quickly began to mount in reaction to the unusual five-year lending authorization sought by the administration.[17] In a leak of information intended to be kept secret after a closed-door session (an all too common occurrence, according to the respondents), it became public knowledge that Passman's Foreign Operations Subcommittee intended to trim $750 million in foreign aid from the Kennedy request. In the full House, $565 million of these cuts were upheld by a vote of 270 to 123, after maneuvering and compromise by the committee and House leadership and a raucous floor debate in which comments like "You can tell Africa good-bye!"[18] were bandied about. The Senate in turn rejected the House cuts by a 62–17 margin, and the two chambers went to conference, as Otto Passman pledged to fight the restoration and cut the Senate position "plenty."[19] As the first session of the 87th Congress adjourned, he delivered on this vague promise as the chambers concurred on a compromise measure (H Rept 1270) that reduced by $860.9 million the administration's request for fiscal 1962. The new measure appropriated just over $3.91 billion for economic and military aid for a 19 percent reduction from Kennedy's position.[20] Kennedy signed the bill on September 30, 1961.[21]

For all of the acrimonious public debate and outright arguments, a clear pattern had emerged. The administration would publicly request a foreign aid figure about 20 percent higher than it wanted, then lobby hard for the amount in closed committee sessions, through formal and informal contacts with the members of Congress, and with the public and the media. The congressional leadership, as well as rank-and-file members so inclined, could then make good political theater by reducing the administration position by 20 percent, leaving everyone satisfied. The consensus among the interviewed House members, House staffers, and administration staff involved in the foreign operations process in the early 1960s was that this public and private dance was expected and that the administration tailored its foreign aid request accordingly.

The events that would lead to the passage of the Foreign Operations Appropriation for Fiscal Year 1963 began with Kennedy's budget request in mid-January of 1962, when he outlined his ambitious foreign policy goals and requested the largest foreign aid budget since Eisenhower's first-year request. Kennedy requested $4.897 billion for foreign operations, an increase of nearly $1 billion over the fiscal 1962 appropriation.[22] The administration's lobbying effort began, in the recollection of one state official involved in the efforts to get the bill passed, with formal and informal meetings at the secretary and undersecretary level between the White House's foreign policy advisors, key congressional leaders from the authorizing and appropriating committees, and state executives. The executive agency would then routinely give formal information briefings to the subcommittee members, outlining the objectives and means of implementation of those objectives written into the Kennedy plan. At the same time, the congressional liaisons would arrange meetings between the editors or publishers of the major newspapers and senior State executives to give the administration's perspective firsthand. The administration had a specific group of senators and representatives judged to be friendly to the White House and knowledgeable and influential on foreign policy issues that it would consult throughout the entire process, from drafting through passage. The White House and state staff members charged with coordinating the administration's efforts on the bill tracked the bill's progress through nightly legislative summaries that went to the president.

However, in the view of respondents who participated in the passage of this legislation, to understand this outcome was to understand the give and take between Chairman Passman and the White House. Although White House and state operatives knew Passman to be a skillful, experienced legislator and outspoken foe of foreign aid, the administration expected Otto Passman to deliver eventually. "We expected Otto Passman to rant and rave for about a month and then tell us what he'd want to pass the program. I told (Assistant Secretary) David Abshire that Otto Passman (for all his yearly blustering) was the greatest benefactor of foreign aid I'd ever worked with . . . the foreign aid subcommittee was his personal avenue to making the administration's bill economically valuable to the state of Louisiana. Every year, the foreign aid bill was about rice . . . rice and other exports from the state of Louisiana . . . rice mattered to him and he made it happen year after year." Without question, however, the Appropriations Committee leaders made it difficult on Kennedy. "JFK would call, and Chairman Cannon would refuse to take the call," one member recollected. "Jackie would invite Passman to parties, and he'd still carve out 1 billion the next day." Furthermore, Chairman Cannon, described as a master parliamentarian, was a "crony" of the Rules Committee chairman, "Judge" Howard Smith (D-VA), and as such could do pretty much as he pleased.

The same day that Kennedy argued in a special message to Congress that if the aid program were to succeed, it "cannot be further reduced," Passman began hearings in his subcommittee. Like his Senate counterparts, Passman used the administration draft as the vehicle for consideration, and his hearings began even before the authorizing committee, the

House Foreign Affairs Committee, started its own work on the bill. The day after Kennedy's special message, Passman used the resources of his position as subcommittee chairman to frame the terms of the debate, denouncing the aid plan figures as "preposterous."[23] Kennedy responded with a rebuke, asserting at a news conference in response to Passman's charges that "This program is just as important as our national defense . . . it's always open season on [foreign aid]."[24]

Secretary of Defense McNamara and the Joint Chiefs of Staff chairman Lemnitzer, were among the parade of administration officials who testified before the House and Senate committees in support of the program in hundreds of hours of hearings. The House foreign aid subcommittee hearings were described by most observers as particularly painful ones for the executive agency personnel sent before Passman to justify the funding of their programs, and as in previous years, the subcommittee negotiated the aid bill's future in closed session. Furthermore, while some respondents described Passman as "dictatorial and arbitrary," he still managed to forge a working coalition across party lines among the eleven members of his subcommittee and as such was able to dictate the terms of the debate to the administration.

Unexpected reductions began to come from other committees as well. The Senate Foreign Relations Committee voted 8–7 to slash the bill's provision for aid to India by one-third, and the House's Foreign Affairs Committee rejected altogether a companion bill seeking $73 million for Philippine war damage claims.[25] The Senate Foreign Relations Committee then reported, by a 14–3 vote, its authorizing bill with a modest $216.5 million cut below the president's original request, generally giving the president the long-term lending authority for development loans the administration had sought.[26] The House Foreign Affairs Committee reported an even smaller $210 million cut. During their proceedings, however, Chairman Thomas "Doc" Morgan (D-PA) highlighted certain "abuses" in the use of the emergency funds in prior years that members in opposition to the plan would later try to use on the floor to attack that funding level.

Nonetheless, after passage in each chamber and ratification of the minor conference compromises necessary to align the two plans, the administration was able to claim a significant victory. The administration had gotten most of what it wanted at that point, both in terms of funding levels and the lending and administrative authorities (including presidential authority to waive prohibitions against aid to Communist countries) granted by the authorizing legislation. However, even as the New York Times printed a transcript of Kennedy's news conference, in which Kennedy trumpeted the victory, the newspaper sounded a pessimistic note on the foreign aid appropriation's prospects, asserting,

"But the battle is only half won. . . . [Foreign Aid's] unreconstructed enemies are already sharpening their axes."[27]

Passman was indeed building his case against foreign aid. He had held over five hundred hours of closed hearings by early August that undoubtedly meant trouble for the administration, and he intentionally delayed the measure in getting to the House floor with the tacit support of the House Appropriations Committee chairman, Clarence Cannon (D-MO). According to fellow subcommittee members, Passman had sought and been awarded the foreign operations subcommittee chairmanship in the first place because Cannon was an opponent of foreign aid himself and knew that Passman would give each administration yearly fits over the program. Kennedy, after warning against "the height of folly" and associated dangers of any "slash" in the foreign aid funding levels, publicly absolved the House leadership of any blame for the delay in bringing the measure to the floor.[28] As Passman attacked the program on the floor of the House in response to the president's remarks, longtime *New York Times* observer Felix Belair described the scene as a "solid cheering section (on the Republican side of the aisle) and . . . scattered applause from the Democrats."[29] Transcripts of the hearings released later showed open clashes between Passman and Secretary of State Rusk and other administration officials over a wide variety of provisions, ranging from broad program objectives such as contingency funds to individual projects such as athletic stadiums. At least publicly, prospects for the foreign operations package were grim indeed.

The politics of this subcommittee, which dominated the next step in the legislative proceedings, are particularly interesting. Despite the larger chamber's southern Democrat-Republican alliance, this subcommittee was seemingly well positioned to make life easier for the nominal Democratic majority and the Kennedy (and later Johnson) administration. A majority of members on the subcommittee were described by their colleagues as "pro-aid." Furthermore, the full committee chairman Clarence Cannon, described by his Appropriations Committee colleagues as "dogmatic, arbitrary, and not very popular," was often openly at odds with the ranking minority member, John Taber (R-NY). Fellow committee members could remember no evidence of personal warmth between the two, and it was the number two Democrat, George Mahon (D-TX), who most often mediated between the Republicans and Democrats on the full committee, though in one memorable incident a respondent recalled him getting into fisticuffs with Taber. In sum, there was little personal warmth and little trust among the full committee leadership and as such, little possibility of any cohesive effort or inclination to change the subcommittee's policy stances.

Comfortable with Passman's legislative abilities and ideological bent against foreign aid, Cannon gave Passman great autonomy in running his subcommittee. Passman himself was described as arbitrary and dictatorial in his public leadership style, but respondents also acknowledged his mastery of the legislative process and his ability to get what he wanted on his yearly legislative centerpiece. While Passman was a vocal opponent of foreign aid in public, subcommittee members remembered him as one who would work with members on both sides of the aisle to build a subcommittee consensus, and they uniformly noted his willingness to seek eventual compromise. Subcommittee members J. Vaughn Gary (D-VA), John J. Rooney (D-NY), William Natcher (D-KY), Hugh Alexander (D-NC), Joseph Montoya (D-NM), George Andrews (D-AL), Silvio Conte (R-MA), and John J. Rhodes (R-AZ) were generally pro-foreign aid, with only Gerald Ford (R-MI), Taber, and Passman generally opposed. Montoya, Natcher, and Alexander worked particularly closely with the Kennedy administration in advocating and assisting the administration position. It was primarily one willful actor, Otto Passman, achieving a working majority within the eleven-legislator subcommittee, who managed the foreign aid process and made it difficult for the administration in the House. Respondents recollected Speaker McCormack and the other Democratic Party leaders as supportive of foreign aid generally but content to let Passman work out the legislation with the administration.

The administration had grim expectations regarding the appropriations battle to come, and Passman certainly did not disappoint. The subcommittee reported a bill (H Rept 2410) on September 18, 1962, slashing nearly $1.5 billion from the administration's request, with the subcommittee incorporating nearly all of Passman's requested cuts.[30] Again, this information was first leaked from a four-hour-long closed negotiating session about which members were asked to remain silent. Furthermore, Passman did little to endear himself to the administration, writing among other pejorative comments in the report that the administration had requested "unjustifiable . . . pie-in-the-sky" figures "to the subcommittee's surprise."[31] As the measure made its way to the floor with the bulk of the huge cut intact, Passman used the floor debate to quote Kennedy first as a member of the House then as a senator condemning foreign aid programs for fraud, waste, and inefficiency.[32] His broadly drawn floor attack on foreign aid focused on three problems: the inefficiency of the administration of the program, the lower-than-American tax rates of some recipient countries, and the usual requests for "bigger handouts" from recipient countries after initial grants of aid. One after another, his fellow subcommittee members rose to support the subcommittee cut, and even those remembered as supporters of foreign aid stood in support of the large reduction. Final passage came on

September 20 by a 249–144 roll call vote, as proponents of the larger package decided to wage their fight in conference rather than make a serious attempt on the House floor. The bill was nearly recommitted with instructions to pare more funds, but that motion was defeated by a 190 to 203 roll call vote. Republicans were split 75 to 83 on final passage, as were southern Democrats (45–51), and the measure carried largely through the support of 129 of 139 northern Democrats. [33]

In conference, largely through Passman's obstinacy and negotiating ability, the Senate agreed to pare $493.9 million off of its original position, while the House added $298.5 million, after Passman met personally and individually with President Kennedy. One administration observer remarked, "Passman would always put highly controversial political limitations on aid that he had little interest in. Then, after all the publicity that would generate, he would publicly make a great show of reluctantly backing off of that position. He knew how to get what he wanted." The resulting net reduction of $1.03 billion from the administration's final request was widely believed to be the result of a "secret agreement" between Kennedy and Passman. Passman addressed the claim in a television interview, conceding only, "Certainly I had a meeting with the president. If we had a secret agreement it was certainly to the advantage of the taxpayers that we did." [34] The conference report (H Rept 2540) was adopted by both chambers with little debate, with a 171 to 108 roll call vote in the House and a voice vote in the Senate, and the president signed the bill into law on October 23 without public comment.

In sum, participants in the process agreed that the passage of the Foreign Operations Appropriation for fiscal year 1963 is best understood as an interaction among a few key actors, willful agents who marshaled and expended legislative capital prior to negotiating the eventual outcome. Over time, Otto Passman was able to forge an ad hoc issue coalition of subcommittee members willing to support his position on aid, a coalition that led directly to policy success. Furthermore, he used his tremendous legislative skills and took advantage of a largely supportive party hierarchy and a House predisposed to support his initiatives in order to dictate his terms to the president, in spite of concerted executive agency and administration efforts to the contrary. Regardless of his public persona as an autocratic chairman in vocal opposition to foreign aid, Passman was able to work smoothly behind closed doors and through a network of personal allies and effective member contacts, using the powers of his subcommittee chairmanship, to realize legislative success on his terms. His leverage in this issue area came from his carefully constructed consensus within the subcommittee, his orchestrated public and private legislative maneuvers, and his unmatched mastery of the issue itself. Considerations of timing were even taken care of for him by the nature of the appropriations cycle, as the administration eventually had to come to him. One administration after another had no choice but to dance the foreign aid dance as choreographed by Otto Passman.

PL88–204: THE HIGHER EDUCATION
FACILITIES ACT OF 1963

The Higher Education Facilities Act of 1963 (HR6143), signed into law by President Johnson on December 16, 1963, represented the first major educational assistance initiative since the National Defense Education Act of 1958. It was the first of the Kennedy education proposals to pass after high-profile failures of broader educational reform propositions in the years prior. In its sixteen pages, the law authorized $1.195 billion for the first three years of a planned five-year program to upgrade the nation's higher educational facilities through a combination of grants and loans, and its passage was inextricably linked with the consideration of broader educational reforms in the early 1960s.[35] The Title I provisions of the legislation included allotments for public technical and community colleges and other types of undergraduate facilities, while Title II provided for grants for graduate facilities. Title III of the law stipulated the terms of eligibility for the loans, while the fourth and final title made general provisions for the loan agreements and means of recoupment of improperly used grants.[36] Previous attempts at passage of essentially the same legislation had died in House-Senate conference in 1962 when conferees were unable to compromise on the two issues of aid to private colleges and federal scholarships.

While the House had approved both grants and loans to private schools in its version of the legislation in 1962, the Senate bill (in line with Kennedy) had only provided for loans to private institutions. Similarly, the Senate, but not the House, supported the Kennedy proposal for federally funded scholarships for higher education. The passage of this law came about after the 1963 conferees arrived at a compromise satisfactory to both sides. In that compromise, Senate conferees agreed to eliminate a controversial Senate-version provision allowing for U.S. District Court judicial review of grants or loans made to private institutions, and House conferees accepted a broadened version of the Senate's categorical undergraduate grants for specific facilities.

The impetus behind this legislation came, as usual, from a variety of actors and interests in the "primordial issue soup" so well described by Kingdon. Aid to higher education for the purpose of facilities construction and upgrade had been the subject of both House and Senate hearings at least as early as 1955, and legislation enacted by both the 81st and 83rd Congresses gave limited assistance to that purpose. Testimony from a variety of education professionals and administrators, medical professionals, education advocacy groups, and state and local executives influenced the consideration of those initiatives. Many observers viewed the National Defense Education Act of 1958, which expanded federal aid to education, as the legislation that signaled a new federal role in education policy.[37] While President Eisenhower remained a staunch opponent of any increased federal intervention into education, viewing education as a local responsibility, he did propose in general terms a "program to stimulate classroom construction by incentives to extend and encourage state and local efforts" in his 1960 State of the Union address.[38] The precedent for federal assistance for educational facility construction existed in the form of the Community Facilities Administration, which already provided low-cost loans for dormitory construction. That program itself was headed for funding trouble in 1960, however, as Eisenhower sought to zero out funding for the program even as it struggled to meet the existing demand for that type of new construction.[39]

At the same time Eisenhower was somewhat vaguely identifying college construction aid as a possible area for increased federal action, the House Education and Labor Committee and the House in general were surprised by Education and Labor chairman Graham Barden's (D-NC) announcement that he would not seek reelection.[40] While seniority rules were routinely observed in both the House and the Senate in the early 1960s, there were no formal rules requiring the chamber to do so. Speaker Rayburn indicated that while it was probable, it was by no means certain that Adam Clayton Powell Jr. (D-NY) would receive the chairmanship. Powell was then carrying much political baggage in the eyes of the Democratic leadership, as he had supported the Eisenhower-Nixon ticket in 1956. Furthermore, Powell irritated southern Democrats as an African American supporting civil rights initiatives, and he had been indicted on income tax evasion charges. Second ranking among committee Democrats by seniority, Powell had never even received a subcommittee chairmanship. Nonetheless, Powell eventually received the chairmanship, and his appointment represented a major ideological shift that would have great implications for the type of legislation that could emerge from the committee later.

In response to the Eisenhower speech, Health, Education, and Welfare Secretary Arthur S. Flemming, interested members, and interested groups all urged the House Education and Labor Committee's Special Education Subcommittee to hold hearings on a variety of initiatives in March of 1960. These topics included an administration-backed proposal (HR4267) and other Democratic bills (HR967, HR2218, HR5467, HR10942, and HR11250), all of which addressed facilities construction. Each proposal sought to expand college construction aid, replacing or expanding the college housing program that Eisenhower had asked to terminate in his budget message.[41] Flemming endorsed the bill offered by Peter Frelinghuysen Jr. (R-NJ) that would provide federal aid for construction with a mix of bonds and grants, but the subcommittee decided to back an approach calling for a broader federal role. The subcommittee hearings lasted through the end of March, with testimony from the American Council on Education, U.S. Commissioner of Education Lawrence G. Derthick, and a wide variety of other professors, education advocates, and state and local authorities.

As this broader Democratic approach made its way to the House floor, and while Eisenhower remained fundamentally opposed to federal "intervention," Vice President Nixon became an advocate of the proposal, despite the administration's solid opposition to the measure. With the upcoming presidential election season in mind, Nixon was seemingly able to convince Eisenhower that, with certain modifications, the Democratic proposal would meet the administration's intent.[42] Ironically, as the measure made its way through the floor proceedings, southern Democrats and Republicans lined up to vote for a Powell-sponsored antisegregation amendment that would likely doom the measure in the Senate. This strategy by opponents of the measure saw them creating an ad hoc coalition of southern Democrats, many of whom ordinarily supported federal aid to education, and Republicans already opposed to federal aid to education to dim the bill's prospects by passing it with the antisegregation provision. The bill's sponsor and author, Democrat Frank Thompson of New Jersey, said, "It's all up to [Senate Majority Leader] Lyndon Johnson."[43]

At this point, it was still also unknown whether or not Eisenhower would sign any aid bill anyway, so prospects for passage were now grim. "Judge" Howard Smith (D-VA), chairman of the Rules Committee, and his like-minded conservative Rules Committee allies took the suspense out of any possible House-Senate conference by refusing by a 7–5 vote to send the bill to the Senate.[44] Backers of the measure were unsuccessful in using parliamentary tactics to circumvent the Rules Committee, and the measure was effectively dead for that Congress, much to the chagrin of both the sponsoring Democrats and Vice President Nixon, who had supported it. Analyzing the defeat, Fred Hechinger of the *New York Times* observed that a major cause of the defeat was the failure on the part of the National Education Association (NEA) to throw its full weight behind the measure. He reasoned that the Rules Committee obstacle in fact served both the Republicans and the Democrats well, given the election year liabilities that the lack of enthusiasm and possible veto might have caused for both parties.[45] The timing was not yet right for the passage of this initiative.

As this attempt at college construction aid was being thwarted, presidential election year politics were heating up, and a variety of educational advocates were making public appeals for an expanded federal role in education. Groups such as the American Association of School Administrators, the American Association of Land-Grant Colleges and State Universities, the American Association of Junior Colleges, and a wide variety of others pushed for strong education planks in the party platforms. Both parties responded to the calls, with the Republicans including planks calling for school desegregation and primary and secondary school construction assistance (supervised by state and local authorities), in addition to a general call for college construction aid.[46] The Democratic platform included those provisions as well as calls for aid for teachers' salaries and federal scholarships.[47] The *Wall Street Journal* responded to both parties' school construction aid planks by calling the perceived need "a political myth," but the Republicans and Vice President Nixon had clearly taken a more liberal approach to federal aid to education than the Eisenhower administration had ever supported.[48] Both candidates reiterated their support for school construction aid in the famous televised debate, with Nixon defending the Eisenhower record on construction aid as well.

Soon after the election, President-elect Kennedy met with Adam Clayton Powell Jr. as the prospective chairman of the House Education and Labor Committee and conferred for an hour in Kennedy's Georgetown home.[49] At the meeting, Kennedy and Powell established a minimum wage increase and a general aid-to-education bill as the committee's legislative priorities for the new Congress. Powell indicated that the education bill, or bills, would focus on aid for teachers' salaries and building construction, and he optimistically hoped for action within the first thirty to sixty days of the new Congress. The committee and the new administration began work on a massive aid proposal immediately after Kennedy took office.

Almost as quickly as they got started on the broad design, however, the administration's education initiatives began to run into opposition. Though Kennedy had planned to submit his multibillion-dollar education aid blueprint on January 31, he and his advisors decided to put those plans on hold when a group of liberal Democratic senators expressed their dissatisfaction with the plan after reading press accounts of its provisions. Chairman Powell also disliked some provisions of the three bills constituting the administration proposal. In particular, he disapproved of the federal scholarships initiative and the somewhat vague language that would give state and local officials wide latitude in determining the distribution of the funds between "teachers' salaries, school construction, and any other education purposes."[50] Powell, the group of liberal Democratic senators, and the administration also realized the need to write into the legislation provisions that would generate support among the southern Democrats in both chambers, a difficult strategic proposition and one which the education reformers had not yet figured out. There was much work to do.

The Kennedy administration submitted three draft bills. The first of these was a three-year, $2.3 billion program of grants to public elementary and secondary schools for classroom construction and teachers' salaries. The second was a five-year, $5.6 billion program of federal grants and loans that would benefit higher education through construction and scholarships. The third provided for an unspecified increase in funds allotted for science, mathematics, and foreign language education as part of an extension and expansion of the National Defense Education Act of 1958.[51] At the same time, as part of a developing strategy to gain southern support for the larger education initiatives, the administration proposed a new formula for the distribution of "impacted" school aid for poor school districts. [52] This last initiative placed the administration in a position to offer either a carrot or a stick to recalcitrant southern Democratic or Republican members of Congress. Furthermore, Kennedy tried to avoid the potential roadblocks of antisegregation provisions and aid to church-related educational institutions that had doomed earlier attempts at education aid by publicly excluding those elements up front. Though Kennedy described the package of bills as a "modest program with ambitious goals," the plan actually represented great change in the federal role in the support of education, both in terms of the levels of funding sought and of the new areas of responsibility accepted.

Immediately, however, opponents and proponents of antisegregation and church-school support enmeshed the bill in the exact controversies that the administration had sought to avoid. In March, both House and Senate hearings on the administration's bills attracted a wide variety of interest group leaders representing religious and educational advocacy groups, all of whom engaged in often bitter attacks on the bills and each other. Interest group activities included frequent member contacts, public information campaigns, and a nationwide "write your congressman" campaign begun in Missouri that gained national attention. As Lawrence Wood, vice president of the St. Louis Chamber of Commerce, put it, "There isn't a week that passes that some of our important people here—a vice president of Monsanto Chemical, say, or a top official from Ralston Purina—[don't] pass through Washington on business. When they do, we urge them to drop in on the senators and congressmen . . . and tell them what they think of the education bill."[53] The education bill attracted diverse interests from church groups to labor to business groups and governmental watchdog organizations, all of which seemed to find something they did not like in the aid-to-education proposals.

In light of the diverse and energized opposition that had emerged, the Kennedy administration reversed course and decided on an omnibus strategy, with the goal being to include in the massive legislative proposal something for everyone without completely alienating anyone. Theodore Sorensen, White House special counsel, met with key Democratic senators, including education reformers Pat McNamara (D-MI), Wayne Morse (D-OR), and Joseph Clark (D-PA), in addition to the Senate's Democratic leaders Mansfield and Humphrey. While Morse, the chairman of the subcommittee handling education issues, was noncommittal, the other senators supported the strategy.[54] The relevant Senate and House subcommittees, chaired by Senator Morse and Congresswoman Edith Green (D-OR) of the Special Education Subcommittee of the House Education and Labor Committee, continued the hearings and markup of the newly combined aid package.

At this point, then, the administration initiative, on the House side, was placed firmly in the hands of Edith Green. Colleagues on that subcommittee described Green, a key Oregonian ally of Kennedy in the nomination fight in 1960, as "intelligent, strong-willed, persuasive, and independent." She had a "standoffish" relationship with the full committee chairman, Powell, who was described by those respondents as a "flamboyant" chairman only fairly attentive to his legislative work and "easily bored . . . he needed fireworks to keep him interested." Powell was said to be cordial to members whose views on the issues lined up with his but indifferent to those whose views did not. While Green was not a close ally of Powell, there was no hostility between the two, and their colleagues viewed the working relationship between the two as a "solid" and "professional" one. At this point, Green's educational philosophy was solidly liberal, though this would change in later years, and she was described by one respondent as a "tiger" who took firm control of this initiative.[55] She began from the start to work closely with Larry O'Brien, the head of Kennedy's legislative liaison and a man with a passion for education issues.

Several members of the subcommittee, in addition to Green, were particularly active on the administration's aid program. These active members included the subcommittee's ranking minority member, Peter Frelinghuysen Jr. (R-NJ), Frank Thompson (D-NJ), John Brademas (D-IN), Albert Quie (R-MN), Carlton Sickles (D-MD), and Sam Gibbons

(D-FL). Frelinghuysen had offered an alternative to the administration bill that limited scholarship and teacher salary assistance, and his approach, which had been supported by the Eisenhower administration in the years prior, still had support among many conservatives. Contrary to the common perception that early termers were "to be seen and not heard," Gibbons (who had chaired a Florida state legislature committee on education for many years prior to coming to Congress), Brademas, and Sickles were all early-termers whom Powell relied upon for a variety of legislative purposes.

Furthermore, Powell tended to skip over more senior and likely more conservative members of the full committee when appointing legislative task force chairmanships and distributing whipping responsibilities on the initiatives that he really wanted to see move forward. Also, while the committee had a reputation for persistent ideological party-line splits on its votes on labor issues, the respondents from the 1960s described this distinction as only partially correct. Members of the committee noted that party alone was not a sufficient indicator of who was willing to work with whom within the subcommittee and the larger committee. Instead, coalitions depended upon the issue, and regional, ideological, and personal factors all determined the composition of each issue coalition. Subcommittee minutes indicate that amendments to the administration bill went on outside the executive sessions as well as during them.

In the House, Edith Green became the administration's primary advocate for its education program, though Powell retained the traditional role as spokesman for the legislation originating in his committee. Green met personally and frequently with a variety of Kennedy operatives, including Douglass Cater, serving as a White House policy advisor, and White House legislative liaison Larry O'Brien. A former public school teacher, Green asserted herself within the committee, and despite the media attention on Powell in relation to the administration's initiatives, fellow members on the committee remember Green being "very much in control" with an "unmatched command of the legislation."[56] "She was very loyal to Kennedy, and she was hard working and strong." While Kennedy was far less "hands-on" than Johnson was in his day-to-day legislative operations, there was direct contact between Kennedy and Green on this legislation, reflecting the importance Kennedy placed upon it.

Green's subcommittee demonstrated its support for the administration by adding $200 million to the program before reporting the bill, and the subcommittee changed the state distribution formula in a bid to win greater support among legislators representing populous northeastern states with large Roman Catholic populations.[57] A few days later,

Senate Labor Committee Democrats, in an informal caucus prior to what turned out to be a pro forma closed-door negotiating session, similarly beefed up the funding over what the administration had requested. This move represented a bid to appease legislators from a number of states who were dissatisfied with the distribution formula.[58] The Senate Labor Committee and the House Education and Labor Committee both turned back attempts to add controversial amendments and reported the measures to their respective chambers relatively intact.

At this point, however, significant problems began to emerge. The Senate passed a modified version of the administration's education plan, by a 49–34 vote. However, the bill's Senate sponsors were forced to scale down the funding levels for the program, and they reduced the constraints on states as they would use the aid in an attempt to appease the growing southern Democratic opposition to the measure. Shortly thereafter in the House, an ad hoc coalition of proponents of aid to parochial schools and opponents of any school aid whatsoever together engineered a delay in the floor consideration of the Kennedy education program. Majority Leader McCormack, a Roman Catholic Democrat from Massachusetts, and House Rules Committee chairman Smith, the conservative Virginia Democrat, led these two factions within the House.[59] While the Kennedy administration, in the person of Abraham Ribicoff, Health, Education, and Welfare secretary, backed the McCormack push for passage of loans to private schools concurrent with the larger measure, Speaker Carl Albert demanded that the larger measure be considered on the House floor first. Chairman Powell supported the McCormack request, which would in fact only require a reauthorization of loans already provided for in the National Defense Education Act.

On the other side of the issue, however, was Judge Smith of the Rules Committee. He viewed the McCormack-administration split as an excellent opportunity to thwart education aid altogether. Smith was able to use the temporary support of two northeastern Catholic Democrats with heavily Roman Catholic constituencies, James J. Delaney of Queens (D-NY) and Thomas P. "Tip" O'Neill Jr. of Boston (D-MA), to stall the education measure in the Rules Committee.[60] To add insult to injury, former President Eisenhower weighed in against the measure as well, warning in a letter read by Minority Leader Halleck on the House floor in a televised press conference of a "permanent" and "ultimate . . . federal control of education" if the bill were to be passed.[61] The bill was clearly in danger, and the House Rules Committee effectively killed the bill when it tabled the legislation by an 8–7 vote on July 18. Kennedy was unable to overcome this outcome despite a variety of parliamentary techniques that the administration hoped might remove the Rules Committee as an obstacle to success.[62]

Despite compromises with the Senate, a radical overhaul of the bill in the House, and an intense lobbying effort by the administration, the bill was dead for this session of Congress. A strange and short-lived issue coalition of southern Democratic opponents of aid to parochial schools and Republican and conservative Democratic opponents to education aid of any kind had defeated the measure. In doing so, they had pleased an outspoken coalition of interests that had worked hard to kill the Kennedy legislative effort, among those interests an unusual alliance between public school education groups desiring to maintain the status quo and northeastern proponents seeking aid to parochial schools.

The House leadership gloomily informed the Kennedy administration that prospects for 1962 were grim as well, in light of the strength of the opposition to Kennedy's plan indicated by the surprisingly solid 242–169 final vote against passage. Additionally, the finger pointing for the high-profile failure began, with many House members blaming Secretary Abraham Ribicoff for the legislative setback. Members accused Ribicoff of "too much flip-flopping on strategy," a needless "ruffling (of) the feelings of Speaker Rayburn," and a disrespectful manner of dealing with Congress while "trying to please too many people."[63] The administration was forced to settle for only an extension of existing education programs in 1961.

Kennedy persisted in 1962, however, calling on Congress in his January State of the Union address to approve the aid package it had rejected in 1961. Ribicoff and Powell differed immediately afterward, however, as Powell said there would be no push for the education plan during the second session, and Ribicoff insisted there would be.[64] But Kennedy removed all doubt in his budget message, requesting $5.7 billion in funding for the full slate of education reforms, and Edith Green's Special Education Subcommittee quickly began hearings and markup on HR8900, a bill covering the higher education construction provisions of the larger package. The proposal avoided the problems caused by the federal scholarships initiative by omitting that provision entirely, and it included in it provisions for loans and grants to private institutions as well. A variety of influential higher education groups, including the American Council on Education, the Association of Junior Colleges, the Association of State and Land Grant Colleges, and the State Universities Association, among them representing all of the nation's eighteen hundred accredited colleges, issued a joint statement. In it, they announced that they would be "giving top priority in the current session of Congress to 'the need for academic facilities.'"[65] With the measure enjoying bipartisan support typified by the endorsements of subcommittee members Albert Quie (R-MN) and John Brademas (D-IN) on the House floor, the measure's prospects looked good.

In his education message to Congress on February 6, Kennedy renewed his call for the broader package of education reforms, but privately congressional leaders expressed doubts that it would go forward. The same day, the Senate passed its college construction bill. Included in it were provisions for federal scholarships, thus dimming the prospects for passage of the initiative given the House's past opposition to that type of assistance.[66] Even as the House Rules Committee this time allowed the college construction measure to go to conference, the combined weight of the Senate's scholarships provision and renewed controversy over the allowance of aid to parochial schools doomed the measure in 1962. Chairman Powell of the conference committee was unable and unwilling to remove the federal scholarships and parochial aid provisions in conference.[67] The House killed the conference report by a 214–186 roll call vote. In this vote, 84 mostly southern Democrats joined 130 Republicans to recommit the bill to conference with instructions to strike the student loan provisions, in spite of the conference compromises worked out between Edith Green and Senator Joseph Clark and signed by Republican subcommittee members Goodell and Quie.[68] The National Education Association, the influential public school teachers' union claiming to represent seven hundred thousand teachers, had sent each member a telegram just prior to the vote urging rejection of the measure as a dangerous precedent of aid to private schools. Anthony J. Celebrezze replaced Abraham Ribicoff as secretary of Health, Education, and Welfare in July as Kennedy sought to stem congressional opposition to Ribicoff, but aid to education was dead again in 1962.

Kennedy, his education advisors, Green, Powell, and other congressional education policy leaders had learned some tough lessons about the feasibility of a general aid package in the congressional climate of 1961 and 1962. Kennedy therefore decided upon a new legislative strategy after the general aid approach had failed twice before. Dropping the "across-the-board" approach to elementary and secondary school assistance that had doomed the broader package in 1963, the administration adopted an "urgent need" strategy, requesting aid for elementary and secondary schools, which could demonstrate significant problems such as overcrowding, inadequate fire protection, or other pressing needs. The goal here was to attract the support of conservative Republicans for a "sound fiscal policy," while enlisting the support of "Roman Catholic churchmen, as an equitable solution to the church-state problem." [69] In his education message to Congress of January 29, Kennedy requested total outlays of approximately $5 billion for the program over four years, and he subsequently submitted an omnibus package of legislative proposals, thus completely abandoning the piecemeal approach he had employed the two years before.[70] The substantive proposals remained essentially the same, but the packaging was different.

The decision to present the entire package of proposals to Congress in one bill immediately drew fire from both Powell and Frelinghuysen, the ranking Republican on the Education and Labor Committee, as Anthony Celebrezze, the new secretary of Health, Education, and Welfare, testified before the full House committee. The two ranking members agreed that the bill would have to be broken up into smaller pieces. Testimony in support of the administration approach came from Education Commissioner-designate Francis Keppel, National Education Association vice president Robert Wyatt, and American Council on Education chairman Charles Odegaard, among others. Opponents included Monsignor Frederick Hochwalt of the National Catholic Welfare Conference and Dr. Edgar Fuller of the National Council of Chief State School Officers.[71] Albert Quie (R-MN) asked pointedly of Wyatt why, with the NEA's "reputation for having killed" the 1962 bill, would the NEA support the 1963 measure? Wyatt replied that while the NEA probably would not oppose the measure again, the group might have to rethink its policy stance if college aid were separated from elementary and secondary school aid in the final legislation.[72] With Speaker (and opposing faction leader) McCormack's statement that he thought there were "excellent chances for good progress" on education legislation in the 88th Congress, prospects for at least some portions of the Kennedy plan were looking up.[73]

As concerns over racial and religious provisions mounted again in April and May, Powell, Green, and other committee leaders settled upon a strategy to break the massive omnibus bill into four smaller bills, despite the administration's desire to keep the bill intact. Furthermore, the committee leaders decided to push first on the bill of the four that had the most support and greatest likelihood of passage, the college facilities proposal.[74] Green took firm control of this legislation on behalf of the Kennedy administration, in the recollection of her subcommittee colleagues, and she was variously described as "the mother of the legislation" and "a tiger." She worked tirelessly on the language of the legislation and in performing the member-to-member contacts necessary to ensure success for the proposal.

After being reported out of subcommittee and committee relatively intact, with a provision pointedly prohibiting any use of college construction funds for "sectarian" purposes, the House passed the measure by a 287–113 bipartisan roll call vote on August 14 and sent the measure to the Senate.[75] After the Senate's passage of HR6143 with amendments, the Rules Committee granted a rule by voice vote on October 29, paving the way for a conference with the Senate.[76] Green's subcommittee members were appointed as House conferees. The two sides negotiated the disagreements in conference, and the conference report (H Rept 884) was adopted by a roll call vote of 258–92 on November 6.[77] After the death of Kennedy later that month, the Senate cleared the conference report on December 10 after pressure from President Johnson, and Johnson signed the bill into law shortly thereafter.

A variety of legislative actors with key positions and diverse resources influenced the long struggle to see this initiative become law. Chairman Smith of the Rules Committee and Speaker McCormack were able to dictate the terms and the pace of the legislative battle after forging a strange ad hoc issue coalition of interests that were, in some cases, directly antithetical to one another in their long-term education policy objectives. Furthermore, Powell, Green, Kennedy, and the other persistent actors seeking education reforms had to content themselves with incremental changes far lesser than the radical changes they had pursued at the outset. Finally, those pursuing college aid had to innovate strategically in the packaging of the proposals in order to realize success. In the view of the participants in the process, this legislative achievement came about largely as a result of Edith Green's patience, persistence, and innovation in the face of adversity and opposing interests.

PL88–365: THE URBAN MASS TRANSPORTATION ACT OF 1964

The Urban Mass Transportation Act of 1964 (S6, HR3881) was signed into law by President Johnson on July 9, 1964, after years of debate stretching back at least as far as the Highway Act of 1944. The six-page law authorized $375 million in spending for a three-year program of federal matching grants for state and local mass transportation projects in urban areas, and it indefinitely reauthorized a $50 million fund for low-interest loans to metropolitan agencies to be used for the construction of mass transportation facilities. The law further provided for an emergency program, relocation allowances, and research and demonstration projects, some of which had been provided for originally by the Housing Act of 1961.[78] Finally, the law required as a condition of the aid that the rights of transit workers be protected by "fair and equitable arrangements" in cases where federal assistance was brought to bear.

While the impetus for urban mass transportation aid came primarily from representatives and interest group leaders seeking solutions to problems posed by America's increasing urbanization in the late 1950s and early 1960s, the legislative push was helped along by the obvious and immediate problems in the District of Columbia.

According to respondents who participated in the passage of the legislation, the problems precipitated by poorly run or inadequate private transit companies were continually brought home to the legislators as they tried with some difficulty and aggravation to move about in Washington, D.C. In fact, the Eisenhower administration, which generally sought to keep the government from encroaching upon the private sector, pushed for "a Government corporation to develop an improved mass transportation system in the National Capital metropolitan area" in Eisenhower's Budget Message in 1960.[79] The message made no mention of any other aid for other metropolitan areas. Later in March, the Commerce Department released a seventy-eight-point plan which, despite its generally conservative reliance on private means to alleviate the transportation problems, proposed to make the nation's transportation system more efficient through some public inner-city transit systems.[80]

In May, a group of big city and suburban mayors, including Mayors Wagner of New York City, Tucker of St. Louis, Dilworth of Philadelphia, and Hartsfield of Atlanta, representing the American Municipal Association, testified before the Senate and House Banking Committees' housing subcommittees. The mayors sought support for a $100 million federal loan fund for urban mass transit systems, claiming that even aid at that level would leave the major cities about $400 million short of their needs.[81] Similar delegations of transit aid supporters including railroad interests and groups of governors testified as well. Key supporters in the Senate included John Sparkman (D-AL), the chairman of the Housing Subcommittee, and Senator Harrison Williams (D-NJ), the sponsor of the proposal. In the House, Albert Rains (D-AL) sponsored the companion legislation. In both chambers, omnibus housing bills dominated the housing subcommittees' 1960 calendars, but the Senate completed a draft of the transit system aid legislation as well.[82] On June 14, the Senate Banking Committee approved the omnibus housing measure, the Williams transit plan, and two other measures, sending them to the Senate floor. The Senate passed the transit aid measure by voice vote on June 27, sending S3278 to the House.

As election-year considerations began to dominate congressional politics, each party included language on mass transportation policy in its platform. The Democratic platform stated that the Democrats would "expand Federal programs to aid urban communities to clear their slums, dispose of their sewage, educate their children, transport suburban commuters to and from their jobs, and combat juvenile delinquency."[83] The Republican platform, on the contrary, pledged to aid small business and the economy in part "by keeping the Federal Government from unjustly competing with private enterprise . . .

(thus allowing) continued improvement of our vital transportation network."[84] Neither chamber got any further with the transit initiatives in 1960.

In early January of 1961, a special Senate task force completed a massive nine-hundred-page, two-year study of the nation's transportation problems.[85] The study cost more than $400 thousand to complete and was commissioned by the Senate Interstate Commerce Committee, and it proposed wholesale changes in the transportation systems and their regulation in America. This report would eventually lead to legislation providing for nationalized rail services, tighter regulation of airlines, and other systemic changes. The report called for "direct Federal loans for capital improvement of railroad commuter services" as well. On January 11, Senator Harrison Williams of New Jersey again introduced his bill calling for federal aid to mass transportation facilities. Similarly, the president commissioned a study of the housing and urban issues. As part of the task force's eighty-seven-page findings, task force chairman Joseph McMurray, a former New York State Housing Commissioner and president of Queens Community College, urged the government to provide "an immediate program for planning grants and $100 million for public facility loans to improve mass transit systems."[86]

In March of 1961, the Senate Banking Committee's Housing Subcommittee opened hearings on the Williams bill, which called for $325 million in aid to transit systems. Williams's initiative had strong evidence of bipartisan support in the form of eighteen cosponsors, six of whom were Republicans, and Williams also enjoyed the support of his subcommittee chairman, John J. Sparkman of Alabama.[87] But in the view of the House members and staff involved in the eventual passage of this legislation, it was not party or regional hostility that was the major obstacle to moving the legislation forward, but rather a general indifference on the part of most members. Respondents noted that many members represented districts or states that needed no mass transit systems, or they already had effective privately run systems in place. The Senate hearings attracted a wide variety of supporters of the legislation, including railroad industry chairmen, labor leaders, and the governors of Pennsylvania, California, and Massachusetts. Only the Chamber of Commerce and a few other business groups expressed opposition on the grounds of the bill's anticipated encroachment upon private businesses.[88] Senator Williams was optimistic about the prospects for the passage of both of his transit initiatives, the $325 million transit aid bill and an additional $100 million authorization for mass transit planning and demonstration projects included in the omnibus housing bill, and he said so publicly.[89]

At this point, however, the focus of the attention surrounding the Senate-passed and House-stalled omnibus housing measure shifted to its mass transit provisions. As the Kennedy administration sought to facilitate the passage of the housing bill in the House, its strategy was to sacrifice any prospects for mass transit spending beyond the $100 million called for in the housing measure rather than jeopardize passage of the larger measure. So while the Kennedy compromise would seek to preserve the planning and demonstration project funding, the Williams measure calling for federal funding beyond that earmarked $100 million would be opposed by the administration, at least for 1961, in the interests of passing the omnibus housing measure. Kennedy stated, "Non-federal government financing will have to provide the preponderant share of the new capital funds needed for mass transportation, and federal assistance should encourage and supplement rather than take the place of such investment." [90] Kennedy sent a letter to Speaker Rayburn asking that any consideration of larger mass transit aid be held off until the "results of (an) Executive Branch study" on the matter were received by the administration. Only last minute maneuvering and compromise between Senator Sparkman and the chairman of the House housing subcommittee, Albert Rains (D-AL), saved $75 million in transit project and demonstration aid in Congress in the omnibus housing bill.[91] The Williams proposal was dead for 1961.

The Kennedy administration would get on board in 1962, though not quite to the degree desired by the rail industry, the American Municipal Association (representing 13,500 municipalities), and other key proponents of transit aid. Deputy Special Counsel Myer Feldman, the top Kennedy aide on transportation policy, expressed the administration's concern over the plight of failing railroads in New York, New Haven, and Hartford. However, the eventual $100 million request made in the president's budget message for 1963 was a far cry from the five-year $1.7 billion program sought by the rail industry and the municipalities.[92] Furthermore, anticipating Kennedy initiatives in the area of transportation industry policy, the Senate Commerce Committee had done nothing to date with its expensive and extensive special study, commissioned in 1958 and completed just prior to Kennedy's inauguration, which proposed regulatory and grant and loan policy changes. Simultaneously, railroad executives began to push for permission to consolidate or cease operations that were money-losers, which would have adverse consequences for urban and suburban commuters.[93]

Proponents of large-scale transit aid were generally cheered, however, by the Kennedy transportation plan, issued in a presidential message to Congress on April 5, 1962. The plan emphasized transportation industry self-help in the short term but broadly outlined future initiatives for loans and grants to facilitate the development of efficient urban and suburban mass transportation systems.[94] Reversing course from his statement of the year before, Kennedy requested $500 million over a three-year period, $100 million of which he had requested in the 1963 budget message. Kennedy asserted, "Only a program that offers substantial support and continuity of Federal participation can induce our urban regions to organize appropriate administrative arrangements and to meet their share of the costs of fully balanced transportation systems."[95] Kennedy would meet the municipalities and the rail industry halfway. An ad hoc issue coalition of suburban Republican and urban Democratic supporters predicted that the requested measure would be passed quickly.[96] With nearly unanimous support expressed in House and Senate hearings from the administration, rail industry executives, labor officials, and state and local executives, the transit aid initiative seemed to be fast-tracked for success.

The measure moved quickly through the Senate Banking Committee, gaining the contract authority that would protect the aid from future cuts and an additional $300 million in loan funding through the stewardship of sponsor Williams of New Jersey.[97] While not providing for the contract authority or the additional $300 million in loan aid, the House Transit Subcommittee, chaired by Abraham Multer (D-NY) of Brooklyn, quickly reported the bill as well. The full committee reported the measure just as expeditiously, warning in a public statement that "urban mass transportation was deteriorating in many places just when the need was beginning to spiral."[98] The refusal of the House Appropriations Committee to appropriate $100 million prior to a completed authorization and the Rules Committee's delay in giving the bill a rule for the floor pending Senate action on the companion bill seemed to be only temporary and minor impediments to transit aid success.

However, the Rules Committee impediment would prove fatal to transit aid in 1962. The mass transportation bill and twenty-one other measures were held up in the newly (January 1961) expanded Rules Committee, with few of the bills given any chance of emerging in the 1962 session.[99] What occurred next was viewed by several respondents as a blatant bid by Rules chairman Howard Smith (D-VA) to force the administration and the House Democratic leadership to "unpack" the Rules Committee in the next session. Smith orchestrated a legislative logjam despite the recent addition of two members chosen for their support of the administration program. On September 19, in an attempt to circumvent the Rules Committee, "a group of House Democratic liberals" led by John Blatnik (D-MN) of the Democratic Study Group and Carl Perkins (D-KY) tried to use the Calendar Wednesday procedures to bring up legislation of interest to each. Smith and other Democrats and Republicans from the Rules Committee defeated the effort through a combination of "procedural roll-calls, quorum calls, and demands that the House Clerk read the *Journal* from the previous day." [100] Transit aid was dead again in 1962.

The growing and broad-based support for the mass transportation initiative and the attention it had garnered in the Smith logjam boded well for the plan's passage in 1963. As one of ten bills that had been identified by the congressional Democratic leaders, unsuccessfully, for action prior to adjournment of the 88th Congress, hopes were high on the part of the bill's supporters that 1963 would be the year for passage.[101] Once again, Senator Harrison Williams Jr. of New Jersey sponsored the measure in the Senate. This time, he proposed a $500 million plan of grants and loans to be authorized over the next three fiscal years, while leaving the remainder of the proposal otherwise in the same form as the years prior. For this iteration, Williams was able to attract twenty cosponsors, and the president's State of the Union address and his Budget Message firmly reinforced the administration's backing of the measure.[102] Kennedy followed up the messages with a draft proposal for a $500 million program, subsequently sponsored by Williams in the Senate and Albert Rains (D-AL) in the House. Both chambers scheduled hearings, and the process was underway again.

However, even as the same industry and state and local governmental witnesses testified in favor of the measure in each chamber, in some cases for the third or fourth time, the aid package began to run into unexpected opposition in the Senate. As the debate had progressed over the years, the bill had acquired a reputation (perhaps justifiably) as a "big city" bill with nothing in it for rural areas or self-sufficient smaller communities. With federal budgetary problems and this perceived lack of a broad distribution of the program's benefits in mind, normally loyal supporters of the administration such as Senator Edmund Muskie (D-ME) and others began to withdraw their support for the legislation.[103] Support and opposition for the measure did not fall along party lines but instead generally depended on whether or not a member's constituents stood to gain from the measure or not. For example, Senator Wallace Bennett (R-UT), the ranking minority member of the Senate Banking Committee, led the Republican opposition to what he described as a "big city giveaway." At the same time, the assistant minority leader, Thomas Kuchel (R-CA), supported the measure, as did Republican senators from New York, New Jersey, Massachusetts, Pennsylvania, and Maryland. Minority Leader Dirksen (R-IL) opposed the measure in spite of pressure from civic organizations in Chicago.

Concurrently, Andrew Biemiller, the chief legislative representative of the AFL-CIO, sent a letter to all senators demanding amendments in the legislation intended to protect railroad employees similar to what the House had included in its version.[104] Williams and subcommittee chairman Sparkman eventually negotiated compromise provisions to satisfy labor demands, and after a $125 million cut of the bill's level of funding to $375 million, they secured Senate passage by a 52–41 vote.[105] Passage was helped along by newly elected Senator Abraham Ribicoff (D-CT). Just prior to the vote on the Senate floor, Ribicoff pointedly asked, "If votes are withheld by states that have little or no present need for Federal funds for commuters, where do these states expect to find support for their own urgent needs?"[106] The House Banking and Currency Committee followed suit on April 9, reporting HR3881. This bill was an amendment in the nature of a substitute for S6, differing from the Senate version primarily by the inclusion of the $125 million cut in negotiations with the Senate.

As it appeared to transportation industry observers that prospects for passage of the urban mass transportation proposals were more favorable than they had been to date, railroad industry rivals intensified their lobbying efforts. *Congressional Quarterly Weekly Report* described a wide array of "pressure groups" engaged intensely in the legislative proceedings, with highway user groups and the automotive industry on one side and "manufacturers of rail transit equipment and other transit enthusiasts" on the other.[107] The intensity of the interest group fight, according to *Congressional Quarterly* observers, had caused enough members "to shy away from the president's proposals to provide federal aid for urban public transportation systems" that those proposals and "the drive for a rail transit system in Washington" had stalled completely.[108]

Diverse interests, and coalitions of interest groups, worked hard to shape the legislative outcome. Among the industries and other interests visiting House and Senate offices during this period were automobile manufacturers, rubber producers, trucking interests, highway officials, road builders, bus company operators, asphalt producers, cement producers, railroad equipment manufacturers, municipal and civic action groups, and other private, industry, and local government groups. The groups operated singly and in ad hoc groupings, depending on the relationships between industry and interest. But without question, interest groups encouraged enough members to avoid the fight that the mass transit initiative stalled again in 1963, despite its seemingly solid glide path toward success. The urban mass transit bill once again remained in the Rules Committee as the session ended.

In his first State of the Union address, President Lyndon Johnson stated, "We must help obtain more modern mass transit within our communities as well as low-cost transportation between them."[109] A close friend of Senator Harrison Williams, Johnson had indicated, according to White House aides, that if prospects for the measure seemed poor, he would consider wrapping the mass transit aid in the upcoming omnibus housing bill in order to help his friend. Other observers characterized Johnson's advocacy of the issue as a bid to gain support among the northeastern states, but regardless of motive, Johnson was squarely on board with the mass transit initiative. Chairman Wright Patman (D-TX) of the Banking Committee, who had Johnson assigned to him as a page in the Texas legislature many years before, could be counted on by Johnson to support him fully. Patman, described by some as a "legislative tyrant," had votes in his pocket.

The administration and congressional supporters immediately began to press again for passage. Dr. Robert Weaver, administrator of the Housing and Home Finance Agency, went public with an information campaign intended to make the case that highway interests and rail interests were not mutually exclusive.[110] Johnson listed the mass transit initiative first on his list of transportation and technology proposals in his Economic Report on the Nation, and he requested $500 million for the program in his Budget Message.[111] House members and House staffers recollected that Johnson notified members of his interest in this legislation through personal contacts that included White House invitations, telephone calls, and personal notes. Lobby organizations on both sides of the issue renewed their member contacts on the proposal in a thorough campaign in the House. Speaker McCormack's whip count indicated that there was enough support to pass the bill, as about forty Republicans had lined up in support of the measure, and the Rules Committee was directed to issue a rule for floor consideration of the measure.[112] Two administration-backed measures, mass transit aid and a raise for federal employees, were cleared on May 20, and House Housing Subcommittee chairman and floor manager Albert Rains moved to get the measure to the floor just after Memorial Day.[113]

Finally, on June 25, after repeated floor maneuvers by Rains, the House passed a modified, $375 million version of the administration-backed aid plan, by a 212–189 vote.[114] It was a hard-fought Johnson victory. Many observers and participants attributed the passage of the legislation in the House to Johnson and Rains, both southern Democrats, who had attracted the support of thirty-four southern Democrats by making the bill seem less of a "big city" proposal. In addition, thirty-nine Republicans delivered as promised, despite the Republican Policy Committee's stance of "unalterable opposition" on the bill. Others attributed some of the credit for the legislative victory to the hard work in drafting, negotiation, and compromise carried out by Rains' trusted staffer, John Barriere. Rains had sponsored amendments on the House floor that broadened employee protection from aid encroachment, reduced the funding level to $375 million, and limited the government's ability to take over even failing private transit companies, and those measures had provided the final impetus needed to secure the victory.[115] One of his peers on the subcommittee said, "Albert Rains, a soft-spoken liberal, was a magician in his ability to work with recalcitrant southern-ers."

Williams and Rains began preparing for the likely conference that they would lead. In a strategy session prior to the actual conference, however, Rains convinced Williams that any attempts to reinstate the funding cut in the House would lead to rejection of the conference report in the House. In convincing Williams of this likelihood prior to the conference itself, Rains avoided the most likely source of major controversy in the negotiations. As is often the case, this negotiation and other key compromises took place outside of the formal conference itself. Deciding to take the bird in hand, Williams and the Senate Democratic leadership then adopted the House-passed version and sent the measure to the president by a roll call vote of 47–36 on June 30.[116] Johnson signed the bill on July 9, 1964.

The key players who determined the shape and the timing of this legislative outcome included two presidents, a multitude of intensely energized interest groups, and a handful of congressional actors. The critical elements of this legislative success included Senator Harrison Williams Jr.'s patience and persistence, Representative Albert Rains's mastery of the legislative process and his skills in building consensus, staffer Barriere's coordination of the legislative effort, and President Johnson's similar skills in personal lobbying. In the several years between Williams's first attempt at aid to mass transportation and his realization of success, it was necessary for the proponents of the legislation to innovate, persist, and compromise. They constructed an issue coalition of members from urban and suburban districts as well as sufficient peripheral support to overcome first indifference and then outright hostility among the members of Congress to see the transit aid materialize. Until all of those elements of success were assembled, it would not happen.

LEGISLATING IN THE 1960S

The portrait of legislating in the 1960s that emerges from the cases is a personal one. In each case, the legislative champions realized policy success after persistently working through opposition ranging from ideologically driven adversaries to organized interests to their colleagues' indifference, among other obstacles. These legislative leaders used hearings, floor debates, various packaging strategies, and procedural innovations to advertise and advance their initiatives, and each relied upon the administration's draft legislation, with its implicit presidential support, as the vehicle to carry their policy goals. But in constructing the issue coalitions that enabled them to eventually achieve policy success, these leaders relied heavily upon interpersonal relationships and personal alliances as the glue that held together those coalitions, often starting with bipartisan relationships forged within their subcommittees. Members in the 1960s took advantage of abundant social opportunities as legislative business opportunities. Agents had to fight the legislative fight in a fluid environment, as they had to contend with both external events that could arbitrarily stymie their efforts as well as procedural obstacles thrown in their way by their opponents.

In the 1960s, legislative success was predicated upon persistent member-to-member contacts, a mastery of the issue, an effective performance during the hearings process and floor debates, presidential support and direction, and the nonopposition (at least) of the chamber and key committee leadership. Without question, doing the homework on the issues mattered. The importance of interest groups in the process varied based upon the issue and the leverage of the groups themselves, and we get the sense that these groups could also "cancel each other out" when lined up on opposite sides of an issue. Similarly, it is interesting to note that none of the respondents to this study from this era couched his or her voting commitments in terms of party affiliation. Finally, it is clear from the cases and the respondents that legislators' personal and often arbitrary motives and alliances consistently and directly influenced the realization of legislative success in the 1960s.

CHAPTER 4

Legislative Histories: The 1990s

The House is more partisan today in the sense that the party machinery is more complex. 'Party cohesion out of necessity' is probably a better way of putting it. It's ironic, since the parties are a lot weaker at the grass roots now.

—House member from the 1990s

PL103–87: THE FOREIGN OPERATIONS APPROPRIATION FOR FY 1994

President Clinton signed the Foreign Operations Appropriation for fiscal year 1994 (HR2295) into law on September 30, 1993, with $2.5 billion of the $14.6 billion foreign operations budget going to the former Soviet Union. In 1993, foreign aid was as unpopular as ever, and the large budget deficit exacerbated the political problem for its proponents. To meet the foreign aid budgetary goals in this difficult political climate, legislators had to use $1.6 billion from unexpended fiscal 1993 foreign aid and defense funds to complement $13 billion in newly appropriated money.[1] The bulk of the appropriated aid was earmarked for a handful of recipients, among them Israel (approximately $3 billion), Egypt ($2.1 billion), the Commonwealth of Independent States ($2.5 billion), and international financial institutions ($1.8 billion). The five-page blueprint was passed in a time of great civil and political unrest in Russia that gave the CIS aid provisions the highest profile of the issues addressed in the enactment of the legislation.

The initiative for the foreign operations appropriation for fiscal year 1994 came, like most appropriations, from a combination of appropriations cycle expectations, pressing current foreign policy objectives, past commitments made, international political events, and the political and policy objectives of the legislators involved. In the case of the foreign operations appropriation for fiscal 1994, and similar to the fiscal year

1963 appropriation described in Chapter 3 and other years, the foreign aid bill had relatively few natural constituents. As such, this appropriation attracted the usual number of opponents, legislators who found it easy to denounce foreign aid in promoting their own reputations for "fiscal responsibility" regardless of the fact that this appropriation represented less than 1 percent of the total budget. Furthermore, foreign aid's recent policy history had been particularly bleak. Prior to the foreign aid appropriation process for 1993, Patrick Buchanan had loudly and frequently attacked foreign aid in 1992 in his unsuccessful bid for the Republican presidential nomination. His attacks included one highly publicized episode in which he had loudly declared to the national media in a congressional hallway that foreign aid was a "Washington insider deal to shovel $25 billion out to the Third World."[2] Lee Hamilton (D-IN) pointed out that anti-aid sentiment wasn't new by any means, but Buchanan's rant resonated in that election year and subsequently in 1993 as many Americans perceived the aid to be contrary to their own domestic interests.

With this in mind, it was unlikely that new monies would be voted to foreign aid in 1992, and with the desire to assist the newly independent Russian republics, some countries would likely emerge as losers in the distribution of aid in 1992 and 1993. The 1992 foreign aid appropriations process, which involved both the leftover appropriation for the ongoing 1992 fiscal year as well as aid for fiscal 1993, first centered on the issue of loan guarantees to Israel and then aid to bolster Boris Yeltsin's Russian government. Given the public's general disinterest in seeing the Israeli loan guarantees granted (only 13 percent of those surveyed supported giving the guarantees outright), President Bush and Secretary of State James Baker felt free to use the $10 billion credits as leverage in their relations with the Shamir government.[3]

In any event, Bush had a clear incentive to downplay the whole foreign aid issue in light of his domestic political difficulties with Buchanan's "America First" campaign. These considerations, coupled with the general unwillingness of members of Congress to rally around foreign expenditures of any sort in an election year given record budget deficits, severely limited the administration's legislative options. It was likely that foreign aid for fiscal 1992, the current year, would be in the form of either an extension of the five-month continuing resolution passed the previous October or as provisions tucked into a supplemental appropriation at the end of the 1992 fiscal year. Furthermore, allegations of an obscene reference to Jews by Secretary Baker and a breakdown in Senate negotiations over the aid to Israel only reinforced those prospects. Legislators were faced with a March 31 deadline, after which U.S. aid missions and other international relief efforts would shut down.

House Foreign Operations Subcommittee chairman David Obey (D-WI) lashed out angrily at certain senators for being "so damned greedy" for Israel that they would jeopardize everything. [4] Other members blamed Congress' inability to pass a new foreign aid measure on factors such as the administration's "domestic policy vacuum," the check-bouncing scandal in the House, and fear of a recorded vote on foreign aid in an election year.

Just as these factors had combined to make the passage of a foreign aid measure seemingly difficult, if not impossible, Yeltsin's situation in Russia was deteriorating further. On March 29, Defense Secretary Richard Cheney announced on NBC's "Meet the Press" that the administration would propose and pursue a comprehensive aid package for the former Soviet Union, in light of Yeltsin's difficulties. [5] It was not coincidence that the Bush administration initiative was announced just after the Buchanan challenge had been turned back and at the same time Arkansas Governor Bill Clinton had emerged as Bush's likely November challenger. Clinton had announced plans to address the need for aid to Russia in a speech in the coming week, and former President Nixon had recently criticized Bush for not acting quickly enough.

With the political cover given them by Bush, Senate and House Democratic leaders quickly pledged to work with the administration on the $24 billion plan of aid to the Russians. [6] Congress gave the administration a $14.6 billion stopgap foreign aid continuing resolution (H J Res 456) on April 1, and it was signed by Bush that same day. Officials from a variety of American Jewish organizations, fearing another Bush administration showdown over loan guarantees, were said to have lobbied Senator Dennis DeConcini (D-AZ) and other supporters of Israel in the House and Senate to prevent the inclusion of the credits in the stopgap measure. These proponents feared Bush's stated intention of vetoing any legislation providing for loan guarantees without territorial settlement limitations. Floor debate on the measure was subdued and perfunctory as few members were willing support the measure though final passage was by a 275–131 vote in the House and a 99–1 vote (Robert Byrd, D-WV was the only nay) in the Senate. [7] The measure provided the balance of funding necessary to operate American foreign aid concerns through the end of the 1992 fiscal year. Attention within the State Department and among foreign aid proponents then quickly turned to the fiscal year 1993 authorizing and appropriating legislation, which had within it $5 billion that the Bush administration had pledged as part of the larger $24 billion package put forth by the Western allies.

With the elections only a few short months away, a wide variety of both generally antiforeign aid legislators and single-issue advocates attacked the authorizing bill, characterized by Gerald Seib as "broad and vague."[8] House Democratic Whip David Bonior (D-MI) mounted a high-profile Buchanan-esque campaign to demand "jobs for Americans . . . first." Conservatives insisted on a variety of conditions for aid, including the return of defector and accused spy Edward Lee Howard, increased Japanese aid to the former Soviet Union, redress of grievances against the Russians for treaty violations, and a whole host of others. All of this went on despite the fact that there were virtually no new direct aid handouts being considered. House Speaker Thomas Foley (D-WA) and Senate Majority Leader George Mitchell (D-ME) avoided linkage of the foreign aid bill with any domestic issues, even as Bonior and others pushed for this strategy. Secretary Baker pleaded with the House Foreign Affairs Committee to prevent this linkage, and its second-ranking Democrat, Lee Hamilton of Indiana, indicated that he concurred with Baker on the issue.[9] It seemed likely that the administration would eventually get most of what it wanted in the foreign aid package, despite the usual problems in even passing any authorizing legislation.

However, on June 25, the House voted a much smaller appropriation, passing a $13.8 billion measure by a solid bipartisan vote of 297–124.[10] In seeking election-year support for a generally unpopular measure, subcommittee chairman Obey had gone along with cuts in a variety of initiatives at each level of consideration so that members could claim to have voted for foreign aid cuts at every turn. Furthermore, Obey had reminded members repeatedly that regardless of cuts in foreign spending, those reductions could not be used to offset domestic spending under the terms of the 1990 budget agreement. On October 6, after House and Senate conference negotiations, and after the Rabin coalition had taken control of the Israeli government, the House approved by a 312–105 vote an amended fiscal 1993 appropriation. This sum included $10 billion in additional Israeli loan guarantees on top of the original amount, and the Senate passed the same measure hours later by voice vote.[11] The tortuous efforts to enact foreign aid for 1992 were complete.

After Bill Clinton was elected and the 103rd Congress convened, both the foreign aid authorizers and appropriators began the preliminary work on the fiscal year 1994 foreign operations legislation. David Obey (D-WI), House Appropriations Foreign Operations Subcommittee chairman, with a reputation as something of a populist among his colleagues, hoped to avoid the bitter partisan fights of the previous Congress by emphasizing bipartisanship from the beginning of the drafting process. The crafting of the draft legislation got underway after frequent meetings among state, treasury, and congressional staffers. Soon thereafter, the Japanese government signaled in March its willingness to provide a greater sum of aid to the former Soviet Union. The Clinton administration then announced that it was considering asking Congress for approximately $1 billion over the $700 million in aid to Russia already projected in the working fiscal year 1994 foreign aid budget.[12] Clinton announced his intentions just prior to his trip to Vancouver, British Columbia, which was to be his first foreign trip as president. On that trip, he hoped to begin to reverse the lack of support for increased foreign aid among the public, who opposed foreign aid by a 75 percent count in the most recent polls.[13]

In April, the G-7 nations' foreign ministers met in Tokyo, emerging with a $28.4 billion plan to aid the former Soviet Union, and Secretary of State Warren Christopher immediately sought to head off likely criticisms. He asserted, "The U.S. effort is in no way a program of charity. The stakes couldn't be any higher for the American people."[14] The congressional leadership and many rank and file members were unconvinced, however, particularly given the nation's continuing deficit woes. Even with public support running higher, with 40 percent of those polled supporting aid to Russia by late April, the Russian aid package had muddied the water for other major administration initiatives, including health care and the other foreign aid programs.[15] Office of Management and Budget Director Leon Panetta expressed concerns that "political reality" was making it unlikely that aid to Egypt and Israel could be reduced. He felt that given the unwillingness on the part of the congressional leadership to cut domestic spending to pay for aid to Russia, there was nowhere to get the money to pay for the package to which the administration had committed.[16] Congressional leaders began talking of a strategy in which they would link a jobs bill and the Russian aid proposals, in order to soften the public consequences of deficit spending for Russian aid.[17] With joint opposition from Obey in the House and Foreign Operations chairman Patrick Leahy (D-VT) in the Senate, however, that strategy was abandoned.

Tapping into nearly 1 billion dollars of unspent defense funding from fiscal 1993, Obey was able to deliver on a complex administration request for $1.8 billion in aid to the CIS and the balance of $13 billion in other aid for fiscal 1994.[18] In a single voice vote, the House Foreign Operation Appropriations Subcommittee cut $1.2 billion from the administration request for fiscal 1994 and $185 million from previously appropriated funds from fiscal 1993. Obey was the central figure in the negotiations, which included Panetta (a personal friend of Obey), CIS ambassador Strobe Talbott, and Defense Appropriations Subcommittee chairman John P. Murtha (D-PA), among other key administration, executive agency, and congressional officials.

While Talbott was the administration's chief negotiator on the CIS aid package, most observers gave credit to Obey for the success of the plan. Talbott gave "an unusual briefing for the subcommittee before markup, . . . (providing) the general outline of the aid program" in order to allay the concerns of subcommittee members who had criticized aid in the past as unfocused and poorly utilized.[19] While Sonny Callahan (R-AL) remained the most vocal opponent of the aid, many observers believed that his main goal was to get on the public record with his opposition, rather than to change the opinions of fellow subcommittee members. Callahan was described as often being at odds with the ranking subcommittee Republican, Robert L. Livingston (R-LA). The early and frequent efforts Obey had made to include Livingston in the drafting of the legislation paid off, as Livingston supported the compromise solution. The bipartisanship begun in the House subcommittee would stand the bill in good stead as it made its way to enactment.

A part of Obey's restructuring of the aid plan was to increase the administration's flexibility in distributing the aid by eliminating earmarks, the practice of specifying the exact levels of aid going to a particular country or program in the appropriating legislation.[20] Nita Lowey (D-NY), an engaged subcommittee member and committed supporter of Israel, agreed to the elimination of the provisions after "tacit" assurances from Secretary of State Warren Christopher that the level of aid to Israel would not be decreased in fiscal 1994. Lowey was also pleased by language in the bill that mandated the payment of the $3 billion aid to Israel in a lump sum at the beginning of the fiscal year, thus allowing the assisted country to earn interest income on the aid.[21] As the negotiators reached a working agreement, staff participants in the process noted that the relationship between Livingston and Obey had been the key to success in subcommittee. They pointed to a trip made by the two legislators to Russia, arranged by the House leadership, during which Obey and Livingston saw things that cemented their support for Russian aid as a primary reason for that positive personal and professional relationship.

On June 10, by voice vote, the full House Appropriations Committee approved the subcommittee measure (HR2295). Respondents recollected little involvement on the part of the full committee chairman, William Natcher (D-KY), but this was not unusual, as Natcher normally gave a great deal of autonomy to each of his subcommittee chairs. Obey and Livingston joined forces in advocating the measure, and the House responded with a rare-enough bipartisan victory for the Clinton administration, approving the package of foreign aid appropriations, including the $2.5 billion in assistance to the CIS, by a 289–140 vote.[22] The most prominent opposition came from the Congressional Black Caucus, which opposed the legislation on the grounds that the funds made available to Russia could have replaced funds cut from the treatment of AIDS patients and recipients in the Head Start program. Callahan and John Kasich (R-OH) each attempted floor amendments intended to reduce the foreign aid expenditures further, but both fell short. Citing the European Bank of Reconstruction's marble floors paid for by earlier American aid and first-class air fares enjoyed by the bank's executives, Kasich was nearly successful in denying $55.8 million in callable aid to the World Bank, losing narrowly on a 215–211 roll call vote.[23] The Senate followed suit by an 88–10 count on September 23, and conferees were appointed to work out a compromise on differences between the two versions.[24]

Unlike previous years, the conference went smoothly and was completed within four hours. Despite there being over one hundred differences in the two bills, the primary substance of the conference debate was over earmarks. Senator Mitch McConnell (R-KY), the ranking Republican on the Senate's Foreign Operations Subcommittee, argued particularly strenuously and at length over the $300 million earmark for the Ukraine. The House and Senate staffers, all of whom had been working nearly around-the-clock for days on end in order to meet the September 30 deadline, had negotiated the vast majority of the "second-tier" issues paving the way for the relatively smooth conference. The House adopted the conference report (H Rept 103–267) by a 321–108 count, and after resolving a parliamentary technicality, the Senate approved the measure with little debate by an 88–11 count. President Clinton signed the measure into law on September 30.

Legislative success, on the foreign operations appropriation law for fiscal year 1994, came primarily as a result of Representative David Obey's deft management of the legislation, his bipartisan inclusion of Robert Livingston in the process, and the administration's efforts on the part of their foreign policy centerpiece. In spite of the usual and incessant denunciations of foreign aid by every legislator with a mind to rail against either "fiscal irresponsibility" or "helping Russians before Americans," Obey and Livingston together were able to maintain the administration program relatively intact except as they saw fit to alter it. The two legislators brought to bear a number of resources in realizing this success, among them the powers of their positions in the relevant subcommittee and an issue coalition encompassing enough legislators within the subcommittee to deliver the legislation. Finally, the two willful agents were able to use the September 30 deadline and the relative autonomy afforded them by the chamber leaders to their advantage as they pursued and achieved legislative success on their own terms. The genuine bipartisan cooperation early in the process between these two legislators provided the momentum they needed to move this traditionally unpopular legislation.

PL103–204: THRIFT DEPOSITOR
PROTECTION ACT OF 1993

The forty-eight pages of the Thrift Depositor Protection Act of 1993 (S714) provided $18.3 billion in closeout funding for the Resolution Trust Corporation (RTC) and was signed into law by President Clinton on December 17, 1993.[25] The final sum appropriated represented only a fraction of the $45 billion requested by Treasury Secretary Lloyd Bentsen on behalf of the Clinton administration eight months before. The 1993 close-out funding was the fourth outlay given to the agency to clean up the thrift mess, though Congress had found the appropriation so unappealing that members had not given additional funds to the agency in almost two years. The law required the RTC to close down no later than the end of calendar year 1995. The law also specified that any remaining assets were then to be turned over to the thrift industry's new deposit insurance fund, the Savings Association Insurance Fund (SAIF). Since the RTC had not received additional funds in the past two years, it had been able to take over failed and failing thrifts, but it had not been able to pay off depositors or sell their assets.

Every respondent who participated in the passage of this legislation, when asked where the initiative for the law came from, responded that it was just an ugly job that had to be done. Given that the federal government had insured the thrift deposits, the members of the House realized that in some form or another they would have to honor the obligations, however politically unpalatable and unrewarding that prospect might be. The final closeout funding legislation was first introduced in 1992, after Treasury Secretary Nicholas Brady and RTC Chief Executive Albert Casey both wrote the House Banking Committee's Financial Institutions Subcommittee requesting funds to keep the RTC operational. Brady requested $55 billion to keep the agency running, without specifying that this sum would close out the funding. The subcommittee instead agreed to $25 billion in additional funds on February 27, after receiving a letter from Casey stating that the lesser sum would keep the agency afloat until April 1, 1993.[26]

While some administration officials were irritated, believing the subcommittee had been on the verge of authorizing the full amount before Casey's letter, respondents said that this was just another example of the usual "high-ball, low-ball" game played by the executive and legislative branches on a variety of funding issues. In the words of one subcommittee member, "It was expected that the administration and the executive agencies would shoot us a figure that was too high. They didn't expect to get everything they asked for." Speaker Foley and some others supported an open-ended approach, with the goal being to reduce the number of appropriations that would be necessary to finish the job. However, the recent General Accounting Office's scathing report of mismanagement at the RTC and the unwillingness of subcommittee members to write a "blank check" meant that this would not happen.

On March 12, the House Banking Committee approved HR4241, which would authorize the $25 billion in new RTC funding and reauthorize the use of $17 billion in unused funds. The only major change from the subcommittee's version was a removal of the April 1, 1993, deadline for the use of the money. With Banking Committee chairman Henry Gonzalez (D-TX) and ranking minority member Chalmers Wylie (R-OH) standing together in opposition to any amendments, the committee voted 34–11 to close off debate before any of nine amendments drafted by other committee members could be offered during the quick one-hour markup session.[27] Both Democratic and Republican House leaders had stated their desire to avoid any fractious debate over RTC funding in the election year, and Gonzalez and Wylie aimed to deliver.

Public Citizen's Congress Watch, a public interest advocacy group founded by Ralph Nader, hammered the RTC for mismanagement and Congress for "contradictory congressional mandates" in a report it issued at the same time the committee was acting.[28] Brushing aside the criticism, on March 26 the Senate approved the next installment of funding for the RTC by a 52–42 vote. With the RTC funding about to expire on April 1, there was some hope that the business would be completed prior to the deadline. However, this was not to be, as an "election-wary" House killed the funding bill altogether by a wide margin. In a vote of 298–125 against the measure, the House rank and file thwarted the objectives of the Bush administration and a bipartisan effort by the House leadership to see the legislation pass.[29] Legislators blamed the bill's floor defeat on a number of factors, including weak administration lobbying efforts, persuasive floor arguments questioning whether the RTC was competent to differentiate solvent thrifts from insolvent ones, and floor criticisms of the bill as "corporate welfare."[30] Additionally, the Rules Committee had prevented Republican amendments on the floor, giving many Republicans another good excuse to vote against the measure.

Gonzalez stated his intent to quickly introduce a stopgap month-long funding measure, but RTC officials argued that with bidding procedures taking as long as they did, a month would not help.[31] Shortly thereafter, the RTC announced that the funding failure would cause it to fall $15 billion short of its $100 billion asset sales goal for the year.[32] The Bush administration, seeking to make up for its generally weak lobbying effort on the first bill, tried to restart the initiative with a letter from President Bush to Gonzalez and other House leaders requesting a new bill for the $42 billion for the RTC.[33] By this time, however, the earlier bipartisan leadership push had given way to election-year partisanship. Amid allegations of RTC thrift-closing slowdowns motivated by election-year politics, illegal job awarding practices, and other forms of RTC mismanagement, funding for the agency was dead for 1992.

As President Clinton took office and the new 103rd Congress convened, the RTC problem loomed large in the House and Senate Banking Committees. Chairman Gonzalez and the new House Banking Committee Financial Institutions Subcommittee chairman, Stephen Neal (D-NC), wanted to get the bailout done quickly and completely. Some Democrats who had voted against what was perceived to be a Bush initiative viewed the problem differently now. In the words of one subcommittee Democrat, "This was our fiscal Vietnam. We'd voted on it in the 102d, and the goal was to get it behind us and move on." Chairman Gonzalez, described by committee members as a very democratic, inclusive chairman, was generally in a no-win situation with this particular legislation. Regardless of whether or not he produced a good legislative solution to the savings and loan mess, he would be the lightning rod for criticism of the problem. This was true even though it was his predecessor, Chairman Fernand St. Germain (D-RI), who was largely to blame for the provisions that led to the debacle in the first place.

In any event, the Financial Institutions Subcommittee members generally did not trust either the RTC leadership or the RTC numbers. While there was not enough time or resources to do a thorough investigation, several respondents noted that they suspected that illegal activities were going on in the agency, so the goal was to fund it, close it out, and stop the problems that way. The problems with investigating and supervising the RTC activities were exacerbated by the generally high turnover among committee members as well as the great complexity of the financial issues addressed by the legislation. Added to this, some subcommittee members, like a number of the participants in the foreign aid appropriation described in the last case, had "single-issue orientations." These members had particular legislative objectives that, once-satisfied, ended their interest in the matter.

Both Gonzalez and probank subcommittee chairman Neal were described by committee members as "respectful" leaders who practiced "inclusive" leadership styles as chairmen, and the two men had a good working relationship with each other. Gonzalez had experience with the major problems in the regulation of thrifts in Texas, and he was very active on the thrift issue and was particularly tough on regulators. Neal, however, was described by some respondents as being less energized and less forceful, with a cordial but weak relationship with the senior Republicans on his subcommittee. Ranking subcommittee Republican

William McCollum (R-FL) was described as generally personable but dogmatic, and he was publicly vocal in his opposition to the thrift bailout. Furthermore, he had made enemies among some committee Democrats for violating the taboo against campaigning against incumbents in their districts. James Leach (R-IA), the next ranking Republican on the subcommittee and ranking minority member of the full committee, was described as a "nice man" but one "principled almost to a fault" and "generally unwilling to compromise." Leach announced to Gonzalez and Neal that he would support their efforts but that he would not work for them.

Other key personalities involved in the passage of this legislation included John LaFalce (D-NY), Bruce Vento (D-MN), and Charles Schumer (D-NY). LaFalce was described as a thoughtful and methodical consumer advocate, while Vento was noted to have been "a smart and strong force" within the committee who had once challenged Gonzalez for the chairmanship. Schumer was closely allied with the securities issues and described by one respondent as a "tough opponent." Additionally, the subcommittee included fourteen other more junior Democrats and ten other Republicans, making consensus that much more difficult. Descriptions of the junior members ranged from "junkyard dog" to "kept a seat warm." Respondents also noted that the senior leadership on the subcommittee managed the consideration of this legislation. However, the leaders' work was made more difficult by a wholesale change in the makeup of the House Banking Committee in the 103rd Congress, featuring an influx of early termers and a shift of interest to the committee's housing and consumer subcommittees. These early termers' "consumerist" predispositions created concern within the banking industry, and the banking industry expected that the committee would be difficult to work with in the new Congress.[34] Despite these concerns, respondents characterized the committee's day-to-day operations as often bipartisan, and certainly more bipartisan than most committees in the House at the time.

President Clinton's first step in dealing with the RTC problem was to accept the resignation of Albert Casey as head of the agency, replacing him temporarily with Deputy Treasury Secretary Robert Altman.[35] Lloyd Bentsen, former senator and newly appointed treasury secretary, then delivered the administration's $45 billion RTC request personally during appearances before Congress on March 16 and 17, visits described as "cordial."[36] Bentsen received immediate assurances of quick action and support on the measure, which asked for $28 billion for direct RTC funds and $17 billion to fund the Savings Association Insurance Fund (SAIF) proposed the year before. The bill did not include any changes in RTC management practices. Both House and Senate committees began work off of the executive branch draft, and frequent coordination and collaboration among Treasury Department officials, Banking Committee staffers, and the committee members became routine over the next several months. This cooperation represented a marked improvement over the situation with the Bush administration a year before.

The Senate Banking Committee acted first, passing the $45 billion request by a 15–3 vote, but the committee attached a variety of strings to the money, which would require Secretary Bentsen to verify at certain points that the funds had been used properly.[37] In anticipation of the pending House action on the bill, the RTC announced that the agency expected lower returns on the last remaining thrift assets to be auctioned away.[38] Later in April, the Clinton administration announced that it would reduce its request by $3 billion in light of new projections on the final cost of the closeout, following a GAO audit that confirmed the smaller figure.[39] Additionally, in anticipation of the pending House subcommittee markup and the subsequent full committee actions, the administration began to press its case with Banking Committee members, with interim RTC chief Altman meeting with many members individually. In particular, Altman spent a good deal of time lobbying early-term African American and Hispanic members on the committee who disapproved of the legislation in light of the failure of the economic stimulus package earlier. Those members' sentiments were summarized by Banking Committee freshman Bobby L. Rush (D-IL), who said, "There is an ignorance of stupidity and insensitivity from the federal government when it says that we can't provide $16 billion for . . . a survival program of stimulus, but yet we can have the luxury of providing $45 billion to the thrift industry."[40]

After administration lobbying efforts and acting on a clever amendment by freshman Herb Klein (D-NJ), the Financial Institutions Subcommittee changed the April 1 deadline to allow funds already appropriated but not used to be spent. At the same time, the subcommittee cut the administration's proposal by $12 billion.[41] Klein's amendment, approved by voice vote, allowed the subcommittee to claim to have resolved the closeout funding without having voted any new money. Part of story here was the usual "high-ball, low-ball" executive-legislative game described by the number of respondents, a routine that would predict a lower authorization than the administration's request even in the best of circumstances. However, the funding levels were also pressured downward by a new GAO report that indicated that the closeout could be accomplished for as little as $7 billion if economic conditions were favorable.[42] A subcommittee clash over the SAIF between senior Democrats Vento and Schumer remained unresolved when the subcommittee reported the bill by voice vote on April 29.[43] On May 6, the House Banking Committee approved the bill by a solid 35–16 margin, leaving intact the $18.3 billion for the RTC closeout and $16 billion for the SAIF.[44] The Senate Banking Committee followed suit, adopting the same reduced version of the request passed by the House Banking Committee, and the legislation was moving forward.

At this point, multiple committee jurisdictions slowed the bill down. The House Judiciary Committee, having jurisdiction over the provisions of HR1340 dealing with the rights of the RTC to sue officials over fraud or "intentional misconduct," differed with the Banking Committee over the length of the statute of limitations in such cases.[45] As the two committees became bogged down in details, and as compromise solutions failed to generate enough support to move the legislation forward, it became clear that the differences between the two committees would have to be worked out on the floor. The House adjourned for its August recess without further action on the RTC funding bill.

Planning to bring the measure to the floor of the House upon return in September, House Democratic leaders immediately began talking up the measure and pushed for passage. Key Republican leaders including Minority Leader Michel and senior Banking Committee member Leach, however, still openly opposed the legislation. While the Democratic whips believed there were enough votes for passage, Speaker Tom Foley (D-WA) hoped to reach some accommodation with the senior Republicans prior to bringing the generally unpopular measure up for a floor vote. Foley hoped to avoid a partisan debacle like the one that had killed the same effort in 1992. With the primary obstacle to success seeming to be the SAIF provisions, one strategy considered and ultimately rejected by Neal and Treasury officials was to allow the SAIF to drop out completely on the floor with the goal of resurrecting the provision in House-Senate conference. Barney Frank (D-MA), an influential subcommittee member, said bluntly, "SAIF is dead . . . it's been dead for a month."[46]

Upon return in the first week of September, the Banking Committee's senior leadership, including Leach, Gonzalez, eighth-ranking Republican Richard Baker of Louisiana, and Neal, struck a quick deal in which they reduced the amount of money earmarked for SAIF to $8 billion. The compromise worked, though not by much, with the measure passing on the House floor by a 214–208 vote on September 14.[47] When given word that the outcome of the floor vote was in doubt, Speaker Tom Foley interrupted his meeting with Palestinian Liberation Organization chairman Yasser Arafat in order to rush to the House floor and rally support for the measure. Subcommittee chair and floor manager

Neal was optimistic, saying, "I think it'll be a fairly easy conference. The differences aren't huge."[48]

It was not to be easy. As usual, staffers meeting ahead of the conference had worked out almost all of the differences between the two versions of the bill, operating on guidance from the principals. However, Senator Alphonse D'Amato (R-NY), who was the ranking Republican on the Senate Banking Committee, and Representative Kweisi Mfume (D-MD) had come to a preconference impasse over language written into the bill by Mfume that assisted minority-owned businesses in securing bailout contracts.[49] In response to this issue, D'Amato, Phil Gramm (R-TX), and other Senate Republicans had blocked the appointment of conferees as a means of acquiring leverage over the conference itself. It was not until November 18 that a compromise was worked out, with agreements and compromises on the minority-contracting language and the statute of limitations provisions.[50] The Senate shortly thereafter adopted the conference report (H Rept 103–380) by a 54–45 vote on November 20, and the House adopted the report by a 235–191 vote. The final compromise measure retained the minority-contracting language, adopted the three-year statute of limitations approved originally by the House, and authorized future funding for the SAIF without providing any funds at present. President Clinton signed the bill into law on December 17, 1993.

Several legislative actors were instrumental in realizing a politically unpopular but important legislative success in the case of the Thrift Depositor Protection Act of 1993. House Banking Committee chairman Gonzalez, Financial Institutions Subcommittee chairman Neal, Treasury Secretary Bentsen, interim RTC chief Altman, and, at some points, Speaker Tom Foley were all critical to the enactment of the RTC closeout legislation. None of those actors was responding to constituent pressure or a chance for popular success in pursuing the closeout funding, but rather each was pushing to clean up a mess that had to be fixed. In order to be successful, the committee chiefs had to work with their Republican counterparts even when there was little common ground, and the executive agency leaders had to work hard at lobbying for individual House and Senate member support throughout the process. Finally, the key willful agents here, as in the other cases in this study, had to content themselves with incremental policy changes if they were to get any change at all. This legislative success would not have been realized, despite the urgent need to fix a nagging problem and get on with other business, if it had not been for the strategic awareness, interpersonal skills, lobbying efforts, and persistence of the key leaders who tackled this politically unrewarding task.

PL103–227: "GOALS 2000"
EDUCATE AMERICA ACT OF 1994

The "Goals 2000" Educate America Act (HR1804) was signed into law by President Clinton on March 31, 1994, and the measure authorized over $400 million in aid intended to improve local schools. A 165-page law, which became a lightning rod for conservative and religious group protests, Goals 2000 was originally a Bush administration initiative dubbed "America 2000" and sponsored by Republicans in both House and Senate. The various titles of the law aimed at achieving eight national educational goals, goals described by most of the legislators involved in the law's passage as being admirable but wholly unrealistic. The education system goals, to be achieved by the year 2000, were as follows: (1) all children would start school ready to learn; (2) at least 90 percent of students would finish high school; (3) students would leave the fourth, eighth, and twelfth grades having demonstrated competence in a wide range of subjects; (4) teachers would have access to programs for the continued improvement of their skills; (5) the United States would be first in the world in math and science achievement; (6) every adult would be literate and possess the skills to "compete in a global economy"; (7) every school would be free of drugs and violence; and (8) every school would promote the involvement of parents in their children's education.

In order to achieve these goals, the law provided for a nineteen-member National Education Standards and Improvement Council. The council was charged with developing voluntary national curriculum content and student performance standards and voluntary "opportunity-to-learn" standards or the specification of the level of resources that a school should have in order to provide a reasonable educational opportunity for its students. Furthermore, the council was charged with apportioning the aid for schools that subscribed to the standards, aid for schools with violent crime problems, and money for research institutes and an oversight panel aimed at assisting the nation with achievement of the ambitious goals.[51] Before enacting the measure, which passed by wide margins in both the House and the Senate, there was frequent, emotional, and partisan debate in committee and on the floor regarding the bill. Topics of debate ranged from essential questions, such as who should write a national curriculum, to ancillary issues, such as the establishment of a national contraception distribution policy, parental consent for psychological examinations, school choice, and school prayer.

The legislative proposal that resulted in Goals 2000 had as its most recognizable ancestor the Bush administration's America 2000 bill, but the debate over national education standards and school performance had raged at least as far back as Sputnik in 1957 and other academic debates over education in the early 1960s.[52] As usual, the initiative for this legislation came from a variety of sources. The impetus for the bill came from state governors, local education authorities, various litigating parties, Bush's own desire to validate his claim as "the education president," and the policy and political goals of the legislators involved in its passage. Additionally, the legislative outcome was shaped by a number of high-profile studies and statistics describing a decline in American school performance, including the famous study "A Nation at Risk" published in 1983.

The Bush administration had pushed for "school choice," a proposal that would authorize federal assistance to lower-income parents who wanted to send their children to private schools, as a key part of its America 2000 education initiatives. Despite Education Secretary Lamar Alexander's lobbying efforts and the fact that only a demonstration project was called for in the Bush bill, the Senate rejected the inclusion of school choice by a 36–57 vote on January 23, 1992.[53] As passed, the Senate bill (S2) would authorize $850 million in general educational aid for the current fiscal year, to be distributed to the states in the form of block grants. Individual schools would compete for "educational improvement grants," with states distributing the funds for teacher training, model schools, and other initiatives.

Later in that same week, a bipartisan panel of thirty-two educators, governors, and education administrators, co-chaired by Governors Carroll Campbell Jr. (R-SC) and Roy Romer (D-CO) and created by Congress the previous June, issued its final report. In the report, the panel called for the creation of national education standards and voluntary exams to measure students' performance against the standards.[54] In fact, as part of a broad education program intended to achieve "world class standards," the Bush administration had already moved forward in the development of the national standards by awarding a $1.6 million grant to the University of California at Los Angeles to develop history standards and another $500 thousand to the National Research Council to develop science standards.[55] Education Secretary Alexander enthusiastically endorsed the panel's conclusions.

The national education policy debate, however, had become focused almost exclusively on the ideologically charged question of school choice. Under pressure from a variety of national teachers' unions and education administrators' lobbies, among them the National Education Association (NEA), the American Federation of Teachers (AFT), and the National School Boards Association, the House Education and Labor Committee had scrapped all reference to school choice. Instead, the committee rewrote the provisions on "reform," giving complete authority to the local school boards and even scrapping S2 in favor of a new bill, HR4342.[56] Ranking committee Republican Bill Goodling (R-PA), himself a former teacher, principal, and school board president, was kept in the dark about the changes. He only found out that his bill (HR3320) had been scrapped after a committee colleague mentioned it in casual conversation, as committee chairman William Ford (D-MI) pulled what was described as an "about-face" on the measure.

With the Bush administration already characterizing the Democrats as "business-as-usual" on education policy, Ford had put himself and the committee on a collision course with the administration. In lobbying for the changes, the National School Boards Association, which represented fifteen thousand school boards with ninety-seven thousand members, held its annual conference in Washington, D.C. Seven hundred of the association's attendees had sought out their members of Congress to personally complain about the school board reform provisions. Additionally, the first rumblings against "national standards" and a "national curriculum" were being felt as the National Education Association repudiated the findings of the congressional panel.[57]

On May 20, the House Education and Labor Committee passed the revised approach by a 23–12 count with the vote generally following party lines, though not one legislator asked said anything good about the bill, and the Bush administration promised to veto it.[58] While the bill provided $700 million in aid and contained most of the elements of the America 2000 plan proposed by the administration, the exclusion of school choice provisions irritated many Republicans. Among them was Education Secretary Alexander, who said, "This bill is worse than awful . . . the only ones who should be happy are those who want the schools to stay forever just like they are."[59] His lament summarized, of course, the goals of the lobbies arrayed against the original initiatives, since the committee-passed measure would provide $700 million in school aid with relatively few strings attached to the money. The National Education Association conducted a national media campaign aimed at both promoting the bill and portraying the union as the protector of the nation's education system.[60]

Despite those efforts, Chairman Ford eventually dumped his own bill, and the Senate approach (S2) was passed in both chambers. In the end, however, S2 never made it out of a late-session conference. In addition to a fundamental lack of ideological and policy consensus described by participants in the conference, Democrats proved unwilling to give the would-be "education president" anything resembling an education policy victory late in an election year. At the same time, Republicans were wary of pushing for legislation that Bush had threatened to veto. Education reform initiatives were dead for 1992, and attention turned fully to the 1992 elections.

It is interesting to note that a *Wall Street Journal* analysis of candidates Bush and Clinton as education policymakers and policy administrators found remarkable similarity between the two, with the major differences being the larger sums that Clinton was willing to spend on new education initiatives and the greater personal efforts he had made in lobbying for education reforms.[61] In fact, as governor of Arkansas, Clinton had been one of the bipartisan group of governors in the National Governors Association who had met with Bush in 1989 to draft the set of national educational goals comprising the America 2000 plan. Upon election, President-elect Clinton quickly nominated Richard W. Riley, a former governor of South Carolina who had enjoyed remarkable successes in reforming the state's educational system, to be his secretary of education. Clinton made his first educational policy decision when he chose to send his daughter to the affluent Sidwell Friends private school. He quickly drew criticism from observers on the left, who asked why public schools were not acceptable, and others on the right, who asked why everyone should not have the same opportunity.[62] At an academic conference at American University hosted by the nonprofit advocacy group Education Commission of the States, outgoing Education Secretary Alexander conceded that the administration's inability to "get our message through more clearly" and the focus on school choice had doomed their education initiatives.[63] Later that week, as his last public act as secretary, Alexander was able to announce that American students had shown a half-grade increase in standardized test scores, reversing the downward trend of the last several years. He attributed the improvement to new math standards developed by the National Council of Teachers of Mathematics. [64]

On February 24, Education Secretary Richard Riley and Labor Secretary Robert Reich appeared before the Senate Labor and Human Resources Committee to outline the administration's education initiatives. Emphasizing the same systemic approach to reform that America 2000 had entailed, Riley described proposals almost identical to the Bush administration's plan, with the key difference being the exclusion of any tuition vouchers or other school choice provisions. Projecting the costs of the program at $400 million for fiscal 1994, with subsequent increases to $600 million in fiscal 1995 and $800 million in fiscal 1996, Riley planned to write into the legislation six explicit national educational goals. [65] Riley, the congressional committees, and the Department of Education began to draft the legislation. Soon thereafter, the National Association of Secondary School Principals issued a call on the behalf of its forty-five thousand members asking Congress and the administration to facilitate the implementation of a fair national program by forcing the states to correct the huge disparities between states and within states in funding per student.[66] Additionally, a number of parents in the state of Missouri sued the state for the same perceived inequity. Providing additional incentive to include this issue in the reform measure was the fact that Representative Patsy Mink (D-HI) had introduced legislation requesting funds for the purpose of aiding poorer school districts in the 102d Congress without success. In light of this and other interest group and constituent interest in the equity issue, Michael Cohen (the Riley education consultant charged with constructing the package) indicated that the problem would be considered in the drafting of the new legislation, now dubbed "Goals 2000." However, up to that point in March, the House Education and Labor Committee had avoided the issue of funding equity, known as the "opportunity to learn" standards.

The momentum began to grow in support of the funding equity issue. By mid-April, committee Democrats had begun to discuss including the opportunity-to-learn provisions in the education package. Jack Jennings, the committee's legislative counsel for education issues, stated, "We do not want to go to national testing until we are sure children have an opportunity to learn the material."[67] Michael Cohen, predicting passage, did not see many problems with the provision's inclusion. At that point, according to respondents, most member discussion centered around the stringency of the national standards, the mix of federal and state control over the proposed funding, and the newly considered opportunity-to-learn standards. The administration stepped up its efforts to coordinate with the Senate and House education committee members and maintain a dialogue on the legislative initiative. Most members of the House committee worked on the legislation while believing, even at this point, that meeting any of the goals described in the bill by the year 2000 would not be feasible. After his draft legislation received a poor reception from both Republicans and Democrats, Riley stepped up his personal efforts to convince the committee members of the merits of the Clinton administration, meeting repeatedly with them individually and in small groups.

Riley was finding it tough going, particularly given the high expectations the administration had created after removing the old sticking point of school choice from the debate. While chairman Ford was described as a partisan, old-style, and somewhat autocratic chairman, he was also a "true friend" of the Clinton administration with several committee votes "in his pocket." Ford was described by some respondents of his own party as overly partisan, and one staffer remarked, "Mr. Ford was very partisan on the Democratic side . . . a liberal who made it difficult to be bipartisan." Ford benefited in his legislative endeavors from a close relationship with Speaker Foley, and "unlike (subsequent chair-

man William) Goodling in the 104th, Ford had a lot of autonomy."
Many Republicans on the committee, including Goodling (R-PA), were
now opposed to the measure merely because it was a Clinton proposal,
while others opposed it for more substantive reasons.

Ironically, Goodling had sponsored the quite similar Bush proposal
in his position as the ranking Republican on the full and Elementary,
Secondary, and Vocational Education Subcommittee. Respondents recollected that Goodling had seemingly become much more conservative
in the new Congress. Similarly, normally stalwart Marge Roukema (R-
NJ) became less cooperative with committee members on the measure.
At the same time, chairman Ford was unenthusiastic about the administration draft, and he opposed the opportunity-to-learn standards in particular. Committee Democrats were beginning to seek amendments that
were causing even more divisiveness among themselves, and the usual
interests were getting energized against the measure. Seeking to counter
these problems was subcommittee chairman Dale Kildee (D-MI). Kildee
was described by respondents as a conscientious and inclusive leader,
having a very close relationship with his fellow Michigander Ford and a
solid working relationship with Goodling. Kildee had counted on the
traditional bipartisan nature of his subcommittee and the full committee (on education issues) to facilitate the bill's progress, but instead partisan rhetoric was beginning to overshadow discussions of the bill's substantive merits.

At this point, as the committee leaders, Riley, and legislative counsel Jennings tried to work through those difficulties, Governor Carroll
Campbell of South Carolina wrote a letter to Riley strenuously opposing the opportunity-to-learn standards. Similarly, other governors
"went ballistic," in the words of one respondent, over what were perceived as stringent, unfunded mandates and unwanted federal intervention. By this time, however, Representative Major Owens (D-NY) had
adopted the inclusion of opportunity-to-learn standards in the larger
measure as his personal mission. Owens would lead the push for these
standards, with some success. As this debate was unfolding, Representative Jack Reed (D-RI) added to the governors' distress by proposing an
amendment adding enforcement provisions to the standards, and his
amendment solidified the Republicans' ideological opposition to the legislation on the grounds of federal involvement in local responsibilities.
The NEA, AFT, and other education interest groups offered support
described by one staffer as "unenthusiastic" and "pro forma," taking a
longterm view of support for the Clinton initiative. It was not usually
the case that business groups would get energized on education issues,
but business groups were taking a higher-profile stance on the national
standards issue. The National Alliance for Business and the Chamber of

Commerce, among other business organizations, strongly supported the Clinton efforts, as they had Bush's before.

Despite the rancorous, partisan debates in hearings and markup, the subcommittee reported the administration bill (HR1804) by a 17–9 vote on May 6. While subcommittee Republicans grudgingly agreed to accept opportunity-to-learn standards in spite of Goodling's warnings about probable future parent-initiated lawsuits, Reed's successful push to include enforcement provisions came at the expense of bipartisan support. The Reed amendment flew in the face of a premarkup agreement made in Democratic subcommittee caucus, cited by Steve Gunderson (R-WI), which was intended to avoid controversial amendments. Gunderson called the amendment a "deal breaker."[68]

Riley and the administration opposed the Reed provision, and subcommittee chair Kildee said that he believed both sides had operated in good faith, promising to try to work something out before the full committee markup. The subcommittee also added a seventh goal, Tim Roemer's (D-IN) proposition that all teachers have access to good training programs, before forwarding the measure. The subcommittee also quickly rejected John Boehner's (R-OH) bid to add school choice back into the bill. Boehner was described by some respondents as a "bomb thrower" with little interest in anything other than derailing the bill. Meanwhile, the perception among some members and staff on the committee was that Goodling was under pressure from Gingrich to oppose the bill, pressure linked to the ongoing struggle between Gingrich and Michel that added another obstacle to passage.

On May 19, the Senate's Labor and Human Resources took the next step forward, reporting the Goals 2000 (S846) measure by a solid 14–3 vote. The Senate committee's version maintained the administration proposal relatively intact at six national objectives, and it included no opportunity-to-learn provisions or occupational skill standards.[69] In the Senate committee's consideration of the measure, however, controversy arose over the wording of a provision that would create a board to develop trade qualification standards.[70] A number of civil rights organizations expressed concern about possible hiring discrimination if the trade standards were put in place. In response, House subcommittee chair Kildee decided to postpone sending the House version to full committee until the issue had been resolved, since that section of the bill had been skipped over during markup.

At this point, Secretary Riley's efforts were geared toward pulling House Democrats "back to the middle," one participant noted. The Congressional Black Caucus was considering the bill closely, as was an informal caucus of Education and Labor Committee women, including Lynne Woolsey (R-CA), Patsy Mink (D-HI), Jolene Unsoeld (D-WA),

Marge Roukema (R-NJ), and Karan English (D-AZ). Occasionally, Susan Molinari (R-NY) would join this group as well, though a few respondents described her as an impediment, rather than help, in the legislative process. Other important negotiators and facilitators mentioned by the respondents included first-termer Xavier Becerra (D-CA), first-termer George Strickland (D-OH), senior committee member George Miller (D-CA), and Steve Gunderson (R-WI).

Over the next few weeks, current and former Education Department officials and academics sought to frame the terms of the Goals 2000 debate with a series of *New York Times* and *Wall Street Journal* editorials. Authors included Diane Ravitch, former Bush administration assistant education secretary (decrying federal intervention in curriculum and opportunity to learn standards), Delaware professor Linda Gottfredson (attacking the plan's alleged "race-norming"), and Clifford Adelman, Department of Education Higher Education director (who applauded the plan's purported ability to make high school diplomas meaningful). [71] Those themes would come into play later when other interest groups that had not yet sought to shape the debate got involved. When the House Education and Labor Committee finally did report the bill on June 23, the 28–15 count represented straight party-line votes on both sides of the aisle.[72] The stage was set for a renewed, and more public-oriented, partisan conflict. Though Reed had toned down the language of his enforcement provisions after negotiations with Goodling and Riley, Goodling summarized the anger of committee Republicans by exclaiming at passage, "This bill is a disaster."[73] The bill's language was opposed by Al Shanker, president of the American Federation of Teachers, as well as other education interest group leaders. Richard Armey (R-TX), another committee member described as one uninterested in consensus but rather seeking to "throw bombs," was defeated in his bid to switch the Goals 2000 plan with a school choice plan by a 7–35 vote.

In light of the various controversies surrounding the bill, HR1804 was placed on hold by the House leadership, while negotiations went on among staffers, members, and administration officials, and interest group leaders continued to lobby for various provisions. A key negotiator remembered that the interest groups' contributions to the debate were primarily informational. Since the sophisticated groups lined up differently on each provision of the legislation, there were no "set" sides on the legislation, and groups could be both allies and adversaries on different portions of the various titles. On September 30, Secretary Riley publicly assailed the lack of progress on the bill, urging the nation to "get serious" about education reform. His comments were seconded by the National Goals Panel, the bipartisan watchdog group appointed by Congress.[74] The panel's chairman, Democratic Governor Ben Nelson of

Nebraska, echoed Riley's sentiments, as did Republican Governor Arne Carlson of Minnesota.

House and committee leaders responded, negotiating a compromise to move the bill to the House floor. After the bitterly partisan fights in committee over HR1804, the compromise reached by Goodling, Ford, Riley, Owens, Reed, and Kildee in a private negotiating session enabled the measure to pass in the House by a wide margin. On October 13, by a 307–118 vote, the House passed the legislation after accepting by a 424–0 vote an amendment by Goodling on the House floor stating that nothing in the bill should be construed as representing federal control over local prerogatives.[75] Rejecting Armey's school choice amendment by a 130–300 count, the House agreed by voice vote to a variety of other amendments, including the addition of another national objective offered by Dave McCurdy (D-OK) calling for increased parental involvement in schooling. Attention shifted for the moment to the Senate, but the Senate would not act on the bill until the following session.

The Senate version of Goals 2000 (S1150) was brought to the floor for consideration during the week of January 31, 1994. Whereas House debate had centered primarily around the opportunity-to-learn standards and Reed's enforcement provisions, Senate debate instead focused on the seemingly tangential issue of school prayer and the oft-considered issue of school choice. Senators Jesse Helms (R-NC) and Daniel Coats (R-IN) offered amendments on the two issues.[76] According to several respondents, as conservative opponents of the legislation realized that they could not change the bill significantly before enactment, they shifted to a strategy of shifting the terms of the debate, regardless of how incorrectly they might portray the legislation. In response to the (false) charge that the legislation would ban home schooling, legislators were inundated with a three-day-long onslaught of faxes, letters, telephone calls, and postcards from the "religious right," all protesting this nonexistent provision of the legislation. One member recollected having to use an unlisted telephone in a D.C. lawyer's office just to get an open outside line. The lobbying efforts notwithstanding, the Senate passed HR1804 by a wide margin of 71–25, after substituting the language of the Senate version (S1150). Each side began preparing for conference.

Prior to the conference, which began on March 15, there was a series of meetings between the education committee staffs of the House and Senate during which most of the "second-tier" issues were worked out in advance of the conference. While members (primarily the chairs of the committees) gave general guidance to the staffs on the breakdown of the issues, the staffs were given, as was ordinarily the case, a fair amount of latitude in working out most of the less controversial issues. Once this was completed, Chairman Ford and Chairman Edward

Kennedy (D-MA) arranged a preconference negotiating session, attended by House members Ford, Kildee, Owens, Reed, and Goodling, as well as Senators Kennedy, Nancy Kassebaum (R-KS) (ranking Republican on the committee), James Jeffords (R-VT), and Claiborne Pell (D-RI). During that session, under the direction of the senior leaders, the major issues separating the two versions were dealt with and resolved. The actual conference was less important in determining the shape of the outcome, though a compromise over opportunity-to-learn standards was worked out there when Senator Paul Simon (D-IL) suggested the conferees include the word *standards* while also making clear that they were *voluntary*. This move pleased both sides of the opportunity-to-learn issue. From one participant's perspective, however, the bulk of the work was actually accomplished by the staff in its earlier negotiating and coordination, and the members only dealt with the higher-profile or "hot-button" issues.

After another choreographed rush of faxes, phone calls, and letters from supporters of the religious right, both chambers ratified the conference report (H Rept 103–446). The House adopted the conference report by a 306–121 vote on March 23 after last-minute objections to the weakened school prayer provision. Helms threatened a filibuster over the same issue in the Senate, and he employed a variety of parliamentary maneuvers designed to slow the floor vote down. However, Senate Majority Leader George Mitchell (D-ME) managed to keep eighty-five senators in town for a rare Saturday morning vote, and the report was cleared by a 63–22 count on March 26 after a vote to invoke cloture that passed by a two-vote margin of 62–23. President Clinton signed the measure into law on March 31, 1994. Had the measure not been enacted by midnight of that day, the authority to spend $100 million allocated for Goals 2000 would have expired. The nation now had eight national education objectives, and legislative success had come just in time.

The enactment of Goals 2000, or the Educate America Act of 1994, came as a result of hard work and skillful maneuvering by several key actors. These legislative champions included Secretary of Education Richard Riley; House Education and Labor Committee chairman William Ford; Elementary, Secondary, and Vocational Education Subcommittee chairman Dale Kildee; legislative counsel Jack Jennings; and several other fully committed legislators concerned about particular aspects of the eventual policy outcome. With impetus from a large number of state governors and local educators, and in spite of spirited opposition from a variety of interest groups, these willful agents persisted over several years to realize policy success. As usual, the resultant change was incremental rather than radical, and compromise and strategic innovation were the order of the day. In the end, however, the legislators realized their vision of a more focused national education effort in spite of the myriad obstacles in their way. Ironically, in spite of the fact that the basic outline of the legislation had originated in the Republican Party, the hardest part of enacting the law had been overcoming the Republicans' partisan opposition to what had once been their own initiative.

LEGISLATING IN THE 1990S

In the portrait of legislating that emerges from the cases of the 1990s, we find a process far more partisan and much less personal than that of the 1960s. Legislative leaders again worked hard to construct policy coalitions in order to realize success, but more often than not, these coalitions fell along party lines throughout the sequence of gates. Furthermore, bipartisanship, even at the subcommittee level, was rare enough to stand out as unusual in the eyes of the respondents. Like the 1960s, each legislative champion in these cases used an administration draft as the policy vehicle most likely to obtain success. But clearly, floor debates, the hearing process, and other traditional legislative activities lost their importance or changed roles in the process viewed generally since the 1960s. The cases and the respondents paint a picture of a modern legislative process highlighted by bitter partisan rhetoric, "bomb-throwing" colleagues, and the absence of the interpersonal relationships so prevalent and useful in the earlier decades. With these characteristics in mind, it is not surprising that would-be legislative champions in the modern era have turned to more mechanical and less cooperative means of achieving their policy goals.

CHAPTER 5

Actors I:
The Internal Actors

How do we make the laws happen? Well, there are plenty of ways
to show the folks back home that you're an "active legislator,"
but it's a lot harder to get to that critical mass that actually makes
it happen. You'll find out there are both "showhorses" and
"workhorses" here, and the workhorses are the ones that get it
done.

—House member from the 1990s

From a theoretical perspective, consequential changes in the internal
House actors since the 1960s could take a whole host of forms. Such
changes among these actors might be indicated by systematic variations
over time in the average House member qualifications, by shifts in the
numbers or seniority of the legislators routinely involved in key activities, or by other changes in the members' voting behaviors, motives, or
actions. Likewise, it is plausible that key changes could have occurred
among the congressional leaders, including evolving leadership strategies, altered levels of leader influence within the process, or changes in
the perceptions of those committee and chamber leaders among rank-
and-file members. Furthermore, the House's other internal actors, the
various staffers working for the members in offices and committees,
might have taken on new roles or experienced an increased or decreased
significance in the process commensurate with their expanded numbers.
The internal House actors of the latter decades might have more or less
policy expertise, might be participating at more junior points in their
careers, or might have different legislative or electoral goals. Finally, the
relative influence of all of those House actors could have changed, with
implications for those actors seeking to realize legislative success.

In the last few decades, a variety of scholars have in fact described
some of these types of variations, and they have regularly argued or
assumed that the consequences of those changes have been serious. Representative of this genre, Samuel Huntington argued in 1965 that several

factors were combining to change the nature of the Congress and the legislative process, including the members' increasing propensity to specialize, their increased tendency to cater to local interests at the expense of national concerns, and even their increasingly "rural" rather than "urban" roots.[1] Sundquist (1981) agreed, arguing, "Underlying the transformation of the Congress in the 1970s was a change in the psychology of the individual members of the House and Senate. . . . The dominant element of the new political order is individualism."[2] He added that "individualism in the constituencies put individualists in the office, and when enough of them were in the Congress, the nature of the place was bound to change . . . he new-style member contrasts with the old in political manners, political vocabulary, interests, and conception of the proper nature of the institution in which he serves. . . . He has no habit of being deferential to the established and the powerful, and he will not be so in the Congress."[3]

Sundquist further argued that these changes in the congressional actors had led to an increase in the power at the subcommittee level. Continuing this line of argument, Kingdon (1981) asserted the need for a revision of his description of member voting parameters in light of "wholesale turnover in the House of Representatives" and corresponding "dramatic changes" in committee and subcommittee practices.[4] Hibbing (1982) attributed this increased turnover and apparent member dissatisfaction with congressional service in large part to the uncertainties associated with the changes in seniority rules implemented in the mid-1970s.[5]

More recent perspectives on the nature of modern legislative actors have continued this theme of individualism and its impact on the processes of the Congress. As Smith (1989) argues in his careful analysis of floor politics in the House and Senate, "It would be surprising if such changes in the policy environment and legislative responsibilities did not affect the kind of people attracted to service in Congress . . . the type of politicians elected to Congress has changed."[6] He characterized this "new breed" by its policy activism, its tendency to self-promote, and its general willingness to challenge the power structure in Congress.[7] Loomis (1988) and Heclo (1989) find similar characteristics in their modern "political entrepreneur,"[8] and Hibbing (1991) argues that the "typical" congressional career and legislative involvement have changed in the modern era, with modern members becoming actively involved much earlier in their careers.[9] Fiorina (1989), reprising an earlier argument concerning member changes precipitated by decreased party allegiance and other factors, argues that legislators are increasingly and successfully focused on district concerns and individual legislative and electoral objectives in the face of a more demanding work schedule.[10]

Ehrenhalt (1992) echoes this theme, describing a professionalization of the legislature that has produced an average modern legislator more "competent, hardworking, . . . serious," intense, and independent than his predecessors.[11] Browne and Paik (1993) characterize the modern members as relying upon "home-style" politics to a greater degree than they had previously, and these authors describe a recently manifested tendency on the part of members to rely on constituent-provided information and local considerations more often in making voting decisions.[12] King (1997) attributes a variety of perceived modern legislative difficulties to a heightened electoral sensitivity on the part of the average member in an American political system he describes as "too democratic."[13]

Other authors seeking to explain perceived changes in the policy-making process point to the great increase in committee and member staffs as a major component of consequential actor changes. Authors arguing in this vein include Heclo (1978), Sundquist (1981), and Kingdon (1981), among others. Heclo identified a nearly three-fold increase in staffers on the Hill from 1957 to 1978 as a source of consequential change within the legislative process, arguing that the value placed upon the specialized staff's expertise (and implicitly, the staff influence in the process) increased along with issue complexity and the scope of governmental reach. [14] Sundquist viewed the large increase in staff as a more indirect indicator of actor change, arguing that the increase in staff reflected a conscious decision on the part of legislators to expand their own workload and a concomitant desire to achieve independence from the encroaching executive branch.[15] Kingdon likewise states that the increase in staffs since the 1960s may "raise the real possibility that staff influence on legislative voting decisions is greater now," a development he felt was probably related to the greatly increased workload of the average member.[16]

Finally, other authors have argued that changes in the significance of the party leadership occurred to cause fundamental changes in the legislative process in recent times. In 1965, Huntington argued that the fragmentation and dispersion of power within the Congress caused by the Legislative Reorganization Act of 1946 had in time led to a "further dispersion of power" that had strengthened the committee chairmen and the executive branch at the expense of the central leadership.[17] However, more recent perspectives on the party leadership largely contend that there has been a resurgence in the power of the central leadership. Davidson (1988 and 1992) attributes this heightened significance of the party leadership to a number of factors, among them a contraction in the net congressional workload, limitations in the number of legislative actors present at key procedural junctures, and a resurgence in party-line voting.[18] Rohde (1991) and Sinclair (1992) support this interpretation.

Cox and McCubbins (1993) add a final cautionary note, arguing that an assessment of party significance leads them to characterize the legislative process as one of "limited party government."[19] In sum, the literature pertaining to the significance of the party leadership relative to other legislative actors moved from one end of the spectrum to the other (and perhaps back) from the early 1960s to recent times.

THE "AVERAGE" HOUSE MEMBER

In terms of the changes in the characteristics of the "average" House member noted in the literature above, the respondents repeatedly emphasized features different than the literature when they were asked to identify consequential changes within the House membership. While this is not to suggest that the literature and the actors' perspectives are necessarily mutually exclusive, the point is that the actors focused on different aspects of the legislators as being most important in under-standing the modern membership and legislating today. Furthermore, their emphasis is supported by the empirical evidence of the cases and the chamber demographics. In fact, looking for changes in the "kinds of people," the legislators' professional and political backgrounds, and other changes cited in the literature, we do not find much in the way of compelling evidence to support those particular assertions of wholesale and meaningful change. While the evidence in that regard is mixed, without question the picture painted by the cases and the actors them-selves is quite different from the literature in its focus.

Demographically, the period from the 87th and 88th Congress (1961–64) to the 103rd Congress (1993–94) saw the average member become less likely to be a lawyer (57 percent to 42 percent), but he or she remained just about as likely to have business experience (31 percent to 30 percent). The average member became moderately more junior in terms of service, with the member's mean term moving from 5.7 to 5.3 terms, and the median number of terms changing from 5 to 4.[20] Elec-torally, over the same period, the number of members with 10 terms of service or more decreased slightly from seventy-four to sixty-seven (17 percent to 15 percent), while the percentage of safe seats increased from an early 1960s average of 61.3 percent to 65.6 percent. In the individ-ual members' general floor voting, party unity on floor votes increased greatly from the early 1960s' average of 50.5 percent to 63.5 percent in the 103rd Congress. The case histories, summarized in tables 5.1 through 5.5, shed further light in this direction, and this evidence also downplays the impact of commonly alleged changes in member attributes.

TABLE 5.1
Committee Legislator Characteristics in the Six Cases, Part I

Case/Year Passed	Committee/ # D and R	Subcommittee, # D and R	Percent with Bachelors Degrees[21]	Percent with Profess'l Degrees[22]	Percent with Graduate Degrees[23]	Percent with Relevant Graduate Degrees[24]
For Aid/ '62	App/ 28–20[25]	7–4[26]	79	56	10	2
Col Aid/ '63	EL/ 19–12	5–3	97	58	16	10
UMT/ '64	BC/ 19–14	8–5	94	70	3	3
For Aid/ '93	App/ 37–23	8–4	93	52	15	10
Goals/ '94	EL/ 24–15[27]	15–99	5	44	38	21
RTC/ '93	BFU/ 30–20[28]	18–12	98	39	15	8

TABLE 5.2
Committee Legislator Characteristics in the Six Cases, Part II

Case	Percent with Military Service[29]	Percent with Prior Public Service[30]	Average # of Terms[31]	Percent with Prior Political Experience[32]	Percent Listing Party Activities[33]	Percent of Carpetbagger[34]
For Aid/ '62	60	81	7.8	15	23	8
Col Aid/ '63	68	77	3.5	42	29	13
UMT/ '64	55	97	4.0	33	24	21
For Aid/ '93	45	95	7.4	12	32	17
Goals/ '94	28	90	4.6	64	36	13
RTC/ '93	21	89	2.9	33	26	20

TABLE 5.3

Aggregated Legislator and Committee Characteristics in the Six Cases, Part I

Cases/ Sample Size	Average Committee # D and R	Average Subc'tee # D and R	Percent with Bachelor's Degrees[35]	Percent with Professional Degrees[36]	Percent with Graduate Degrees[37]	Percent with Relevant Graduate Degrees[38]
'60s/ 112 MCs[39]	22D-15R	7D-4R	88 (99)	61 (68)	10 (11)	4 (5)
'90s/ 160 MCs	30D-19R	14D-8R	96 (153)	45 (72)	21 (33)	12 (19)

TABLE 5.4
Aggregated Legislator Characteristics in the Six Cases, Part II

Cases/ Sample Size	Percent with Military Service[40]	Percent with Prior Public Service[41]	Percent[42] with Prior Political Experience	Percent[43] Listing Party Activities	Percent[44] of Carpetbaggers	Percent of Advanced Degrees, All Types
'60s/ 112 MCs[45]	61 (68)	85 (95)	28 (31)	25 (28)	13 (15)	71 (79)
'90s/ 160 MCs	32 (51)	91 (146)	33 (52)	31 (49)	17 (27)	66 (105)

TABLE 5.5

Legislator Formal Activities by Number and Seniority for the Six Cases

Case/Year Passed	House Sponsors/Average Seniority[46]	Committee-Subcom'tee Amendments/Seniority[47]	House Floor Motions[48] and Amendment/Seniority	Number of Different Floor Speakers/Seniority[49]	House Conferees/Average Seniority[50]	Multiple Jurisdiction/Additional MCs[51]
For Aid/'62	1/8	Executive Session[52]	10/5.2	46/7.1	5/12.8	N/A
Col Aid/'63	1/5	8/3.8[53]	7/3.3	56/5.0	9/4.1	N/A
UMT/'64	1/10	Executive Session[54]	9/8.0	48/4.4	No conference	N/A
For Aid/'93	1/13	0	6/7.7	33/6.6	14/9.2	N/A
Goals/'94	39/4.5[55]	6/3.5	6/6.4[56]	59/4.8	33/6.2[57]	EC, FA/88[58]
RTC/'93	8/8.1[59]	11/4.8	3/12.0	23/5.1	17/9.5[60]	Jud, Gvt O/77

Examining the members' education and relevant experience represented in the three standing committees comprising this study, we find that while the paired committee samples show members with 8 percent more bachelor degrees in the modern era, we also find an average member less likely to have a professional degree in the 1990s (45 percent versus 61 percent in the 1960s). The member of the 1990s was more likely to have a graduate degree (21 percent in the 1990s to 10 percent in the 1960s), though conversely about 95 percent of the members' professional degrees were law degrees in the early 1960s. The average member's graduate degree was more likely to be relevant to the committee's policy jurisdiction in the 1990s cases, though this average still remains somewhat low at 12 percent. The average member of the 1990s was also more likely to have had the benefit of prior public service and prior political experience in achieving his or her policy objectives on the committee, as those averages remained high in both periods. As we might expect, the modern member is more likely to be a carpetbagger, and, perhaps surprisingly, is more likely to have considered his party activities as significant in his pre-House career. The average member of the 1990s is far more likely not to have served in the military (32 percent versus the 1960s' 61 percent) and, again perhaps surprisingly, is less likely to have an advanced degree of any type whatsoever (66 percent compared to the early 1960s' 71 percent).

In terms of legislator activities, table 5.5 quantifies the legislators' formal activities in the cases by average seniority, from sponsorship to conference. Analyzing these data, we find an average of twelve more members involved in the committee charged with reporting each law in the 1990s versus the 1960s, as well as an average of eleven more members involved at the subcommittee level. Table 5.5 also shows that sponsorship of legislation remained an activity open to and exercised by legislators of all tenures, as did committee and subcommittee amending, floor speaking, and conferring, evidence contrary to some assertions within the literature. Floor motions and amendments actually became a somewhat more senior activity in the 1990s, which we might expect given the much greater incidence of restrictive or closed rules and the relative seniority of the floor managers in the latter cases. Finally, multiple committee jurisdictions in two of the three cases from the 1990s meant that an average of eighty-three more legislators had the opportunity to influence (or seek to prevent) those eventual outcomes, even above the increase in legislators involved in passage that resulted from the uniform expansion of the committees.

Consistent with these chamber characteristics, the respondents identified other changes and continuities they viewed as crucial in describing the attributes of the "average" legislator in the two periods. Taken collectively, the evidence indicates five consequential changes and four essential continuities, and these features encompass the most essential attributes of the membership in the opinion of the legislative actors themselves. Likewise, each of these changes and continuities has associated implications for the construction of supportive majorities:

Change: The propensity of the average member to form significant interpersonal relationships is less, and there is far less civility among the members.   The six respondents with House service in both periods identified a general "lack of civility" among the legislators of the 1990s as a critical difference between the members of the 1960s and those from the 1990s. They also described this characteristic as a significant hindrance to the conduct of the House's legislative business. Modern members are less likely to have the breadth or depth of personal relationships among their colleagues that members of the early 1960s enjoyed, and they are also less likely to be naturally "civil" in policy debates, a trend apparent from the cases. Respondents described the members from the 1990s as more contentious and more often cynical or negative in their dealings with their House colleagues, particularly those across the aisle. Consistent with this assertion, the 1990s' respondents frequently included phrases such as "absolutely did not trust X" or "didn't really know Y at all" when describing some subcommittee colleagues, unlike the respondents from the 1960s.

As another indicator of this trend, respondents from the 1960s were far more likely to couch their accounts of the passage of the laws in personal terms, citing fellow subcommittee members' policy goals and opinions while demonstrating a solid working knowledge of the personalities and district concerns of their colleagues. As one member with service in both periods put it, "The personal relationships and friendships (of the 1960s) might not have been all that cogent (to the bill being deliberated) by themselves, but favors and consideration certainly helped the process along." Respondents from the cases from the 1990s, on the contrary, were much more likely to describe the policy outcomes in terms of policy properties and relevant interest groups, rather than the personal stakes of their colleagues. Given the critical importance of member-to-member contacts as a factor in realizing legislative success, this change clearly made the construction of issue coalitions more difficult in the House in the modern era.

Change: Bitter partisanship predominates in the House now, and members come to the House with much stronger policy predispositions.   As a member with service in both periods asserted, "The House member of the 1990s comes to Congress thinking he has the answers already. Ideology drives too many of these folks, and they just don't want to listen or learn." Former Representative Lee Hamilton (D-IN), citing a recent *Congressional Quarterly* study, noted that chamber activities had been "overwhelmed by the excessive partisanship" that would evidence itself in "more party line votes in this Congress than in any since the Taft Presidency."[61] Identifying this trend as one that had developed over several Congresses, he asserted that the average legislator of the 1990s had become "too negative, too bitter, (and) too contentious."[62] Conversely, respondents with service in the 1960s at times described stronger relationships with members across the aisle than with members of their own parties.

As an interesting aside, the respondents with service in the 1960s frequently mentioned their common service in the military and the general respect for authority engendered by that service as a key facilitator of member-to-member relationships and cooperation with each other and committee and chamber leaders. The three-committee sample shows evidence of this decline, as the average member did become much less likely to be a military veteran (59 percent to 36 percent). Many of the members of the 1960s had World War II–era military service, and a number of respondents asserted that the common experiences and challenges of World War II ensured that almost every legislator had been involved in issues "much larger than ourselves," as one respondent put it.

In any event, the floor debates in the cases also provide strong evidence of the bitter partisan rhetoric that respondents see as all too common in the modern House. The respondents and cases clearly indicate that an increase in partisanship and a membership generally less willing to listen to one another have had significant and adverse consequences for the construction of the ad hoc issue coalitions necessary for policy success.

Change: There is heightened racial, gender, and social diversity in the House. Another consequential change in the House membership, highlighted by respondents with service in both periods, has come as a result of the increased racial and gender diversity in the House of the 1990s. The average House member in recent times has become much more likely to be a woman or African American than a counterpart from the early 1960s, as the percentage of African American members increased from under 1 percent in the early 1960s to nearly 9 percent in the 1990s and the percentage of women simultaneously moved from 4 percent to 11 percent. This change has meant that there is a greater opportunity for members to introduce (at the very least) racial and gender issues into the public forum and that more members are inclined to do so. Issues of these sorts were successfully introduced into the policy debates in two of the three cases in the 1990s, and the influence of the Congressional Black Caucus and existence of informal women's caucuses at the committee level evident in the cases attest to this trend as well.

To elaborate, Adam Clayton Powell Jr.'s abortive attempt to include desegregation language in the college aid bill serves as the only example of any attempt to address racial or gender issues in the 1960s cases, and it was used by southern Democrats and conservative Republicans to club the bill to death. On the contrary, two of the three laws considered in the 1990s cases had racial or gender issues as a key part of the general debate and the committee and conference activities. In the consideration of the Goals 2000 law, the debate included Major Owens's (D-NY) opportunity-to-learn standards, and an informal caucus on gender issues, consisting of Karan English (D-AZ), Jolene Unsoeld (D-WA), Susan Molinari (R-NY), and Marge Roukema (R-NJ), screened the bill for gender acceptability in committee. In the Resolution Trust Corporation closeout-financing bill, one of the more significant issues negotiated in conference was Kweisi Mfume's (D-MD) call for specific minority-contracting language. Setting aside the positive normative aspects of this heightened diversity, the net effect of the change has been to make the construction of policy coalitions somewhat more difficult, since these members represent additional interests that now must often be satisfied to achieve a working majority.

Nonetheless, one member cited this trend as the most positive member change he observed between the two periods, noting, "Today's House is more representative . . . women, blacks, and Hispanics bring different viewpoints to the debate, and that's healthy." Heightened racial and gender diversity in the House has provided new opportunities to introduce racial and gender issues into the public policy debate in the modern era, with corresponding challenges for would-be legislative champions.

Change: The average member has widely expanded issue opportunities. With greatly expanded committee memberships and the increase in multijurisdictional consideration of legislative initiatives, the average member has far greater opportunities to involve himself or herself in a wider range of issues or to introduce items of personal interest into the policy mix. Sponsorship, subcommittee and committee amendment, and floor activities other than floor amendments remained about the same in both periods, while committee memberships increased over the period. Therefore, the net opportunities open to the rank-and-file member of the House to serve in the chamber and to become involved in issues of personal interest have greatly increased over the period from the early

1960s to the early 1990s. The net effect of this change is to have made it more difficult to construct a supportive majority, given the additional viewpoints routinely considered and the additional members needed to achieve a majority at a variety of junctures.

Similarly, these expanded issue opportunities have encouraged the growth of "point specialists" among legislators. These members aim at making relatively minor changes within a whole host of bills, rather than focusing their legislative energies on the broad policy products of one or a few committees. They can take one aspect of policy in general, such as minority contracting provisions or the promotion of a particular industry, and intervene throughout a variety of committees to further the prospects of that particular specialized policy concern.

Change: "Bomb throwing" is far more widespread now than in the 1960s.   House members in the early 1990s are more likely to view their party activities prior to entering the House as significant career activities, and their predisposition is more toward party unity than their counterparts from the 1960s. Members were generally described by those respondents with experience in both periods as much less likely to listen, less likely to be interested in compromise or negotiation, and generally much more partisan than the average member of the early 1960s. Members were far less likely to "throw bombs" for bombs' sake in the early 1960s. Even high-profile Otto Passman, as he vocally and publicly attacked the Kennedy foreign aid plan, still worked hard and collegially behind the scenes to achieve legislative objectives. A variety of respondents from the 1990s' cases identified members whom they viewed as merely seeking to deny others' legislative efforts with no other goal than making a public name for themselves. Unlike the House of the early 1960s, respondents in the 1990s felt that a necessary step in constructing a working majority was to identify and isolate as much as possible these "bomb throwers," thus making the legislative task more difficult as a result.

The evidence reveals four fundamental continuities in the House members as well.

Continuity: The average House legislator's qualifications are not significantly different in the modern era.   The average House legislator of the early 1990s, when compared with his counterpart of the early 1960s, is less likely to have formal legal training, and he or she has slightly less House legislating experience. Conversely, the modern legislator has slightly more prior public service experience and more graduate education. He has about the same chance of having business experience but is more likely to have some graduate training in an area of jurisdiction on his committee. In general, the average House member is more likely to have an undergraduate education but is actually less likely to have an advanced degree of any type. He is slightly more likely to have prior policy experience in the policy areas covered by his committee work and slightly more likely to be a carpetbagger. All in all, the qualifications of the average House legislator seem to be a wash. The evidence indicates that changes in the average legislator qualifications over the two periods generally offer neither help nor hindrance to the actors seeking to put together an issue coalition.

Continuity: The impact of seniority on the legislative process has not changed significantly. For the average member, the impact of seniority as a determinant of influence and opportunity at the various levels of the legislative process did not change significantly since the 1960s. Referring to table 5.5, the case evidence shows no trends in the importance of seniority over the period, as measured by sponsorship, committee and subcommittee amendments, floor speaking, or conference participation. Floor motions and amendments have become a more senior activity, likely a result of the restriction in floor amendments altogether. Respondent accounts support this assertion of continuity as well, with both junior and senior legislators having prominent roles in the passage of all six laws considered.

Continuity: Reputation, interpersonal skills, and integrity remain critical in the realization of legislative success. In both periods, legislators continually categorized fellow participants in terms of their knowledge of the relevant policy area and the legislative process, their willingness to work with colleagues, and their perceived level of integrity. The respondents uniformly named these characteristics as crucial identifiers that would lead to legislative success, and many related stories of legislators of opposing party or conflicting ideology who had (perhaps grudgingly) earned their respect for these personal characteristics despite their policy differences. While difficult to quantify, these personal traits of policy and parliamentary expertise, "contractual" honesty, and interpersonal skills were commonly attributed to the willful agents who achieved success in the six cases. Respondents viewed these attributes as critical legislative resources in both periods, in spite of the contextual changes that had occurred by the 1990s.

Continuity: Legislators continue to pursue the same self-determined goals. Respondents from both periods of interest to this study mentioned the same legislator goals so well described by Mayhew, Fenno, and Kingdon. The primary legislator goals of the 1960s, as in the 1990s, remain reelection and the satisfaction of constituents, the pursuit of intra-Washington or intrachamber influence, and the search for good public policy solutions. Respondents did add one more goal to that list, however, an additional legislator objective identified occasionally in the interviews by respondents and usually attributed to others. This fourth motive was the goal of assisting or thwarting a colleague's policy aims for purely personal reasons. This goal was a consistent feature of the accounts of passage from both periods, and it seemed no lesser or greater in either period. This motive certainly is treated as a serious operating assumption by legislators.

THE CHAMBER AND COMMITTEE LEADERS

Regarding the chamber and committee leaders, we might expect to see a general centralization or decentralization of the chamber leadership function or some other pattern of change in the importance of seniority that would emerge as a result of the reforms of the early 1970s. We might expect to see either greater or lesser involvement of the chamber leaders in the passage of individual laws in the two periods, or we might look for changing goals on the part of the House and various committee and subcommittee leaders. And certainly, we might expect some change in the leadership styles employed by the various House leaders, in light of the common perception that the stereotypical "autocrat" of the 1960s would have necessarily given way to some other more collegial kind of committee or subcommittee leader.

As it turns out, the evidence offered by an examination of the passage of the six cases and the respondents to this study demonstrates no systematic changes of any of the above sorts. Beginning with the respondent descriptions of the chamber leadership's centralization, table 5.6 summarizes the respondent characterizations of leader styles at the chamber, committee, and subcommittee levels for each of the six cases. After Speaker Rayburn's tightly centralized control of the chamber until his death in November of 1961, Speaker McCormack was far more decentralized in his management of the House's legislative business, according to all respondent accounts. This decentralization was characteristic of Speaker Foley in the 103rd Congress, though Speaker Gingrich reversed the trend in the 104th, more closely resembling Speaker Jim Wright before Foley. Similarly, there was no evidence of any systematic propensity on the part of the sampled committee and subcommittee leaders to be more or less inclined to inclusiveness. Committee or chamber leadership styles, in the view of the respondents, are primarily a function of the personality of the leader in question. Similarly, the hierarchical chamber and internal committee support for the leader, in addition to the mix of personalities and interests represented in the organization led, determine the opportunities available to each leader.

Similarly, there was no apparent systematic difference in the seniority of the key leaders relevant to the passage of the six cases, as table 5.7 indicates. Instead, we see similar levels of seniority in the two periods for the Speakers, the majority leaders, the minority leaders, and the committee chairs, and a wide variety of tenures represented among the ranking minority members and chairs of the committees and subcommittees. The Rules Committee of the 103rd Congress had a more junior though still senior membership, and also a less independent one, but otherwise there were no systematic differences. The most junior member represented in a leadership position was Albert Quie (R-MN) in the position of ranking minority member on Edith Green's (D-OR) Special Education Subcommittee in the 88th Congress, and the most senior member represented was the 103rd Congress' Appropriations Committee chairman, William Natcher (D-KY), with twenty-one terms.

Table 5.8 offers an overview of the actions, influence, and goals of the key leaders and other internal actors evident in the case histories, and as the respondents noted, any number of actors could turn out to be critical in the success or failure of a legislative initiative. Viewing the snapshots of these key actors, their evident goals, and their actions in the passage of the laws, the most important pattern that emerges from the chart is no pattern at all. That is, in both periods, from the early 1960s to the early 1990s, there were no distinctive patterns of actions, goals, or influence that would predict legislative success in general. Put another way, the key leaders were at times involved in the process for personal, district, or national policy reasons, and their actions ranged from only casual interest to intense involvement in the process in the cases from both periods. Three fundamental continuities emerge from the evidence:

Continuity: Committee and chamber majority party leader support or, at minimum, nonactive opposition remains a critically important element of legislative success.   Every respondent, from all six cases in both periods, identified the subcommittee, committee, and chamber leadership's support, or at least nonactive opposition, as essential to the realization of legislative success. The cases provide evidence of this necessity, as in each case the bill did not become law until at least the majority leadership was in support across the board, with the exception of Rules Committee chairman Howard Smith's (D-VA) continued opposition to the Higher Education Facilities Act of 1963. Even so, the combined efforts of the chamber and committee leadership, as well as the personal efforts of President Johnson, were successfully brought to bear to overcome that one leader's opposition. Not surprisingly, legislative actors seeking policy success view the majority leadership's support or at least indifference as a critical element of that success.

TABLE 5.6
Respondent Assessments of Leader Management Styles for the Six Cases

Case/Year	Speaker	Style[63]	Cmtee Chair	Style	Subc Chair	Style
For Aid/'62	Rayburn/ McCormack	Centralized Decentralized	Cannon	Decentralized	Passman	Mixed
Col Aid/'63	McCormack	Decentralized	Powell	Decentralized	Green	Centralized
UMT/'64	McCormack	Decentralized	Patman	Centralized	Rains	Centralized
For Aid/'93	Foley	Decentralized	Natcher	Decentralized	Obey	Centralized
Goals/'94	Foley	Decentralized	Ford	Centralized	Kildee	Decentralized
RTC/'93	Foley	Decentralized	Gonzalez	Decentralized	Neal	Decentralized

TABLE 5.7

Key Leader Seniority in the Six Cases, by Number of Terms

Case/Year	Speaker	Maj Leader	Min Leader	Rules Chair	Cmtee Chair	Cmtee RMM	Subc Chair	Subc RMM	Chief Sponsor
For Aid/'62	18	8	14	16	20	20	8	20	8
Col Aid/'63	19	9	15	17	10	6	5	4	5
UMT/'64	19	9	15	17	18	13	10	8	10
For Aid/'93	15	9	19	11	21	16	13	9	13
Goals/'94	15	9	19	11	15	10	9	10	9
RTC/'93	15	9	19	11	17	9	10	7	10

TABLE 5.8

The Evident Actions, Goals, and Influence of the Key House Leaders in the Six Cases

PART I

Case/Year	Key Actor[64]	Key Actions in the Passage of the Case	Evident or Attributed Goals	Relative Influence[65]
For Aid/'62	Passman (Sub chr)	Championed the bill Hearings and negotiat Vocally opposed aid Negotiated w/Kennedy	Opposed foreign aid District benefits Agency oversight Report product on time	Significant
For Aid/'62	Cannon (App chr)	Supported Passman	Opposed foreign aid	Moderate
For Aid/'62	Smith (Rules chr)	Reported the rule	Supported Passman	Low
For Aid/'62	McCormack (Spkr)	Brought bill to floor	Supported Kennedy plan	Low
Col Aid/'63	Green (Sub chr)	Championed the bill	Educational policy goals Kennedy administration supporter	Significant
Col Aid/'63	Powell (EL chr)	Vocal supporter Negotiation w/ admin	Educational policy goals High public profile	Significant

(continued on next page)

TABLE 5.8 (continued)

PART I

Case/ Year	Key Actor[64]	Key Actions in the Passage of the Case	Evident or Attributed Goals	Relative Influence[65]
Col Aid/ '63	Smith (Rules chr)	Delayed floor consider	Opposed federal school aid	Significant
Col Aid/ '63	McCormack (Spkr)	Exacted local benefits Bill to floor after delay	District benefits Parochial school aid goals Avoid legislative defeat	Significant
UMT/ '64	Rains (Sub chr)	Championed the bill	Mass transit policy goals Supported Johnson goals	Significant
UMT/ '64	Patman (BC chr)	Hearings and negotiat	Supported Johnson goals	Significant
UMT/ '64	Smith (Rules chr)	Reported the rule	Supported Johnson goals	Low
UMT/ '64	McCormack	Brought bill to floor	Supported Johnson goals	Low

(continued on next page)

TABLE 5.8 (continued)

PART II

Case/Year	Key Actor[64]	Key Actions in the Passage of the Case	Evident or Attributed Goals	Relative Influence[65]
For Aid/'93	Obey (Sub chr)	Co-championed bill	Foreign policy goals Report product on time	Significant
For Aid/'93	Natcher (App chr)	Bill reported by committee	Report product on time	Low
For Aid/'93	Moakley (Rule chr)	Reported the rule	Supported Foley/Clinton goals	Low
For Aid/'93	Foley (Spkr)	Brought bill to floor	Avoid legislative defeat	Low
Goals/'94	Kildee (Sub chr)	Hearings and negotiation	Educational policy goals	Significant
Goals/'94	Ford (EL chr)	Championed the bill	Educational policy goals	Significant
Goals/'94	Moakley (Rule chr)	Reported the rule	Supported Foley/Ford/Riley	Low
Goals/'94	Foley (Spkr)	Brought bill to floor	Avoid legislative defeat	Low

(continued on next page)

TABLE 5.8 (continued)

PART II

Case/ Year	Key Actor[64]	Key Actions in the Passage of the Case	Evident or Attributed Goals	Relative Influence[65]
RTC/ '93	Neal (sub chr)	Hearings and negotiat Co-championed bill	Complete S&L debacle	Significant
RTC/ '93	Gonzalez (B chr)	Hearings and negotiat Co-championed bill	Complete S&L debacle	Significant
RTC/ '93	Moakley (Rule chr)	Reported the rule	Supported Foley/Gonzalez	Low
RTC/ '93	Foley (Spkr)	Brought bill to floor	Complete S&L debacle Avoid legislative defeat	Significant

Continuity: The power of position remains clearly evident.   The second fundamental continuity to emerge from the examination of the case histories and the corresponding respondent accounts of the chamber and committee leaders is the universal respect for the power of position. In both periods, the primary power of the chamber leaders revolved around the agenda-setting, caucus leadership, and appointment functions, while the committee and subcommittee leaders were recognized as the masters of their particular policy domains. The committee and subcommittee leaders, regardless of the will of the majority, maintained the ability to schedule hearings or to dictate committee consideration of legislative initiatives. Alternatively, they also were empowered to not do any of those things, and these leaders were recognized by all of the respondents from both periods as key actors with unique powers that must be respected by those seeking legislative success. Position mattered in both periods, and it continues to matter.

Continuity: Committee and chamber leadership style is a highly individualized trait primarily dependent on the incumbent's personality. The various leaders' styles greatly influence both the shape and the likelihood of legislative success.   For each of the key legislative leaders in all six cases, respondent accounts and the case evidence demonstrate that while the chamber and committee leaders share the same general goals as the other legislators, there is no algorithm to explain the miscellaneous differences in their leadership styles. There are no patterns of change or continuities over time in the chamber or within the committees to allow prediction of style or likely committee characteristics. As one staff member responded flatly, "Much of the legislative process is personality-driven, and the personalities of the leaders matter most." As another staffer with service in both periods noted, "Committee chairs want to produce the product on time, and controversy slows it down and risks a veto. Most chairmen are more than willing to make life hard for members who slow things down." In any event, almost every respondent in both periods, when asked to identify the elements necessary to the realization of legislative success, first mentioned securing the support of the committee leaders. Chamber and committee leadership remains largely a function of personality and circumstances, even as it is judged by all respondents to be a critical determinant of legislative success.

THE HOUSE STAFFS

The House staffs, whether one is referring to institutional, committee, or personal staffs, grew explosively over the period from the early 1960s to the early 1990s. In light of the tremendous increase in staffers of all varieties reflected in table 5.9, we might expect changes in the staffers'

TABLE 5.9

House Staffs in the Early 1960s Compared to the Staffs of the 1990s

Case/Year	Cmtee[66] Staffers	Total House[67] Employee	Library of Cong[68] Employee	Cong Research Service	General Account Office	Cong Budget Office[69]	Office of Technol Assess
For Aid/'62	59	2,441	2,779	183	5,074	—	—
Col Aid/'63	25	2,441	2,779	183	5,074	—	—
UMT/'64	14	2,441	2,779	183	5,074	—	—
For Aid/'93	227	7,400	5,033	814	4,958	230	143
Goals/'94	112	7,400[70]	5,033	814	4,958	230	143
RTC/'92	100	7,400	5,033	814	4,958	230	143

actions in the legislative process, the staffers' relative influence in the legislative process, or in other characteristics related to these additional actors. The case histories and the respondent accounts provide evidence of some basic, though not radical, changes in the influence and actions of staff members in the passage of legislation over the period of interest.

Individual staff members were cited by several case respondents as critical agents of the resultant legislative success in two of the case histories, including the passage of the Urban Mass Transportation Act of 1964 and the passage of Goals 2000 in 1994. John Barriere, director of Albert Rains's (D-AL) subcommittee from 1949 through the passage of the mass transit law, was described by member respondents as having had "the complete confidence of Rains" and was instrumental in forging the ad hoc issue coalition that eventually led to passage of the mass transit measure. Similarly, education issue legislative counsel Jack Jennings was described by one respondent as "an incredibly strong leader," singularly dynamic in assembling the eventual language acceptable to both sides of the aisle and helping to forge the eventual bipartisan passage of the ideologically-charged Goals 2000 measure. While other staff members were mentioned as having made important contributions in the passage of the six legislative initiatives, these two particular staff members were mentioned repeatedly as key actors.

In general, an examination of the cases, the House staff composition, and the respondent accounts indicates that, like the expansion of the committee and subcommittee memberships, the net result of the increase in staffers has been to add additional actors into the mix of individual policy outcomes. Issue complexity and diversity increased, partly in response to the government's foray into new policy areas since the 1960s and partly just a result of simple arithmetic growth in federal regulation. In any event, these factors and others created a need for many of the newly created positions, and several member respondents with service in the Congress of the early 1990s indicated that some of the additional staff members felt as though "they're here, so they have to do something."

With the staff in the 1990s still responsible for the negotiation and reconciliation of second- and third-tier legislative issues, and given the increases in issue complexity and breadth of the federal statutes, there remains a great deal of room for personal policy authorship in the details of most initiatives. It was in this part of the policymaking process that many respondents felt that the staffers' role had changed. While the members continued to address the high-profile and politically charged issues themselves, and while the staffs generally performed the same functions in the same professional manner in both sets of cases, increasingly, both bureaucratic agents and congressional staffers are able and eager to influence the process through the statute details. Out of this, two contextual changes and one fundamental continuity emerge.

Change: The House staffs have grown explosively in the period since the early 1960s.   As table 5.9 illustrates, the various House staffs in support of the legislative effort in the District of Columbia expanded astronomically over the period from the early 1960s to the 1990s. As a quick illustration, imagine being the Banking Committee chairman in the early 1960s, with fourteen individuals working for you on banking issues. By the 1990s, however, your staff had increased to one hundred people, most of them talented and energetic individuals. Furthermore, each of the one hundred has his or her own ideas about good banking policy, and each has some point of access into the policymaking process. While you would still be in control of the eventual outcome, there is no way that you could know all of the details of the staffers' actions, the deals they had made, or the entirety of the legislative language written. By definition, the huge increase in staff numbers takes some control of the process away from the principals.

Change: "I have (and want) to do something."   While the staff grew at least partly in response to the increase in breadth and depth of issues across the policy spectrum, part of the increased influence of the staff on second-tier issues is of their own doing. Former and current members of the House uniformly described the staff as professional, hardworking, and energetic public servants. But the respondents from the latter period also identified the staff members as legislative actors seeking to influence at least the second-tier issues in accordance with their own views of good public policy. While this is unlikely to be a new phenomenon, the vastly increased numbers of staff members and the impossibility of close supervision by the principals with concurrent issue growth means that those staffers have more opportunity to do so. Similarly, with so many new actors seeking a niche in the legislative process, there is plenty of incentive to "do something" regardless of whether anything needs to be done, a phenomenon noted by respondents from the early 1990s.

Continuity: Members alone deal in the first-tier issues.   A commonality between the two periods is the fact that staff members still are not generally authorized to deal in what the members describe as "first-tier issues." First-tier issues are generally defined as the politically charged or high-profile issues of controversy between House factions or between the House and Senate prior to conference. Both staffers and members understand and acknowledge this fine line. As one member put it succinctly, "Staff is staff . . . those who forget, aren't staff." The key party or chamber staff negotiators, those individuals doing the often late-night coordination and negotiation in advance of a conference, committee, or floor consideration of a bill, are generally given guidance from the chairmen or key leaders for whom they work. This guidance involves policy preferences as well as information regarding what topics are on limits and what ones are not. Essentially, the politics of the process have remained the same for the members, while the staff has expanded to meet the demands of increased issue diversity and complexity. The staff in each of the six cases involved had important negotiating and coordinating roles at various junctures of the process, but the member respondents did not list the staff actions as a significant cause for concern in the pursuit of legislative success.

THE WILLFUL AGENTS

As I interviewed respondents regarding the importance of the various actors and components involved in the pursuit of legislative success, every respondent focused on a small set of key legislative champions who had pursued the legislation relentlessly. These willful agents were the actors who had pushed the legislative initiative through to fruition, against all obstacles. In each of the six cases, particular names kept coming up as we talked through the events leading to passage of the case laws, and as one member summarized, "Every piece of legislation needs a champion."

Table 5.10 lists the key legislative actors, or the willful agents, identified by the respondents as those individuals who were instrumental in enacting (or temporarily thwarting) the six laws examined in this study. The list of actors includes key House members and administration officials, in addition to the presidents mentioned by the respondents or prominent in the case histories. The key interest groups are identified only by industry or activity and are addressed in greater detail later in the book. The main theme of table 5.10 is that the willful agents are self-selected, and they come from a variety of sources. While the case histories describe the actions of these willful agents in some detail, the following fundamental continuities emerge from the analysis.

Continuity: "Every initiative needs a champion." For each case law, there was a small group of key actors who had set their minds on seeing a legislative initiative become law. In each of the six cases, hundreds of actors had the opportunity to push for something similar, and any number of other actors had the chance to influence the outcome sought by these willful agents. However, the respondents uniformly attributed the realization of that legislative success to the efforts of a handful of key leaders working together toward a common objective. While there have always been "showhorses" and "workhorses" in the House, as respondents noted in both periods, the legislative champions are the workhorses that do the chamber's legislative heavy lifting.

Continuity: Persistence, patience, hustle, and a willingness to compromise are the common characteristics of the willful agents who realize legislative success. Regardless of the period, and regardless of the level of background noise, the ability to stay focused on the political objective is necessary in order to realize legislative success. Senator Harrison Williams Jr. (D-NJ), for example, doggedly pursued mass transit aid for New Jersey despite a whole host of reversals. He worked at the project for at least five years and suffered numerous setbacks when agonizingly close to success, but he kept at it until the law was enacted. One current (and senior) member of the House noted having "about ten major pieces of legislation" ready to go if the opportunity for success were to arise, and he claimed to have been routinely working those issues through the relevant committees for many years. He was waiting to see if external events or shifts in member support would create conditions that would favor success. In sum, all members agreed that legislative champions who demonstrated persistence, patience, the willingness to compromise, and hustle were critical to the realization of legislative success.

THE NET RESULTS

The net effect of these changes and continuities in the internal House actors in the House over the last several decades has been to make the construction of supportive majorities more difficult. With a more contentious and less civil membership inclined toward fewer and more superficial interpersonal relationships, and given an ideology- and party-driven unwillingness to compromise among its members, the House of the early 1990s became a chamber less friendly to legislative initiatives. Furthermore, as a greatly expanded staff and expanded issue opportunities further fragmented legislative control, the fractious predispositions of the members and the heightened use of bomb throwing as a personal strategy clearly combined to present new challenges to actors pursuing policy goals in the modern House. Even as they highlighted key continuities between the periods, the respondents emphasized these consequential changes and the associated changes in the nature of member-to-member contacts that they have meant as critical aspects of contemporary policymaking.

TABLE 5.10

The Willful Agents in the Six Cases

Case/Year	The Willful Agents	Position	Most Significant Activity
For Aid/ '62	John Kennedy	President	Set policy and lobbied personally
	Otto Passman	Subc chair	Championed bill w/intense efforts
	Clarence Cannon	Approps chair	Appointed Passman, tacit support
	John Taber	RMM subc	Worked w/Passman, Repubs
Col Aid/ '63	John Kennedy	President	Set policy objectives
	Lyndon Johnson	President	Adopted cause, lobbied personally
	John McCormack	Speaker	Opposed until rec'd concessions
	Howard Smith	Rules chair	Opposed until pressured by P and Ds
	Adam Powell	EL chair	High-profile lobbying/negotiation
	Edith Green	Subc chair	Championed the bill w/intense efforts
	Higher educ. lobbies		Sought aid for facility construction
UMT/ '64	John Kennedy	President	Sacrificed bill for omnibus housing
	Lyndon Johnson	President	Adopted cause, lobbied personally
	Harrison Williams Jr	Senator	Championed bill years of effort in S
	Wright Patman	BC chair	Facilitated House passage for LBJ
	Albert Rains	Subc chair	Championed bill w/intense efforts
	John Barriere (PSM)	Rains's PSM	Acknowledged facilitator/negotiator
	Local transit companies		Opposed federal transit aid
	Subfederal authorities		Sought aid for transit improvements

(continued on next page)

TABLE 5.10 (continued)

Case/Year	The Willful Agents	Position	Most Significant Activity
For Aid/ '93	Bill Clinton	President	Set policy and lobbied personally
	Strobe Talbott	Ambass, CIS	Gave briefings and lobbied intensely
	David Obey	Subc chair	Championed bill, bipartisan approach
	Bob Livingston	Subc RMM	Negotiated w/Obey
	Mitch McConnell	Senator, RMM	Conference negotiations
Goals/ '94	George Bush	President	Set initial policy goals
	Lamar Alexander	Educ secretary	Drafted original policy and lobbied
	Bill Clinton	President	Revised policy goals and lobbied
	Richard Riley	Educ secretary	Lobbied intensely for passage
	William Ford	Educ/Labor chair	Championed bill despite 1st setbacks
	Dale Kildee	Subc chair	Assisted Ford /managed subc
	Jack Jennings (PSM)	Ford's leg/cnsl	Important compromise/negotiation
RTC/ '93	Lloyd Bentsen	Treas secretary	Lobbied intensely for closeout funds
	Roger Altman	RTC chief	Replaced Casey, cleaned up RTC
	Henry Gonzalez	BFU chair	Championed the bill, lobbied hard
	Stephen Neal	Subc chair	Assisted Gonzalez, managed subc
	Thomas Foley	Speaker	Lobbied hard for final passage
	S&L/banking officials		Sought support for industry bailout

CHAPTER 6

Legislative Actors II: The External Actors

So many members get told now, "You're out of touch." The truth is, today we're way too "in touch."

—House member with service in the 1960s and 1990s

Few would dispute the fact that a wide variety of legislative actors external to the House, ranging from the president to the electorate, have profound influences over the eventual shape of most public policy outcomes. Like the internal actors described in the last chapter, many of these actors have also been alleged to have changed significantly since the early 1960s. In theory, there are a number of ways that these actors may have changed that could have had process-altering consequences. The president and executive agencies may have systematically and consequentially modified their specific functions in the legislative process, or those actors' relative significance to the realization of legislative success could have changed over time. Changes in the numbers of these various actors, among them executive agency personnel, interest group members, and constituents, could have had serious consequences for the nature of the legislative process. The nature and amount of media coverage could also have changed with implications for the construction of supportive voting majorities. Constituent pressures, relationships, and activities might have changed over the period from the early 1960s to the 1990s as well. Any or all of these external actors could have changed consequentially in their legislative strategies, motives, methods, or influence.

A number of authors have identified external actor changes of these varieties. The most frequently posited or implied actor change in the literature regarding the period since the 1960s is variation in the legislative process caused by changes in interest groups. Gross (1953) predicted a coming increase in interest group numbers and influence, noting "the probability is that private organizations will extend their scope and that increasing power will be concentrated in the hands of the dominant groups."[1] Bauer and colleagues (1972), however, demonstrated that interest groups were already a potent force in the legislative process in the early 1960s, claiming that "hundreds" of groups were interested in the passage of the Trade Expansion Act of 1962 while citing by name the most active thirty-two.[2] Huntington (1965) continued this theme of expanding interest group influence, arguing that an "organizational revolution," in the form of an "emergence of other large, national bureaucratic organizations (such as) manufacturing corporations, banks, insurance companies, labor unions, trade associations, farm organizations," and others, had confronted Congress with "an institutional 'adaptation crisis.'"[3] The clear expectation was that the increasing numbers of interest groups active in the policy arena would have significant implications for the shape of the legislative process in the years to come.

Subsequent scholars observing the state of the legislative process in the 1970s and 1980s generally claimed that these expectations had proven correct. Heclo (1978) argued that even as government administrative need contributed to the phenomenon, the "almost inevitable tendency of successfully enacted policies unwittingly to propagate hybrid interests" helped encourage a growth of groups to more than eighteen hundred organizations with forty thousand employees headquartered in Washington by 1977.[4] While Heclo was careful to avoid speculating on any concurrent change in interest group effectiveness, he clearly felt that the increase in numbers and the increasingly fragmented nature of the legislative system had altered the public policy processes. Sundquist (1981) echoed this theme, noting that a general change from "party regularity to political individualism" was evidenced in a similar change in the nature of interest groups from older style "professional" groups to "relatively undisciplined, essentially individualistic (groups)," characterized best by an increasing number of single-issue interest groups or an "organized individualism."[5] Walker (1983) analyzed the increasing numbers of interest groups and their strategies for sustaining themselves, noting that while few comprehensive statistics were available, all evidence pointed to a marked increase in interest group numbers in the 1970s.[6] He further argued that the importance of patronage to the groups, and the focus of those patrons on public policy outcomes, meant that those groups had incentive to become even more actively and directly engaged in the policymaking process.[7]

More recent accounts of changes in interest group significance or their strategies have continued these themes. Heclo (1989), in describing the "factionalism" of the modern era, argues that interest groups "have been growing in number, are more prone to open conflict, (and) are less stable in their alliances."[8] Similarly, Peterson (1990) describes a "riot of pluralism" in the contemporary political process, seeing an "expanding range of policy demands, heightening political discord, and (weakened) integrative capabilities of partisan coalitions" since the early 1960s.[9] Much of the blame, in his view, rests upon the interests that threaten to "overload the political system with competing and sometimes antithetical group demands that resist coherent executive management," echoing the concerns of E. E. Schattschneider (1960).[10] Hrebenar and Scott (1990) summarize this view of change in the interest group roles, citing estimates of between 10,000 and 20,000 lobbyists working in the D.C. policy community as part of about 2,000 professional and national non-profit trade organizations, a far cry from the estimated 1,180 lobbyists there in 1946.[11] These authors also identify changes in interest group strategies intended to make them generally more effective in achieving their policy aims, including increased use of the media and direct appeals to legislator constituents.[12] Only Hall and Wayman (1990), in contrast, argue that despite the increase in the number of groups, the evidence for resulting change in the nature of the legislative process as measured by floor voting results is slim.[13]

Another commonly cited category of external actor change includes those explanations of legislative change that focus upon the increasing relative size and significance of the executive branch. These accounts include both claims of presidential encroachment and executive agency dominance. Gross (1953) predicted an executive branch and federal governmental ascendance, arguing that "the long-range outlook seems to favor continued expansion of executive agencies and stronger Federal government as compared with state and local governments." He predicted that the "dominant role . . . will continue to shift back and forth between executive officials and members of the Congress."[14] Huntington (1965) argued that this phenomenon had already manifested itself, noting, "The legislative function of Congress has declined in importance, while the growth of the federal bureaucracy has made the administrative overseeing function more important."[15] He added, "No longer is Congress the source of major legislation. . . . The president now determines the legislative agenda of Congress almost as thoroughly as the British Cabinet sets the legislative agenda of Parliament."[16]

Writing later in this period of supposed change, Sundquist (1981), Peterson and Greene (1993), and Schneier and Gross (1993) had mixed perspectives on variation in the relative significance of the executive branch. While Sundquist viewed the relationship between the executive and the Congress as one characterized by a congressional decline in authority and preeminence followed (in the 1970s) by a congressional resurgence, Peterson and Greene characterized the relationship as one in which (from 1947 to 1990) there was relative stability in the relationship between opposite party members and executive officials and a concurrent decline in same-party member-official conflict.[17] Schneier and Gross (1993) argue that the bureaucracies have taken the lead in the legislative process due to their unique suitability in meeting the challenges posed by increased legislative scope, complexity, and size.[18]

Another frequently cited category of external actor change involves an altered role of the media in the legislative process. Sinclair (1989) attributes changes in issue salience and the creation of a "more open, less bounded, and less stable" system in the 1970s to a decline in political parties and an increased importance of the national media.[19] Heclo (1989) sees similarly democratizing progress in the legislative process in the form of "media-saturated coverage of politics, hyperactive polling and reports on public responses to poll reports, talk shows," and the use of other media.[20] Patterson and Caldeira (1990), however, found no "severe systemic consequences" in Congress from an increase in media coverage (and attendant drop in the public esteem for the institution) since the 1960s. Each of these authors viewed the cited changes as consequential ones.

THE PRESIDENT

Reviewing the evidence, it becomes apparent that just as the various leaders within the House differ widely in their leadership styles and the manner in which they conduct their day-to-day legislative business, the presidential role in the legislative process is a highly personalized one. The House membership, the chamber leadership, the administration personnel, and outside interests and influences, along with presidential preference, combine to define the nature of the president's relationship with the congressional actors. An examination of the evidence provided by the case histories indicates that the president is an extremely important actor, with significant influence over the establishment of the policy agenda and the subsequent direction of the legislative initiative. Furthermore, in each of the six cases, all of the presidents involved in initiation or passage of a policy initiative made frequent use of the office's unique resources in seeking to further their policy aims. In each of the six cases, the first significant definition of the policy objective that would eventually became the case law originated with a presidential statement, however vaguely defined, indicating a personal interest in seeking that policy outcome. Presidential actions in each case included public statements, policy guidance, personal (and usually private) negotiations with key congressional proponents and opponents, and various efforts to track the progress of the legislative outcome in question.

While this pattern of activity was consistent over the period and across all six cases, and though presidential support was an essential element of legislative success in all cases, the resources available to each president varied greatly in the five presidents mentioned in the passage of the case laws. These resources included political or interpersonal skills, popular support, and "mandates." For example, respondents uniformly acknowledged Lyndon Johnson's consummate political skills as a determinant of his frequent legislative victories, while another respondent noted, "Kennedy's election margin was so small, he didn't have the same control that LBJ did." Similarly, party differences and their electoral consequences, among other factors, limited the ability of Dwight Eisenhower and George Bush to realize political goals in the fiscal 1961 foreign aid bill and America 2000 respectively. In sum, while the presidential actors were critical in determining legislative success or failure, their measure of influence was a function of their personal political skills, contextual events, and the support or nonsupport of the congressional actors.

Presidential motives varied throughout the cases as well and ranged from the pursuit of reelectoral goals to the desire for "good" public policy to doing personal favors. Regardless of motive, however, the first significant indicator of success for each case law was the broad policy guidance and emphasis provided to Congress by the president. This guidance took the form of messages to Congress, State of the Union addresses, party platforms in presidential election years, the formal Budget Messages, or personal and telephonic conversations. For each case, the president himself began the real progress toward policy change by issuing a broad call for movement on an issue, which was then shaped by the interest group, legislator, staff, and other forces into a legal expression of the idea. While Presidents Eisenhower, Kennedy, Johnson, Bush, and Clinton evidenced very different styles of congressional interaction in each of the cases and in their policy precursors, the evidence indicates that all five were energetic, personal participants in the realization of legislative success. This was true even though Kennedy and Johnson seemed to enjoy far more in the way of resources such as connections and friends within Congress than the others. All five presidents, from Eisenhower to Johnson and Bush to Clinton, made personal and public appeals seeking passage of their policy aims, lobbied the Congress personally when necessary or advantageous, and issued guidance to Congress and the executive agencies to that end. The following continuities emerged.

Continuity: Presidential direction is critical in setting the legislative agenda.   The president's support was a crucial element of eventual success in each of the six cases examined in this study, and a lack of presidential support would clearly have been fatal for each in the policymaking process. Furthermore, at least in part due to the legislators' recognition of the criticality of presidential support, the president provided the legislative branch with needed direction in the policymaking process in all six cases. Table 6.3 provides a broad summary of the support for the policy initiatives by category of key actor for the six cases. In each case, the president supported the initiative at the time of passage, while earlier opposition in some of the cases had been the key factor preventing earlier passage.

Continuity: Presidential support equals about seventy-three votes on the floor.   Without question, the respondents described presidential support for a legislative initiative as being a critical element of legislative success. Setting aside the other implications of presidential support for an initiative and applying the average legislator's simple working premise that legislative success comes through the construction of a supportive majority sufficient to deliver 50 percent of the vote plus one at each gate, presidential support offers the equivalent of 73 votes in the House. Conversely, presidential opposition increases the difficulty of the task, since a veto-proof House majority equals 291 votes, and a simple majority equals 218. While active presidential opposition can be overcome, it is unlikely, all else being equal.

The Administration

Respondents nearly unanimously described the administration and executive agency officials as hard-working supporters of the president's policy objectives. Whether this view reflected presidential adoption of agency or cabinet policy perspectives, or vice versa, respondents described the administration and executive agency actors as active and energetic proponents of the president's policy objectives in each case. Administration and executive agency personnel lobbied, liaised, coordinated, informed, and negotiated. Of all of the actions of the administration officials involved in the passage of the six cases as indicated by the respondents and supporting accounts, only one official, RTC chief Albert Casey, sticks out as unusual. In fact, his exception (and his eventual fate) confirms the rule. Casey was accused of mismanagement, and his agency was alleged to have committed a variety of illegalities in the distribution of contracts and other RTC activities. As such, his continued presence in the agency was viewed as a major stumbling block in the push to pass the funding closeout legislation. After a clearly despondent Casey testified before the House Banking Committee, during which (to paraphrase) Casey asked the committee members "why any of it mattered since they were going to take his job anyway," Casey was replaced by Deputy Treasury Secretary Altman. Altman's interim appointment was intended to facilitate the passage of the legislation after it became clear that Casey was hindering rather than helping the administration's efforts. A similar circumstance saw Health, Education, and Welfare secretary Abraham Ribicoff leave that assignment after he was blamed by many for the Kennedy administration's failure to meet its educational reform policy goals, though there were no allegations of the agency mismanagement or violations of the law to color Casey's departure. These examples are illustrative in that they represent the only examples of the executive agency officials not publicly marching fully in step with the president in the six case initiatives, and both were removed from their positions in the administration soon after this became evident. Several administration officials were noted as key willful agents in the realization of legislative success, and the evidence suggests the following continuities:

Continuity: The administration generally carries out the policy objectives of the president and his cabinet, as carefully selected representatives charged with doing so. As noted above, in all six cases the administration officials were energetic, consistent, and competent supporters of the president's policy positions, or they were soon unemployed. Table 6.3 summarizes this support. Member and staff respondents in both periods also acknowledged the administration's lead role in establishing the terms of the policy debates.

Continuity: Involving the administration personnel early and often in the policy drafting process is critical to legislative success. One participant in the passage of the foreign operations appropriations law of 1962 noted, "We had frequent contacts with the executive branch and the Foreign Service officers. We traveled to conferences with them, and this enabled us to build pretty strong relationships with them. Our friendships went across party lines. We'd all get together on the weekends for parties, informal gatherings, and the assistant secretaries were invited." Administration support and close coordination with the executive agency officials from the beginning of the legislative effort were noted by the majority of respondents as critical elements leading to legislative success, and the evidence from all six cases supports this assertion.

THE INTEREST GROUPS

A wealth of interest groups were evident in all of the cases except the foreign operations measure of 1962, in which interest groups' contacts were limited to personal pleas for pet amendments. Furthermore, the groups in evidence in the formal processes, national media accounts, and member recollections represent only a fraction of the groups involved in the process, as many respondents in both periods referred to various locally organized groups that sought to influence the respondent member alone. The cases and the respondent accounts from both periods give evidence of a diverse array of interests, aligned differently on each issue and even within portions of the same legislative packages. That is, staff and member respondents in both periods noted that interest groups, or the 1960s' respondents' "pressure groups," were often arrayed in different coalitions on different provisions of the same legislation.

While Walker (1983) and others have noted a probable increase in the number of groups active in Washington, the interest groups largely used the same lobbying techniques in both periods. The interest groups of the 1990s, however, are far more sophisticated and more efficient in their efforts. A common technique in the 1990s is a variation on the phone calls of the early 1960s. "The big interest groups energize their hard-core activists to send a blizzard of faxes to the subcommittee and committee members about to vote on an amendment important to their cause. Then they send faxes, emails, letters, and phone calls every day for three days before the floor vote comes." Another member acknowledged the power of this technique, saying, "You tell yourself that these letters and faxes only represent a small fraction of your constituents, but it's hard not to take a couple thousand letters on one subject into consideration when you cast a vote, and maybe you should anyway." David Broder terms this phenomenon "demo-sclerosis," asserting that interest groups have made tremendous gains in sophistication and efficiency, thus adding to their disproportionate influence in the legislative process.[21]

Organized interests had significant influence over legislative outcomes in both periods. The NEA's lukewarm support for the college construction aid in 1960 was blamed for its defeat, and the passage of the urban mass transit aid package in 1964 could be used as a case study in the influence of well-organized interests in opposition to change. The NEA killed the 1962 college construction and general education aid package by its timely telegram, sent just prior to the vote on the conference report that had earlier passed the House. After the Congress gave the group what it wanted in the 1963 version, the NEA's support helped that iteration to pass. Similarly, municipal associations, railroad interests, and highway interests defined the policy battle over mass transit aid. Orchestrated visits were clearly part of interest group strategies in both periods, as well.

In the 1990s cases, it was the NEA again, in conjunction with the American Federation of Teachers (AFT), the National School Boards Association, and other education groups, that provided panel members, conducted studies, and lobbied in support of the aid and goals package. These groups nearly pulled off the feat of receiving hundreds of millions of dollars in public school aid with no strings attached in one interim iteration of the legislation. During the consideration of Goals 2000, one interest group tactic was to send students to each member's office, with the students requesting visits with the member to discuss tuition difficulties. Staff and member respondents identified the interest groups as key legislative players in both periods, and the groups were the source of important information that shaped the eventual policy outcomes in both periods.

As a longtime staffer with service in both decades of interest to the study noted, "I had worked there for so long, and so had the interest groups, that I had dealt with them over decades on a daily basis. Each legislative issue has a different alignment of interest groups, and each sorts itself out such that no easy generalizations are possible." On Goals 2000, a staff respondent noted, "Most of the education groups were not enthusiastic about the legislation . . . they gave pro forma support to Clinton, as they were taking a long-term view." Said another member from the 1990s, "Moneyed interests can afford to do the research, and they want to do it. You need their information, and the door is always open." Table 6.1 summarizes both the numbers of interest groups identified as publicly active in the passage of the cases as well as the various techniques identified by respondents and in the background research. The following changes and continuities were identified from the evidence:

Change: Interest group lobbying techniques in the 1990s are similar to those of the 1960s, but the applications of those techniques are much more sophisticated today.   Both the case evidence and the respondent accounts indicate that interest group lobbying methods were more sophisticated in the 1990s than they were in the 1960s. In a sense, interest groups are doing the same things they have always done, but now there are more groups all doing those things a lot more effectively. One respondent from the largest independent lobbying firm in Washington noted significant changes in his fifteen years with the company, including changes in the level of sophistication of the lobbying operation and techniques as well as the cross-fertilization of those techniques. Others noted change in the general prevalence of interests in most phases and aspects of the legislative process in the modern era. Lobbying firms now often have efficient and advanced polling and sampling operations, advertising departments, and public affairs and public relations experts, in addition to the traditional member contact operations and other Hill activities. Representative Lee Hamilton tells a story that illustrates well the increased sophistication of organized interests, describing an incident in which he made remarks criticizing an amendment being considered in the Foreign Affairs Committee at 10:30 A.M. Within two hours of his remarks, he began receiving complaining constituent phone calls.[22] Another respondent with service in both periods noted that whereas he used to deal with two or three farm groups in the 1960s, now there are twenty or thirty vying for his attention.

A lobbyist respondent remarked, "The nod and a wink days are over, if they ever existed. All of our employees go through ethics seminars and disclosure instruction . . . a strong compliance program. Our job is to put together a network of support for and with our clients. We need a strong champion (from among the legislators), a motivated member, but that usually comes from finding the right niche on the Hill . . . the member who is already interested in our project." The lobbyists and their clients are usually present at the on-site walk-throughs and in many of the meetings between the Hill staffers and executive agencies. A lobbyist noted, "We have both formal and informal meetings with

TABLE 6.1
Interest Groups Publicly Active in the Passage of the Cases

Case/ Year Passed	Interest Groups Noted[23]	Lobbying Techniques Employed During Case Consideration, Noted from Public Documents, Media Analysis, and Respondent Accounts
For Aid/ '62	2	Member contact
Col Aid/ '63	34	Testimony, member contact, letters
UMT/ '64	40	Testimony, member contact, media campaigns, public speaking, studies, letters, phone calls
For Aid/ '93	58	Testimony, member contact, media campaigns, public speaking, studies
Goals/ '94	38	Testimony, member contact, media campaigns, public speaking, studies, letters, faxes, phone calls
RTC/ '93	11	Testimony, member contact, studies, letters

them, both here and in the district. We talk to both the executive branch and the legislative, because a lot can be lost between them." Even in the 1960s, interest groups would work through a member's constituents. Said one early 1960s respondent, "Those special interests would take you out to dinner and entertain you, but at the same time somebody else was getting your constituents to call about the issue." However, interest group techniques have become much more responsive, efficient, and widespread.

Change: More insiders lobby now.   In the view of many of the respondents, a key change in the interest group operations is the increasing numbers of House and Senate staff members who now turn to lobbying after short service in government. This phenomenon facilitates lobby organizations' efforts at member contacts and policy drafting. As one respondent, himself a former Senate staffer and now a lobbyist, noted, "There has been an explosion of professional lobbyists over the last fifteen years. Most of the new lobbyists in Washington are former staffers. Now, the norm is to do a short stint on the Hill and then come to the private sector to get better pay. The debate doesn't change much from year to year, and 80 percent of our job is informational anyway."

Important continuities emerged as well.

Continuity: In mediating legislation, interest group support is critical. When the legislative initiative primarily involves the mediation between competing organized interests, the groups' support and satisfaction is critical. In this particular and common kind of legislative initiative, compromise and accommodation are viewed as the keys to the realization of legislative success, though in other cases the interest groups have more of an incidental role in the construction of supportive voting majorities.

Continuity: Information is still power.   Respondents from both periods cited information as the primary resource and means of influence for interest groups involved in the legislative process. As one respondent noted, "The lobbying firms today have very specific, focused interests. They are often concerned about specific provisions within a larger piece of legislation, and they know everything about those provisions. It's proactive advocacy." Respondents also identified a quick willingness to exclude prevaricators from the debate, an outcome that would hinder, if not kill, interest group efforts to influence legislative outcomes in their favor. This feature serves as an incentive for the interest groups to provide accurate information, even as they place that information in the best light possible.

Continuity: Interest groups with leverage use it.   In every instance in each case, if an interest group had a particular source of leverage with which to influence an outcome, it used it. This characteristic of the groups was true even in the instances when interested groups like the National Education Association in the early 1960s and the "Christian Coalition" in the early 1990s were only moderately interested in the ongoing policy debates. Even if only to demonstrate their continued ability to influence some feature of a working legislative initiative, groups exercised that ability. Respondents viewed interest groups as a vital part of the legislative process in both the early 1960s and the 1990s, though they were most influential in cases when the legislative initiative involved mediating in policy areas involving organized groups in tension.

THE MEDIA

The media are described by many today as a coherent, willful, interventionist, and broadly influential set of actors in the policymaking process. A number of observers have identified changes in the role of the media in American politics, and others have argued that the impact of the media on the pursuit of legislative success over the last several decades has changed as well. In all, it is possible that consequential changes in the media's actions and levels of influence, types of coverage, and types of political coverage took place over the last several decades. As I examined the cases and spoke to the legislative actors, I found that while some of the stereotypes and arguments were justified, other aspects of the media's performance were rather surprising.

As one might expect, the respondents from the 1990s concurred that whether the media represent a collective willful intent or not, their polling activities matter today more than ever before. The polls count today regardless of their validity or relevance. As one current staffer noted, "The media polls matter. We track them, and we expect to hear from constituents on the stuff that's said back home." But a member with service in the 1990s reflected the sentiments of many when he said, "Too often, the media are uninformed. They don't quote correctly, or they don't understand the policy. They're generally either inaccurate or sensationalized or both." Another member from the 1990s added, "The media back home get it wrong all the time. I'm always reacting to inaccuracies that were flashed back home."

Rather than viewing the media as a collection of coherent, autonomous actors bent on the pursuit of any ideological, policy, or personal agenda, most respondents with congressional service saw the media quite differently. A member respondent with service in both periods stated flatly, "There are no reporters anymore. They all have to be commentators." Media insiders shared these views. Two members of the media asserted that any problems with ideological bias or a lack of objectivity among the media, trends often alleged in the modern era, are less important in describing problems with the media's coverage of politics than the inherent problems associated with the competition for viewer market share. The evidence from the cases and respondent consensus suggested the following systematic changes and continuities.

Change: The media cover politics differently in the 1990s, in terms of both quantity and objective.   Media insiders attribute some of this phenomenon to the altered relationships between reporters and politicians. As one discussant put it, "There used to be a real bonding between the reporters who covered the Hill and the politicians. The Pentagon papers, Watergate, and other events of the '70s made the development of those kinds of relationships a lot more difficult." Similarly, another journalist noted, "We are competing with a lot more news sources now, with Internet news providers, CNN, and other immediate news sources. With that in mind, print journalists are increasingly providing more than 'just' the news." Table 6.2 summarizes the amount and nature of case media print coverage in the *Wall Street Journal* and the *New York Times* in the six months prior to the passage of the cases, and there is clear evidence of this change from "fact reporting" to "analysis." Not only did the average number of articles about the cases in the two major publications decline over time in general, but the number of "fact-heavy" articles declined four-fold. At the same time, the number of "analysis-heavy" articles increased three-fold over the period, with the average number of "mixed" articles staying about the same.

Change: The story is the strife now, not the policy. Similarly, the evidence of table 6.2 supports respondent assertions that there was a clear trend in the coverage over the period that saw a shift from a focus on policy to a focus on politics and personalities. Whether the trend came about as a result of competition for market share with CNN, Internet, and other "fact-providing" news sources or not, the story has become the partisan and personal strife now, rather than the policy outcomes themselves.

Some media continuities emerged.

Continuity: The average member still has a dim view of the media's accuracy, influence, and grasp of the relative significance of events.   As Clem Miller succinctly put it in the early 1960s, "With newspaper, radio, and television deadlines demanding that interesting news be found—or, if not found, made . . . it will be."[24] He added, "By and large,

TABLE 6.2
Wall Street Journal/New York Times Case Coverage
in the Six Months Prior to Passage

Case/Year Passed	Number of Articles	Number of "Fact-Heavy" Articles	Number of "Analysis-Heavy" Articles	Number of Mixed Articles
For Aid/ '62	16	14	1	1
Col Aid/ '63	5	4	0	1
UMT/ '64	14	8	2	4
For Aid/ '93	7	3	4	0
Goals/ '94	12	4	4	4
RTC/ '93	4	1	2	1
1960s average	11.7	8.7	1.0	2.0
1990s average	7.7	2.7	3.3	1.7

the reporting is quite perfunctory with little of the shading which gives political life its validity . . . the press has no time for shading today. This is the age of the 'headline' and the 'news capsule.'"[25] Member and staff respondents in both periods echoed this theme. The respondents uniformly described the media actors, particularly the local ones, as having only a cursory understanding of the policy and the politics at best before meeting the inevitable deadlines and producing the required "news."

Continuity: The chamber leadership, the president, and the administration still make concerted efforts to inform and influence the media as part of every national legislative initiative, seeking their support. The uniformly dim view of the media's collective ability to get the story right did not translate into any unwillingness on the part of the various legislative actors to seek to influence the media story in their favor. This was true in both periods according to the respondents. "Going public" was a common strategy in the early 1960s, and it remains a common feature of the pursuit of legislative success in the early 1990s and today. So while legislative actors seek to enlist media support for the major legislative initiatives, and while significant media opposition, like the opposition of other actors, can doom a policy goal in the making, the legislative actors were generally disdainful of the media's ability to "get the story right." All in all the media were not discounted, but they also were not considered to be as important as other key players in the pursuit of legislative success, even in the contemporary House.

THE CONSTITUENTS

Since the early 1960s, the same increasing sophistication that shaped the relationship between the Congress and interest groups has in some ways altered the dynamic between the representative and the represented. As I examined the case and respondent evidence for meaningful changes or key continuities in constituent activities and significance, it became apparent that the Congress is far more directly accessible to the average constituent in the modern era than in any time before. Furthermore, the average House member today must contend with many more constituents than his predecessors, and those extra constituents and their peers are writing, calling, faxing, stopping in, and e-mailing with specific requests for information and advocacy that the members' counterparts from the 1960s would not recognize. In general, not only are there more constituents, but constituents have increased their level of activity in the legislative process, and more mail is flowing both ways in the relationship. The following changes were in evidence.

Change: Far more constituents contact their legislators in the 1990s than in the 1960s, and they do so with much more sophistication.   By one member's count, his constituent mail is now running at about five hundred letters per week, and his staff answers each letter. That same member reported receiving just about twenty or twenty-five letters per week in the early 1960s. Added to that total are the communications received over the Internet by the members who have opened that gate, as well as those received through fax, telephone, and personal visit. Additionally, one respondent with House service in both periods noted, "Constituent mail used to be pretty simple, and I could respond with a 'thank you for your concern' letter. Now I get letters advocating complex policy positions or requesting detailed information on an issue. Those letters have to be researched and answered carefully."

Members returned the favor to their constituents, too, sending out 200.7 million pieces of mail in the first session of the 103rd Congress, effectively doubling the amount of mail sent during comparable sessions in the early 1960s. Furthermore, the members employed more than three times as many district staffers, with over 3,100 staffers working in the districts in 1993 and another increase to 3,335 in 1994.[30] Related to this phenomenon is the increased sophistication of the lobbying effort, as one lobbyist noted: "A lot of our efforts go to energizing the constituents, through information campaigns back in the districts. That effort, along with our Hill activities, is more likely to get the members interested in our clients' interests."

Change: Polling is fast and efficient, and it matters now.   Polling techniques are faster and more accurate, and polling results are disseminated more widely in the 1990s. An indicator of this trend is the fact that while public opinion is referenced only sporadically in the early 1960s cases (and not at all in the passage of the foreign aid appropriation for fiscal 1963), frequent references are made to public opinion in the floor speeches and other activities of the members in the 1990s cases. Similarly, respondents in the 1990s cases were generally quicker than their 1960s counterparts to cite concerns about public opinion in their descriptions of case passage. In fact, many of the respondents from the 1960s did not mention those considerations at all. Among other effects, this change has exacerbated already heightened electoral sensitivity in the modern House.

Change: There are half again as many constituents per House member in the 1990s.   The average House district in the early 1960s represented approximately four hundred thousand constituents, while the average member today represents close to six hundred thousand people. All else being equal, this alone increases the average member's casework, constituent contact, and other constituent interactions by about 50 percent. Whether as a result of increases in technology and decreases in the cost of a telephone call or as a result of the sheer increase in constituents per member, the average member's constituent workload is much greater today.

Change: The innovation of electronic voting, with a concomitant increase in recorded votes, has fundamentally shifted the average members' primary voting accountability concerns from his colleagues to his constituents.   An interesting byproduct of the technological advance in electronic voting, identified by several of the respondents with service in both periods of interest, is a shift in the primary accountability relationship of concern to the member as he or she casts the legislative vote. The average member casting a standing, teller, or oral roll call vote in the early 1960s was usually primarily concerned (at least initially) with the reaction of his or her peers to his or her public stance on a particular issue. However, with the advent of electronic voting, including its tendency to cloak the member's vote on the floor while providing C-Span-generated instant accountability back home, the legislator's primary accountability concern has shifted toward constituents in the 1990s. While not all of this phenomenon can be attributed to that dynamic, at least part of it can be.

Key continuities emerged as well.

Continuity: On the issues that generate the most mail, constituent desires matter.   As one member related, "There are two issues that matter to my constituents and generate 90 percent of all of the mail I get. I know that I have to be careful on those two issues, which I happen to share the majority opinion on anyway." Another member put it this way, "The (identified) issue is the big issue in my district, and I am held accountable for that issue in the mail and in person back home. Other than that, though, I usually have the freedom to vote the way I see it on other issues without my constituents getting too energized. They elected me to do that." Legislators still have a great deal of latitude on a wide variety of issues.

Continuity: There is very often a disconnect between a legislator's national policy interests or committee work and local constituent concerns.   John Brademas noted that "during twenty-two years in the House during which time I had been chief sponsor or co-sponsor of nearly every education bill enacted into law . . . neither the . . . [NEA or AFT] . . . gave significant support to my campaign. I describe this history only because so many observers of Congress are quick to charge its members with championing legislation chiefly to ingratiate themselves with a 'special interest' or in Pavlovian response to constituent demands."[31] He added, "Ultimately it was only through 'taking care of business' in my district . . . that I was able to gain the latitude I needed to be a policymaker in the national arena."[32] In the pursuit of legislative success, respondents felt that constituents most often mattered on the relatively few issues that they had clear-cut, consistent, and clearly expressed views. As few issues generated this kind of constituent response, constituent support was not viewed by the respondents as being particularly critical in the pursuit of legislative success.

OTHER EXTERNAL ACTORS

Respondents mentioned several other external actors as having occasionally significant influence within the legislative process in the House, such as "think tanks" like the Brookings Institution, the Center for Strategic and International Studies, and the American Enterprise Institute, as well as academics and interested senators. While academics from a variety of universities and colleges testified in support of college aid in the 1960s, groups such as the Center for Public Integrity and Congress Watch influenced the passage of the RTC funding closeout, with clear evidence that members were affected by the groups' public statements on RTC mismanagement. Similarly, state governors, among them Bill Clinton, were given credit for the largest push in support of national education reform. Other state and local officials worked very hard for the mass transit initiative in the early 1960s, making yearly treks from their cities, counties, and states to meet with legislators and lobby for assistance. One change and one continuity emerged from the evidence:

Change: Think tanks have become more advocacy oriented.   As one member with experience in both periods put it, "We used to get policy analysis from the universities and the think tanks. Now, often as not, we get slashing attacks . . . people disagreeing disagreeably." Another current staffer noted, "Think tanks are always sending me things they think I need to know. I've figured out who's reliable and who isn't, and I have good working relationships with the people who've delivered before."

Continuity: External, and often arbitrary, events matter.   Not all of the process is under the legislators' control. While this almost goes without saying, events ranging from Kennedy's death to the House check-cashing scandal to the phrase *education president* to Baker's alleged obscene reference to Jews and Boris Yeltsin's travails affected the various political outcomes represented by the six cases. In military parlance, it is a fluid battlefield.

TALLYING THE SUPPORT

Finally, in terms of the actors' assessment of the influence of these external actors on the pursuit of legislative success, table 6.3 summarizes the support for the laws at the time of passage by category of major actor. The evidence in the table supports the respondent assertions regarding the relative importance of each of the types of actors involved directly or indirectly in the passage of the legislative initiatives. To summarize, consequential changes in the external actors clearly have affected the legislative process since the 1960s through the addition of increasingly numerous and sophisticated players to the policy mix, at the same time the average member's basic constituent responsibilities have increased dramatically. Legislators from the 1960s revisiting the House of the 1990s would recognize the essential ingredients of success among those external actors, including the basic necessity of winning support from the president, the administration, and the majority party leadership in the Congress. However, while those former members would recognize the rules, they would be surprised by the elevated level of competition among increasingly savvy and numerous external players.

TABLE 6.3
Support for the Laws at the Time of Passage

Case Year Passed	President	Administration	Constituent[33]	Interest Groups	House Majority Leadership[34]	House Minority Leadership
For Aid/ '62	Yes	Yes	Mixed	Unknown	Yes	No
Col Aid/ '63	Yes	Yes	Mixed	Majority yes	Yes	No
UMT/ '64	Yes	Yes	Unknown	Majority yes	Yes	No
For Aid/ '93	Yes	Yes	No	Majority yes	Yes	Yes
Goals/ '94	Yes	Yes	Unknown	Majority no	Yes	Yes[35]
RTC/ '93	Yes	Yes	No	Majority yes[36]	Yes	Yes

CHAPTER 7

Legislative Procedures

Today you can get away with saying anything on the floor.

—House member from the 1990s

Back then, it seems like we could actually get things done. You could pull people together and work it out.

—House member from the 1960s

The House became anti-intellectual, anti-evidence, and pure ideology.

—House member with service from the 1960s to the 1980s

Legislative procedures are the formal "rules of the game," or the chambers' standard operating practices in initiating, considering, and passing laws. Since this category of potential change encompasses a variety of readily accessible features of the policymaking process, the congressional literature is rife with documented instances of procedural changes that have occurred in the last several decades. Viewing these documented changes and other potential procedural changes from a theoretical perspective, it is not hard to imagine changes in the features of the formal legislative procedures as having associated and major repercussions for the policymaking process viewed as a whole.

Within this category of plausibly consequential change, we include variations in the procedures of sponsorship, the type and use of policy vehicles, referrals and jurisdiction, committee and subcommittee markups, reports, and the conduct of executive sessions. Additionally, we might find that consequential changes have occurred in the influence and roles of the Rules Committee, within the floor activities, or during conference committees. Key changes in the legislative procedures might also have taken the form of a change in the place where the real legislative "action" takes place within the committee system, or we might find a shift in the relative importance of the committees and subcommittees. Other potentially meaningful changes might be evident as a result of fluctuations in the average member's workload and workday, the relative significance of some standard operating procedures, the average legislative timelines, or other characteristics of the formal procedures. Mirroring these possibilities, students of the Congress have in fact identified a wide variety of procedural changes that occurred over the last several decades.[1] It is useful to categorize this literature by the type of impact that the documented changes are claimed to have had. Variations in legislative procedures are generally argued to have had important consequences for the *committees*, the *floor*, or *member constraints*.

The first of these categories, *committee*-impacting procedural changes, includes reforms and institutional reorganization affecting committee jurisdictions, the partitioning of authority between committees and subcommittees, and seniority rules. In each case, the reforms are argued to have affected the ways that power is distributed through the committee structure. While Fenno described relatively routine lateral changes in several committees' policy jurisdiction already in 1973, Tiefer (1989) notes that recent years have seen change in the form of an increase in conflict over committee jurisdiction.[2] In addition to "chronic jurisdictional ambiguity," the referral process was altered significantly by the practice of multiple referral, the result of changes suggested by the Bolling committee on reform in 1974.[3] Tiefer, Sinclair (1992), Davidson (1992), and others argue that the system of multiple referral has been part of the transformation of the legislative process. Sinclair notes, "Such a momentous development in processing legislation cannot help but transform the legislative process, especially the House."[4] She further argues that multiple referral in part led to a diffusion of power, changes in the Speaker's prerogatives, variation in the workings of the Rules Committee, and an increased incentive for members to engage in more broadly inclusive legislative negotiation.

Other committee-impacting procedural changes include variations in committee and subcommittee rules, meetings, and procedures that led to the widely argued devolution of power to the subcommittees. Interestingly, Huntington (1965) foreshadowed this phenomenon even though many have argued the trend emerged as a result of reforms in the 1970s. He wrote in 1965 that "power has become dispersed among many officials, committees, and subcommittees. Hence, the central leadership has lacked the ability to establish national legislative priorities."[5] Citing the Reorganization Act of 1946, he added, "The net effect of the Reorganization Act was thus to further the dispersion of power, to strengthen and to institutionalize committee authority, and to circumscribe still more the influence of the central leadership."[6] He quoted a staffer, who said, "Given an active subcommittee chairman working in a specialized field with a staff of his own, the parent committee can do no more than change the grammar of a subcommittee report."[7] Polsby, Gallagher, and Rundquist (1969) observed a similar power shift from the party leadership to the committees, blaming the seniority rule as an "automatic" mechanism for strengthening the committees at the expense of the central leadership.[8]

Observing the results of reform, Sundquist (1981) picked up this argument, writing that in the 1970s "the time-honored seniority system was at last shorn of its absolutism . . . breaking the power of committee chairmen, . . . (thus giving greater power to) subcommittee chairmen and individual legislators."[9] While Sundquist noted that the seniority rule had been circumvented in the past in deposing two southern conservative chairmen as early as 1965, he wrote, "Members noted the 'new responsiveness' of committee chairmen."[10] Modified rules on the distribution of committee assignments also contributed to this trend. More recently, Smith (1989), Tiefer (1989), and Strahan (1990) argue that the phenomenon is still in place, as all cite the weakness of the committee chairmen relative to their early 1960s counterparts as an agent of major change within the legislative process. As a special subcategory of committee changes, the conference committees changed in size and composition over the period, becoming much larger and much more open at times than they had been previously. However, the conferences saw little or no accompanying formal change, remaining largely ad hoc in nature.

The second category of legislative procedural change often cited in the literature is that of *floor* innovations, or modifications in floor scheduling, agenda setting, floor procedures, floor management, and the range of acceptable floor activities. Various reforms occurred in this area in the early 1970s, such as changes in the rules governing floor debate, conference report debate, and roll call voting.[11] Smith (1989) and Tiefer (1989) both emphasize the importance of these changes, highlighting the increase in floor amendments (in the Committee of the Whole) in recent times and corresponding modifications to bill manager strategies as the key consequences.[12] Smith and Tiefer identified other floor rule changes as having had important implications for the legislative process, including the permitting of television onto the House floor, the use of electronic voting devices, and other technical innovations. Additionally, floor scheduling changed as a result of reforms and institutional reorganization, as the floor rules were changed to modify the circumstances under which the rules could be suspended and to include use of modified open rules on a routine basis.[13] Other variations of this sort included altered rules on legislative and limit "riders."

The third category of legislative procedural changes, often blamed for corresponding significant changes in the broader legislative process, are those that affect members directly, or *member constraints*. These reforms include those rules changes argued to have altered the legislative process by having made the legislators' voting records and the legislative process more open to public scrutiny, the "sunshine laws." The changes in recorded voting included, significantly, the ability to call for a recorded vote in the Committee of the Whole. Sundquist (1981) argued that this innovation changed the legislative process by sacrificing "the honored tradition of logrolling, the secret pledging and delivery of votes that may not be in the interest on one's constituency to serve the cause of party."[14] Smith (1989) argues that this change had the effect of redistributing influence in the chamber but stops short of arguing that the change had the effect intended by the reformer who proposed it in 1970. Representative Richard Bolling believed that this procedural change would "massively change the way in which this institution works."[15] Rohde (1991) and Sinclair (1992) share this perspective on the effects of the increased number of recorded votes.

Similarly, sunshine laws that opened up committee, conference committee, and subcommittee proceedings to public scrutiny are argued to have had profound consequences for the legislative process. Sundquist (1981) wrote that while "the endemic weaknesses of Congress—its inability to act quickly and its inability to integrate policy—were by no means remedied," progress was made toward these goals of the reforms.[16] Heclo (1989) also argues that these reforms resulted in "a more open, democratically organized Congress," though it was one more difficult to manage as a whole.[17] Strahan observes a decline and resurgence in Ways and Means Committee members' ability to maintain their role as fiscal watchdogs as a result of reforms of this nature. Davidson (1992) and Rieselbach (1994) echo these themes, describing a resultant legislative process in the postreform House that is "more open (and) participatory" and in some ways "democratized" and more "accountable."[18] Observers blamed a great deal of broader process change on the various procedural reforms, including a decentralization of power, alternative apportionments of legislative jurisdiction and committee assignments, modified scrutiny of the legislative process, and an altered member context for decision-making.

THE CONGRESSIONAL WORKDAY AND WORKLOAD

In order to assess the impact of these documented changes in the formal procedures of the House over the period since the early 1960s, our logical point of entry into the analysis is an examination of the demands placed upon the legislators in general. We might expect to find changes in the day-to-day activities of legislators or their basic job requirements that could directly affect their pursuit of policy goals. Key differences in the legislator workday might take the form of changes in length or time available or in the number and type of responsibilities accruing to the average lawmaker.

Without question, the legislative workload and workday have undergone a transformation, with important consequences for the realization of legislative success. To paraphrase one respondent, "A Washington reporter told me, when I first got to Washington, to take a half an hour every day to stare out the window and think about the country." He noted, "Today there are no more quick trips to the golf course after a one o'clock adjournment . . . the pace is quicker, votes come more frequently, deadlines and emergencies are commonplace, constituents flood our offices, and mail and fax messages inundate us. I now need to schedule time to meet with my scheduler." Another member added, "Nobody has time to get to know one another." The period from the early 1960s to the early 1990s saw a 20 percent increase in the number of hearings between the two periods, as well as an increase in committee assignments from 1.5 standing, 3.2 subcommittee, and 0.4 other committee roles from 1.2, 1.6, and 0.2 respectively in 1956.[19] Table 7.1 summarizes this trend. The case and respondent evidence indicated the following changes and continuities.

Change: The "money chase" takes a tremendous amount of time. Every respondent with service in both periods noted "the money chase" as a profound change, the necessity on the part of today's House members to raise money continually. Respondents from the 1960s viewed fund raising as a minor concern, if one at all. One member equated the

TABLE 7.1
The Congressional Workload from the 1960s to the 1990s

Period/ Congress	Cmtee and Subc Meetings	Public Laws Enacted	Pages of Statutes Enacted	Days in Session	Hours Per Session Day	Recorded Votes	Campaign Expenses, Estimated
1960s/							
87th	3,402	885	2,078	304	4.0	240	$30,000[20]
88th	3,596	666	1,975	334	3.7	232	$30,000
1990s/							
103rd	4,304	465	7,542	265	7.1	1,122	$408,240

required effort in the modern Congress to a need for $10,000 per week, every week, regardless of where the incumbent is in the electoral cycle. Another respondent recalled fund-raising efforts and techniques as a common lunchtime topic of conversation in the 1990s. As another member put it, "There is no such thing as an off year anymore." One former member, blaming television costs for the increase, noted that in 1960 he had run and won on a budget of $15,000 but had managed to lose in 1980 after spending $670,000. Other respondents offered similar stories. Adjusting for inflation, the member's costs had risen from about $16,900 to $271,000, after converting both figures into 1967 dollars, an incredible sixteen-fold increase in real terms. The money chase absorbs a tremendous amount of time in the modern Congress, and this chase has come with corresponding challenges for those seeking to achieve policy goals.

Change: The majority of members are now "ITOTs," or "In Tuesday, Out Thursdays." A number of respondents cited the increasing propensity of members to fly in for the votes on Tuesdays only to leave by Thursday as one of the most significant impediments to legislative success in the 1990s, a phenomenon far less common in the early 1960s. Given that member-to-member contacts are critical to the realization of legislative success, this tendency to service the district, regardless of motive, has limited the number of opportunities for extra-chamber or extracommittee meetings, whether formal or informal.

Change: There are far fewer legislative days, and those days have many more meetings and other requirements packed into them. Members are less likely to attend subcommittee and committee meetings. One respondent remarked, "As the committee sizes increased, members began to serve on more than one committee, and multiple committees also meant multiple subcommittees. With so many subcommittee meetings and hearings, people would try to get on the record with a question. That meant that the staff had to attend the meetings to keep the member informed." For several reasons then, the impact of this phenomenon is to have made the construction of supportive voting majorities all the more difficult.

Change: There is less time for social activities. One of the effects of all of these changes has been to limit the legislators' time for social activities. Respondents with service in the early 1960s frequently referred to having been able to conduct business and build relationships at numerous weekend social events and afternoon golf outings and the like that would enable them to realize success in future endeavors. With a longer workday and with members in town for only a few days per week, these opportunities to build interpersonal relationships and to get work done outside of the formal legislative processes are severely limited compared to the Congress of the early 1960s.

Change: There is less time spent on the floor, allowing for fewer professional and personal opportunities for member-to-member contacts. Go into the average House office these days, and there is at least one television tuned to C-Span in that office. Members and staff alike loosely track the floor proceedings through that means, rather than having to expend the resources of time and attention needed to track the proceedings on the floor itself. Once again, this development limits the opportunities for business and personal contacts between members. In the 1960s, members routinely took advantage of the opportunities for personal and professional contacts afforded by daily roll calls and other formal business that was attended by most members. For each of the six cases, the *Congressional Record* evidence, in the form of quorum calls, shows that members frequently remained on the floor for extended periods in the 1960s. In the latter period, however, members only routinely go to the floor when summoned to vote. Table 7.4 summarizes member attendance and other floor activities in support of this assertion. In sum, the net effect of the increased congressional workload, changes in travel habits, and other member workday activities has been to seriously limit opportunities to develop the interpersonal relationships and member-to-member contacts viewed by all respondents as a critical part of coaltion building.

SPONSORSHIP

Examining the cases and respondent accounts for evidence that the importance or attractiveness of sponsorship had changed consequentially over the period since the early 1960s, the following change and continuity emerged.

Change: Members sponsor fewer bills, and cosponsor more. In terms of the individual members' general floor activities, the average number of bills each member introduced fell drastically, from an early 1960s' average of 32.6 to a 1990s' mean average of 15.3. All of the respondents agreed that bipartisan cosponsorship could serve as a useful indicator of "real" bipartisanship, thus enhancing a legislative initiative's prospects. However, the recent case respondents noted that cosponsorship of all varieties is more prevalent in the modern Congresses in part because there are fewer opportunities to "get your name on something" in an era of fewer independent or stand-alone measures. The cases reflect this trend, with single sponsors in each of the three cases from the 1960s but multiple sponsors in two of three of the 1990s cases, including 39 sponsors for the Goals 2000 initiative. There were multiple sponsors of both parties on the Senate side in the urban mass transit issue. Table 7.3 provides a summary of the sponsor numbers and description.

Continuity: Members still sponsor bills as a credit-claiming activity. Not surprisingly, many members view sponsorship as a quick means of "doing something." As one current staffer described it, sponsorship "is an opportunity to show 'I'm an active legislator' to the folks back home." While this activity has reduced significantly (by over half) over the last several decades, the current fifteen bills per legislator per year still represents a significant number of initiatives to introduce. In summary, respondents generally viewed bipartisan cosponsorship sponsorship as an asset in seeking legislative success, but sponsorship itself was not viewed by the actors as being a significant element of the larger process in either the 1960s or the 1990s.

THE POLICY VEHICLE

The policy vehicle is the initial legislative draft off of which the various actors work. Because of the influence that the rough draft has over the eventual shape of the end product, the most significant changes in the policy vehicle would be changes in its drafters or a change in the usual source of the vehicle. Table 7.2 summarizes this phenomenon for the six cases. The following change and two continuities emerged from an examination of the evidence:

TABLE 7.2
The Policy Vehicles for the Six Cases

Case/Year	Policy Vehicle for the Legislative Initiative That Was Eventually Successful
Foreign Aid, 1962	Administration draft
College Aid, 1963	Administration draft
Urban Mass Transit, 1964	Administration draft
Foreign Aid, 1993	Administration draft
Goals 2000, 1994	Administration draft
RTC Closeout, 1993	Administration draft

Change: The budget process and the appropriations bills are where most of the legislative action is.   The authorization process is dying in the modern era, in the view of some respondents. Furthermore, with the leadership and many members pursuing omnibus strategies more often than not, the legislative action takes place most frequently and successfully during the consideration of today's major yearly policy vehicles, the appropriations bills.

Continuity: Bills based on administration drafts have the highest probability of legislative success.   Clem Miller estimated this figure as 80 percent of all successful bills in the early 1960s, and other respondents concurred in that assessment.[21] Interview respondents from both periods noted a tremendous increase in the legislative prospects of policy initiatives initiated or adopted by the administration, and the case evidence supports this assessment as well. For example, as soon as the Kennedy administration got on board with Senator Williams's (D-NJ) mass transit initiative, the Williams-authored version of the bill was scrapped in favor of the administration's new version. As table 7.2 demonstrates, each of the six laws came to fruition having ridden through the process on an administration vehicle.

Continuity: Since the underlying details of any bill are rarely debated, the actor who controls the drafting process generally gets 90 percent of what he wants in the final legislative outcome.   As table 7.2 shows, as a result of this continuity, more often than not the executive agencies usually get what they want. Since staffers and executive agency officials routinely dealt with all of the second- and third-tier issues, or the underlying details of the legislation under consideration at a variety of junctures, control over the policy vehicle and the negotiation of the details confers de facto control over 90 percent or more of the legislation that is finally enacted. This phenomenon was consistent in both periods. The implications of the policy vehicle to the process as a whole did not change fundamentally over the period and was identified as an important feature of the process but one usually dominated by the administration on successful initiatives.

REFERRAL AND COMMITTEE JURISDICTION

The next legislative procedure to consider was that of referral and committee jurisdictions. I was interested in any significantly increased or decreased leadership involvement in the referral decision or patterns of significant changes in committee jurisdictions that might have serious consequences for the process as a whole. Additionally, it was important to examine the evidence for any altered perceptions among the respondents that this aspect of the process had either gained or lost significance in the legislative process. Consequential changes in this procedural consideration had occurred, and once again the net effect of the resultant change was to make the construction of policy coalitions much more difficult. Two consequential changes and one essential continuity were indicated.

Change: Multiple jurisdiction means more decision makers providing input into policymaking, with more legislators able to slow down the process when so inclined.   Multiple jurisdiction has increased dramatically in the House over the last several decades. This practice increased from affecting only 5.2 percent of major legislation considered in the 94th Congress to 14.5 percent of major legislation in the 103rd Congress and 16.7 percent of major legislation in the 104th.[22] Both the Goals 2000 and RTC closeout legislation were multiply referred. However, as we might expect, the main effect of multiple jurisdiction in the RTC case (to the Judiciary and then Government Oversight Committees) in conference committee, aside from bringing to bear more expertise in the consideration of the bill, was to bog the process down. Consideration of the RTC funding closeout legislation was protracted months longer than otherwise necessary when the House's Judiciary and Banking Committees could not agree on a few provisions of the bill. In simple arithmetic terms, thirty-five additional legislators from the Judiciary Committee had the opportunity to influence the process as a result of the multiple referral on the RTC funding, and fully eighty-eight additional legislators had points of access into the debate over Goals 2000. The net effect of multiple referral was to make the construction of supporting majorities that much more difficult.

Change: The increasing breadth, depth, and diversity of federal regulations create more jurisdictional overlap.   The nature of modern federal statutes virtually ensures that many more bills will overlap in jurisdiction. Charles Tiefer writes, "Committees have several arenas for contesting jurisdiction: drafting bills to fit within their jurisdiction rather than another committee's; obtaining help from the leadership, particularly in arranging multiple referrals; negotiating special floor arrangements through House complex special rules; and securing the appointment of multiple-committee referees."[23] In sum, the expansion of scope and depth of federal regulation adds to the burden of the 1990s' legislator seeking to realize legislative success. The almost inevitable jurisdictional overlap means the likely involvement of more legislators than before in the consideration of any measure. At the very least, the bill's authors have to spend time working to secure the committee referral they want. Bill authors have responded by carefully writing measures to avoid multiple referral whenever possible, thus retaining more control over the consideration of the bill and making the realization of success easier.

Continuity: Referral is rarely controversial, given the clearly stated jurisdictions in the committee rules and the fact that the Speaker usually rubber stamps the parliamentarian's recommendation on assignment to committee.   Most respondents indicated that referral is rarely an issue, since almost all are routinely handled by the House parliamentarian. This House officer was described as studiously nonpartisan, receiving an almost automatic approval from the Speaker on his committee assignment recommendations. While this step in the process, like the others, could become an unexpected stumbling block for any particular legislative initiative, it was not viewed by any respondents as a particularly critical element of the general process.

COMMITTEE AND SUBCOMMITTEE ACTIVITIES

The next step in the formal legislative procedures of the House included the formal activities of the policy committees and subcommittees. Possible consequential changes within these committees could have included changes in the conduct, nature, or perceived significance of the markups, reporting, and executive sessions held by the committees and subcommittees. As we might expect, there were both changes and continuities in the way that committees and subcommittees do their day-to-day business. Chairmen remain vitally concerned about "producing the product" on time, in order to qualify for the coveted label as a chairman who can "get it done." In both periods, the committees and subcommittees held formal and informal party caucuses prior to meeting to work through the legislation. Even Chairman Ford of the Education and Labor Committee in the 103rd Congress, despite a reputation for being somewhat autocratic, held frequent formal and informal committee gatherings and party caucuses in order to disseminate information. Chairmen generally do not have carte blanche to do as they please. As one member from the early 1960s wrote, "While the chairman's influence is decisive, he needs support. If he has offended members of his own subcommittee, or if he disregards significant points they want to make, they will hammer in wedges that will widen as the bill proceeds along the legislative ways."[24] The following key changes and continuities were indicated by an analysis of the evidence.

Change: The most significant difference in the committees and subcommittees of the 1990s is their increased size.   In the analysis of the cases and respondent accounts, the most obvious change in committee politics over the decades is the greatly increased committee and subcommittee memberships and the corresponding higher average number of committee assignments per member. There is a clear sense from the available records of the committee and subcommittee proceedings, as well as from the respective quality of the respondent recollections, that subcommittee and committee colleagues of the early 1960s knew each other far better than their counterparts of the 1990s. Edith Green took her subcommittee members to Russia, and John Brademas routinely had members to his office to discuss policy and other topics. Prayer breakfasts and after-session gatherings were cited as popular activities for some subcommittees' members, as well. In sum, the increase in committee sizes, as well as the increased demands upon legislator time and other contextual factors, combined to add greatly to the burden of those seeking to realize legislative success in the modern era.

Change: The committee activities of the 1990s are generally pro forma and poorly attended by the committee and subcommittee members.   In the 1990s, more of the critical negotiation, compromise, and consensus-building activities get done outside of the formal committee hearings, markups, and executive sessions than inside them. For a variety of reasons, the formal activities of the committees and subcommittees have declined substantially in importance, according to the respondents with service in both periods. Sunshine laws have had the primary effect of causing willful agents to go outside of these formal activities, and therefore off the public record, when cutting deals.[25] Most respondents from the House in the 1990s viewed the formal legislative activities, including the House floor action, as frequently desultory and insignificant media performances by electorally or personally motivated showhorses.

Unlike the hearings of the early 1960s, described by Representative Clem Miller as events for which "[w]itnesses will sell their souls for a five-minute appearance,"[26] modern hearings are poorly attended. In fact, the two most active lobbies in the passage of the Goals 2000 legislation, the NEA and the Christian Coalition, did not even bother to testify before the committee, choosing to influence the outcome through other means. A comparison of the different styles and activities of Otto Passman and David Obey, both chairmen of the Appropriations Committee's Foreign Operations Subcommittee, illustrates this difference particularly well. Passman's hearings were a grueling marathon, and they produced a detailed investigation of the why and what of money spent on the foreign operations budget. Administration witnesses were required to give excruciating detail in describing their agencies' use of the funds appropriated in previous years and plans for the use of funds in the coming fiscal year. Over hundreds of hours, Passman and his closely collaborative subcommittee colleagues probed the foreign operations budget from one side to the other. Obey's hearings, on the contrary, were dreary, sparsely attended, perfunctory events. The witnesses generally offered short statements thanking the chair for the opportunity to appear before quickly retiring after submitting lengthy reports for the written record.

Similarly, the Special Education Subcommittee chairwoman, Edith Green, even as she presided over hearings much friendlier in tone, gave clear guidance and received informative and meaningful input. House Banking Committee chairman Wright Patman's hearings were fairly scripted, but Albert Rains directed them in a manner that indicated the hearings had a purpose in gathering support for the mass transit measure in question. All three sets of hearings from the 1990s cases, however, are marked by brief, often tedious testimony, followed by tens, if not hundreds, of pages of reports submitted as part of the record.

Change: The authorizing committees have broken down and no longer perform their gatekeeping function. In the eyes of the respondents with service in both periods, a significant change in the committees' activities is the failure of the authorizing committees to perform this vital function with any consistency. The House Foreign Affairs Committee did not authorize foreign operations spending for fiscal 1994 prior to the Appropriations Committee's appropriation, continuing a trend that had developed over several years. Respondents from the 1990s generally agreed that while the "action" was taking place within the money bills, the real action was on the appropriations bills, not the authorizing ones.

Continuity: The same activities occur in committee and subcommittee in the 1990s as occurred in the 1960s. Even if the mix of emphasis and relative significance of the various legislative activities have changed, the same committee and subcommittee activities take place in the 1990s as took place in the 1960s. As one subcommittee chairman from the 1990s put it, "Both the formal and [the] informal activities matter. Everything that goes on in the House, from the dining room to the cloakroom to the floor, plays a part. Whichever environment you're in, and whichever issue you're dealing with, that's the issue you work on at that time. Member contacts are wherever you find them."

Continuity: Research still matters for all of the participants. Otto Passman's floor attacks on the administration's foreign aid plan worked, because he had the credibility of having held exhaustive and detailed hearings into the problems of the foreign aid program. He knew what he was talking about, and the members knew he knew. Describing the difference between success and defeat in general, a member from the 1960s wrote that "you must know your subject. The chairman did, and his opposition did not (and thus failed)."[27] As a modern lobbyist noted, "We spend most of our time on the analysis and the writing. When it comes down to it, that's what's important."

Continuity: Closed sessions weren't, anyway. In the words of one respondent, "All markups were in executive session, and we were told sometimes not to get into the substance of the markup with the press. Members with a reason to not like the pending outcome might say something anyway." In the passage of two of the cases from the 1960s, newspapers printed the substance of supposedly closed negotiating sessions. One effect of the sunshine reforms, from the respondents' general perspective, was to bring accountability to the formal proceedings of the committees and subcommittees, but the more important impact was to shift the opportunities for horse-trading that had once gone on in those venues to informal meetings. In any event, newspaper accounts of the passage of the cases in the 1960s commonly disseminated information from supposedly "secret" executive sessions, and most respondents from that era noted that they expected that information to leak from executive sessions whenever it suited someone's political objectives. The secret meetings weren't secret anyway. But now, members have to find other venues in which to accomplish member-to-member contacts and compromising, opportunities once afforded them by the closed executive sessions, closed markups, and occasionally closed hearings of the 1960s.

Respondents generally viewed the committee and subcommittee activities in both periods as critical components of legislative success but did not feel that the changes in the formal procedures of those committees and subcommittees were particularly important. Once again, however, the net effect of these changes in sunshine laws and committee size has been to make the realization of legislative success more difficult for the reasons noted above.

THE RULES COMMITTEE

Every House bill, before emerging from the relevant policy committee, must receive a rule under which it will be debated on the House floor, and this process has been a popular focus of legislative scholars looking for meaningful changes in the legislative process since the 1960s. Changes in the Rules Committee over the decades have been well documented, though the evidence for the implications of those changes is less clear. Consequential changes in the Rules Committee's practices and products might be indicated by changes in the perceived importance of the committee and the rules process or by a shift in the committee's independence or its use as a leadership management device. Other possibilities could include variations in the number of rules granted, the nature of those rules, or the means through which willful agents sought the rules they wanted. Charles Tiefer, both a student of parliamentary procedure and a deputy House counsel, writes, "When bills come to the floor, the chambers tend to devise ad hoc procedures rather than following their rules."[28] The following changes and continuities were suggested by the evidence.

Change: The Rules Committee is less independent in the 1990s than it was in the 1960s.   Part of this difference can be attributed to the early 1960s' failure of the Rules Committee-packing plan and the independent personality and conservative nature of its chairman, "Judge" Howard Smith (D-VA). One respondent described the Rules Committee as the "green ramp," or jumping off point, where the forward progress of chamber bills was managed by the House leadership generally and Judge Smith personally. If anything, the Rules Committee became more responsive to the party leadership between the early 1960s and the 1990s, with the net result of making legislators seeking a rule slightly less concerned with the personalities and preferences of the Rules Committee's leadership. Most respondents still acknowledged that the rules process could unexpectedly become a serious impediment to legislative success in the latter period, however, regardless of who was now managing it.

Change: Structured, restrictive rules are now the norm.   From the 95th Congress, which had only 32 restrictive rules out of 211 total rules (15 percent), the 102d Congress' 72 restrictive rules out of 109 reflects the steady increase in restrictive rules over time.[29] Seventy percent of the 103rd's rules were closed.[30] Even more important, the recent trend is toward structured restrictive rules, in which the only amendments considered for floor inclusion are those submitted to the Rules Committee in advance. From the majority leadership's perspective, this takes all of the guesswork out of the floor debate, thus avoiding any potential "blindsiding." Even so, getting a favorable rule is a daunting task. Currently, when a policy committee wants a rule, the committee must first write a letter requesting one. The policy committee staff director then calls the Rules Committee staff, who schedules a hearing. The Rules Committee then contacts the leadership within seven days, in order to avoid any possible "hijacking." Germaneness waivers and other technical points are handled by the staff.

Even then, the policy committee might need help. As a long-time

Rules Committee staffer remarked, "If you're not on the Rules Committee or in the leadership, you have to have an advocate for you on the committee. The committee keeps track of who votes for the rules, and who votes against them. They don't forget, and committees have reputations over here. The leadership assigns members with safe seats to this committee, so they can do obnoxious things."

The following essential continuities were in evidence.

Continuity: The Rules Committee still serves as the majority leadership's traffic cop.   The Rules Committee was used in both periods of interest as the majority party leadership's "traffic cop," or as the leadership's means of controlling legislative movement within the chamber. Various respondent references included the phrases *traffic cop*, *gatekeeper*, and *traffic control* as descriptors of the committee's agenda-controlling function.

Continuity: Chairman-to-chairman contact and the personal relationships between the committee heads are still critical in realizing legislative success.   The Rules Committee, viewed in both periods, confirms the importance of interpersonal relationships seen in other aspects of the broader legislative process. As a longtime Rules Committee member and other House respondents noted, over and above the formal staffing of the rules process and the usual member-to-member contacts, the nature of the personal relationship between the Rules Committee chairman and the sponsoring committee would figure prominently in the likelihood of a favorable rule. Personal relationships matter, and "committees have reputations."

TABLE 7.3
Number of Amendments Authorized by the Rule
and Amendments Offered for the Six Cases

Case/Year Passed	Amendments Authorized under the Rule	Amendments Offered on the Floor
Foreign Aid/1962	Open	10
College Aid/1963	Open	6
Urban Mass Transit/1964	Open	8
Foreign Aid/1993	5	5
Goals 2000/1994	6	6
RTC Closeout/1993	1	1

In general, the respondents viewed the Rules Committee with less trepidation in the early 1990s than in the 1960s, and the case histories support this assessment. The Rules Committee of the 1990s, while far more demanding in terms of the requirements for prior disclosure of intended amendments, is more of a known quantity in the latter period than Judge Smith's Rules Committee of the early 1960s was. In this sense, the Rules Committee is less of an impediment to legislative success in the modern era than it was in the past, though in both periods the chamber's party leadership could and did use the committee to shut down or slow down legislation.

FLOOR ACTIVITIES

Turning our attention to the House floor, consequential changes and essential continuities in the floor activities could be indicated by shifts in the influence of seniority, in the quality and duration of debate, or by changes in voting and floor management practices. As has been well documented, and as we might expect in the age of C-Span, sunshine laws, and other innovations, there have been a number of significant changes and continuities in the nature of floor activities in the two periods. The primary difference identified between the two periods was in the nature and importance of the floor activities. Floor activities, like the committee and subcommittee hearings, became much more pro forma over the period. As one respondent put it, "Floor debate doesn't matter anymore . . . go to the floor, and all you hear are bitter, partisan exchanges . . . or ethics charges flying back and forth." Another added, "There're no intellectual challenges anymore . . . get your licks in on the 'role-of-government' question." The evidence indicated the following changes and continuities in the House floor activities.

Change: Nobody spends significant time on the floor anymore, except when the membership is called to vote. With members spending far less time on the House floor in the 1990s, there are far fewer member-to-member contact opportunities, again causing the construction of policy majorities to be more difficult. Furthermore, the leadership's absence limits legislative opportunities. As one respondent with experience in both periods put it, "Carl Albert sat on the House floor every day. He was there whenever the Committee of the Whole met. From Tip O'Neill on, we never see the Speaker anymore. I go days without seeing him." Most respondents from the early 1960s noted the excellent opportunities that the frequent floor sessions offered. As one member remarked, "To be successful, you have to talk to everybody. . . . [M]ember-to-member contact is the key, and we got a lot of business done on the floor during roll call." Table 7.4 offers a rough measure of this shift in floor attendance, as measured through counts taken for quorum calls at various junctures in the floor consideration of the case laws. Clearly, the trend in the 1990s, confirmed by the respondents and by C-Span or a trip into the chamber on any given day, is that members spend far less time on the floor. This change has made the construction of supportive voting majorities that much more difficult.

Change: Floor debate in the 1990s is about "getting your licks in on C-Span," as rancorous partisan and personal attacks happen more often than serious discussions of the issues.   While the floor debate in all six cases included some level of discord among the various speakers, the floor debate in the 1960s cases was both more issue-oriented and more civil. Even when Otto Passman slyly inserted into the debate quotations of John Kennedy's earlier opposition to foreign aid (that Kennedy had expressed on the floor of the House and then the Senate), and despite his often rabid public statements of opposition to the whole concept of foreign aid, Passman went out of his way to at least appear respectful to the president. He also gave a reasoned, step-by-step accounting of the

TABLE 7.4
Length of Debate, Floor Speakers, and Member Attendance for the Six Cases

Case/ Year	Length in Hours, Floor Debate	Number of Speakers, Congressional Record	MCs on Floor at First Quorum Call	MCs on Floor after Quorum Call	MCs Voting on Final Passage
For Aid/ '62	3	46	80	377	393
Col Aid/ '63	3	56	396	396	400
UMT/ '64	4	48	212	404	401
For Aid/ '93	1	33	25	415	420
Goals/ '94	1.33	59	N/A	N/A	427
RTC/ '93	1	23	N/A	N/A	422

mismanagement and lack of clarity in the foreign aid program. Soon after each member of his subcommittee and Speaker McCormack rose to pay tribute to their retiring Republican colleague, John Taber of New York. The other two cases from the 1960s had similar episodes. Conversely, the floor debate of the 1990s was usually marked by less reverence and more pointed language in the form of partisan mud slinging. The "debate" of the 1990s represented in the cases also often included general antigovernment rhetoric, and it frequently stooped to the level of negative and personal exchanges.

Change: There is less floor debate, due in part to less time allotted per issue and the restrictive rules. As table 7.4 illustrates, episodes of significant legislating got far less floor time in the 1990s than comparable episodes in the early 1960s. Reflecting this trend, and in a fashion similar to the hearings process, many speakers in the 1990s cases were recognized merely in order to allow them to express opposition or support and then insert a lengthy speech into the *Congressional Record*. While the impact of the reduced length of debate itself on legislative outcomes is unclear, the net effect of the reduced time spent meeting with colleagues on the floor is once more a reduction in the opportunities for member-to-member contacts, thus again tending to increase the obstacles to legislative success.

Change: The innovation of electronic voting, with a concomitant increase in recorded votes, has fundamentally shifted the average members' primary voting accountability concerns from his colleagues to his constituents. One advantage of the teller, standing, and roll call voting of the early 1960s, in the view of several respondents, was that members knew where the others stood on particular issues. That knowledge, coupled with the additional time they spent on the floor, afforded the members the opportunity to "gravitate to those with similar interests and floor voting records." One respondent added, "The voting machine makes the voting decision hurried, and the members today are far less likely to know what they're voting on." Another offered, "There was something special about standing, stating your name, and announcing your vote." Again, the impact of the change has been to make the solicitation of colleague support more difficult in recent times.

Change: The increase in recorded votes has taken away negotiating room for members in general, making the construction of supportive majorities that much more difficult. Last, the apparent advantage of increased accountability afforded by the rise in recorded votes has had a converse effect on the legislators' ability to negotiate and compromise to advance the legislative function. Heightened electoral sensitivity constrains most members, and with the nearly instantaneous accountability created by electronic voting, C-Span, and a variety of watchdogs in the district and in Washington, the net effect of the increase in recorded votes has been to make most members pause carefully before casting votes that they would have considered unimportant in previous years. Many leaders have responded to this situation by carefully crafting votes in a way that enables any member to say anything about the vote necessary to justify their preference. In sum, at the same time the quality of floor activities has declined, members have become much more cautious about compromise in the form of voting favors.

CONFERENCE COMMITTEE

In assessing change and continuity in the formal procedures of the conference committees as they bore upon the pursuit of success in the six cases, there were several directions in which to look for possibly important changes. The conference committees could have changed in their common procedures, in their composition, or in their role within the larger process. In general, however, the conference committees remained well known for their routinely ad hoc flavor. As Tiefer (1989) notes, "Conference bargaining does not follow any procedure—it is as pure an exercise in negotiation as can be found."[32] Describing the typical conference committee of the early 1960s, Clem Miller wrote, "Conference committees make their own rules. The watchword is informality. Committee meetings are bargaining sessions between principals who know the game. The preliminaries are out of the way. Now is the time to hammer out the final product."[33]

Even so, the conference committee reports are not automatically passed, as the 1962 college aid initiative illustrates. Though the conference report reflected carefully negotiated compromises on key issues, the House rebuffed the Senate's scholarships initiative, ultimately recommitting and killing the initiative for the year. The following points emerged from the evidence.

Change: Conferences have many more conferees in the 1990s, and the net result of this increased size and the sunshine laws has been to force the action elsewhere.   For example, only a few of the principal actors conducted the critical preconference negotiations in the House-Senate treatment of Goals 2000 that really shaped the conference report. These actors settled the differences in the major sticking points, namely, the opportunity-to-learn standards and enforcement provisions, prior to the beginning of the conference, as noted in the case history. Like the effects of multiple referrals, the net result of the increase in conference committee participants has been to move the "action" elsewhere, while concurrently allowing more participants into the process and making the conference proceedings that much more challenging for those seeking to move the legislation forward.

Continuity: The same general activities take place in the conferences and preconferences, with members negotiating first-tier policy and political considerations while the staff works out the rest. The key battle in the foreign operations conference of 1993 was the debate with Senator Mitch McConnell over earmarks. Almost all of the other differences were negotiated by staff after guidance from the respective chairs. Similarly, Edith Green negotiated provisions regarding scholarships and aid to private schools in the 1962 education bill conference, to the exclusion of almost all other issues. These same activities took place in each case, even including the preconference decision to avoid conference in the case of the mass transit measure, and the only thing that changed was the venue. Today, the preconference negotiations are usually more important than the actual conference, in the eyes of the respondents. In any event, the conference principals only address a few of the thousands of possible issues touched by new legislation in any conference, with the staff negotiators generally achieving agreement on the myriad second- and third-tier issues beforehand.

THE LEGISLATIVE TIMELINE AND THE NET EFFECTS

Changes in the legislative timeline, or the length of time from a case's introduction to presidential signature, would not only represent a change in itself but could also serve to measure the influence of other procedural impediments or advantages resulting from the other procedural changes documented in the literature. Examining this last formal procedural consideration for any systematic lengthening or shortening of the process yields two continuities.

Continuity: The legislative timeline, from first mention of a legislative idea to passage of the law, is comparable in the two periods and generally independent from one law to the next. Respondents from both periods emphasized the importance of patience, persistence, and vigilance. One staffer from the 1990s remarked, "Timing is everything. You have to hit the process at the right time. Sometimes success comes quickly, but most often it comes slowly, and you have to persist . . . for decades in some cases." Another member described the passage of Goals 2000 as "a rolling conversation. There was strong debate from beginning to end, and the prospects were up and down until the end." In sum, the evidence presented by these six cases gave no indication of any systematic change in legislative timelines over the periods.

Continuity: Deadlines help in the pursuit of legislative success, and they attract business.   A variety of legislative deadlines, from the natural fiscal year deadlines of the appropriations process to the impending deadline of the RTC agency authorization and the expiring budget authority that shaped the passage of the urban mass transit law in 1964, all helped those legislative initiatives move forward. This feature of the process probably explains part of the current attraction of the appropriations process as the place to go with district projects, as a legislator can tack "small" projects onto the larger vehicle that funds it with good prospects for the law to actually make it to passage.

In general, while the respondents categorized the various events that led to legislative success by their place in the formal procedures of the legislative process, none of the respondents identified any of these procedures as being crucial to policy success. That is, while the subcommittee, committee, Rules Committee, floor, and conference actors were all identified as important in advancing legislative initiatives, the internal procedures themselves (and documented changes in them) were not viewed by the respondents as being particularly critical in shaping the eventual outcome. As always, any one step in the process can rise up to become an obstacle to success, but generally speaking, members seeking to realize their policy goals were not as concerned about the changes in the formal procedures of the House as they were about other potential impediments to victory. Put another way, while legislative procedures are tools to be used by the legislators, people trump procedure in importance in the eyes of the actors.

CHAPTER 8

Actor Strategies

Leaders are buying leadership positions with "leadership PACs" now.

—House member from the 1990s

I never had a press secretary back then—only the leaders had them. Now, everybody has one.

—House member from the 1960s

Too often, the media are uninformed—not quoting positions right or saying anything correctly. Most often, they are inaccurate or too sensationalized.

—House member with service in both periods

Actor strategies are the recurring methods or common tactics through which legislative actors seek to realize legislative success. This term also encompasses the unwritten "rules of the game," or rules and norms not codified into formal procedure but routinely observed by most legislative actors. It is sometimes argued that these informal actor strategies have changed in tangible ways in recent decades in response to a variety of stimuli, as observers have described shifts in these House norms and techniques. In theory, these changes could include altered actor strategies of persuasion and packaging, and consequential changes in the actors' strategic premises could also take the form of altered perceptions of the party and committee leaders' ability to deliver votes or an increased or decreased reliance on member-to-member contacts to realize policy goals. Alternatively, the forms of these member-to-member contacts, or the informal rules regarding those contacts, might have changed as well with corresponding consequences for the construction of policy coalitions.

While some of the scholarship related to legislators' strategic premises does posit change in those strategies over time, many of these accounts instead provide snapshot accounts of successfully employed strategies at a particular point in time. Furthermore, observations pertaining to legislator strategies can be classified as either *parliamentary* or *personal* strategic changes. In reacting or adapting to formal institutional procedural rule changes, legislative actors could have responded with altered tactics within the chamber's procedural framework, or they could have reacted by changing approaches in the way they built coalitions outside of the procedural considerations. Put another way, parliamentary strategic change represents change within the procedural "box," while personal strategic change represents modified strategies outside of that box.

There are accounts in the literature that argue for both types of strategic changes. Examples of *parliamentary* strategic changes include modified amending and referral strategies, increased use of omnibus packaging, and changes in the use of rules and suspension of the rules for the floor treatment of desired legislation. Tiefer (1989) notes developments in the strategic use of amendments, including both "saving" and "killer" amendments, as well as amendments in the nature of a substitute.[1] Weingast (1992) describes the increase in the use of restrictive rules, multiple referrals, and amending as adaptive strategies of floor management.[2] Likewise, Smith (1989) views the omnibus packaging of bills, and in particular new uses of appropriating legislation and reconciliation bills, as a strategic innovation by the Democratic leadership intended to effectively compel the Republican minority and the White House to consider its legislative initiatives.[3] A related technique involved the tacking of legislative "riders" onto these big-ticket bills to get some desired policy outcome. Tiefer notes that this strategy was nicknamed the "four bill system" by members and included the budget resolution, continuing appropriations, supplemental appropriations, and reconciliation package of spending cuts.[4] Additional techniques of this variety include legislative or "limitation riders," an increased use of special rules, the incorporation of legislative vetoes into policy proposals, and increased use of the suspension of the rules.

A number of changes in the *personal* strategies that members use in seeking legislative success have been argued to be indicators of significant process change as well. These modified strategies include member attempts at decreased traceability, blame avoidance, increased legislative oversight, an increased aggressiveness among younger members, and a variety of altered institutional norms. Other personal strategic changes identified in the scholarship include a tendency of the leadership to avoid conflict, strategies of "going public," and heightened efforts at secrecy. Arnold (1990) describes the first of these, what he calls a "weakened traceability," in his analysis of legislator strategies in the recent Congresses.[5] He argues that members and coalition leaders work to avoid constituent blame for unfavorable legislative costs, and he notes that this effort has increasingly taken the form of broad grants of cost imposition to executive agencies in the form of legislated oversight.[6] The increasing use of this strategy is implied by the four-bill system as well as the recent focus on deficits and the politics of the budget. Related to these strategies is the strategy of secrecy, which Arnold describes as a return to the prereform practices of secret committee proceedings as another technique to avoid the blame for legislative outcomes.[7] David-son (1992) echoes this theme that legislators increasingly seek to dis-tance themselves from unfavorable legislative costs.[8]

Other authors concur in this assessment of broad institutional change in response to strategic changes. Matthews described a Congress in 1960 in which a young senator was "expected to keep his mouth shut" and "to postpone his maiden efforts on the floor (rather than) appear overly aggressive."[9] Similarly, Clapp (1963) described a Congress of the early 1960s in which a new member was "expected to serve an apprenticeship," and he noted that "the junior member should defer to the elders of the House and the leadership."[10] Huntington (1965) agreed, writing, "The newcomer to Congress is repeatedly warned that 'to get along he must go along.' To go along means he must adjust to the prevailing mores and attitudes of the Inner Club."[11] Smith (1989), however, argues that this "apprenticeship" is a thing of the past, and he argues that this norm's demise has contributed to an increase in amending activity within recent Congresses, as deference to seniority and the committee leadership waned.[12] Heclo (1989) echoes the theme, depicting the modern regime as "much more open, fragmented, self-crit-ical, nondeferential, and fluid in its attachment."[13]

These posited changes in institutional norms imply the need for new strategies on the part of the party leaders. Sundquist (1981) argued that the party leadership embarked on a strategy of conflict avoidance, with the leadership tending to "avoid trying to impose its will, or at least to choose its fights very carefully, so as not to risk defeat and expose its weakness."[14] Kernell (1993), writing about the president as a legislative leader, describes the executive's increased tendency to go public in a bid to build popular support for his legislative proposals.[15]

AD HOC ISSUE COALITIONS

In assessing this literature in light of the evidence, I first looked for signs of an increasing or decreasing reliance upon party or interest groups or changing assumptions about the ability of actors or interests to "deliver" policymaking support. The evidence indicated the following continuity.

Continuity: Legislative success depends on the construction of ad hoc issue coalitions, because parties and single-issue interests alone could not deliver policy change in either period. In each of the six cases, the eventual legislative champions built ad hoc issue coalitions that eventually grew large enough to create the resultant policy successes. At first glance, this finding is not all that provocative. However, this fact has substantial implications for both the literature and practitioners interested in the actors' operating assumptions. In both periods of interest, I found no evidence to support the commonly lamented assumption that the "decline of the parties" had translated into a decreased ability of parties to deliver on policy promises. Similarly, even distinctly arrayed specific interests could not deliver policy changes without broader general support for policy initiatives. Even in their heyday, or in the Truman and Schattschneider years, parties and aggregations of interests were only proxies for the real ad hoc issue coalitions of actors and interests that achieved policy successes. The evidence here indicates that state and regional interests, policy history and past benefits conferred, ideology, and existing personal relationships are as important as parties and interest groups in explaining individual outcomes. While it is possible that the array of interests or the internal homogeneity of the major parties has declined since the 1960s, the respondents never couched their descriptions of the events that led to the passage of the cases in these oversimplified terms. At the ground level, neither parties nor interest groups unilaterally produce legislative victories.

The cases from both periods provide a variety of examples of actors displaying legislative independence and extraparty policy goals. One member described the Democratic Study Group, formed in the early 1960s, in these terms.[16] Political scientist and serving House member David Price notes, "No one understands or cares about home like one's home state colleagues, and collegial relationships within a delegation can be a tremendously important personal and political resource for a member."[17] Price further notes, "[A]n important fact about congressional party organizations: though they perform crucial institutional functions . . . , members retain a great deal of independence in their voting behavior on the floor and in how they relate to the broad range of party functions and activities."[18] Clem Miller noted the same independence in the early 1960s, describing the "cold, hard vote," "the close friend you were grimacing with not two minutes before votes with the other people . . . 'voting his district.'"[19] In sum, a close examination of the passage of the cases indicates that, for each, it was an ad hoc issue coalition, rather than any enduring aggregation of interests or party influences that led to the eventual legislative success.

METHODS OF PERSUASION

Another key area of inquiry centered on the methods of member-to-member persuasion. Again, it was one major fundamental continuity that emerged from the analysis.

Continuity: The methods of persuasion have not changed over the decades, and they still include threats, bribes, personal appeals, public policy logic, and public service appeals. Respondents indicated that each of the six ad hoc issue coalitions that eventually realized policy success were constructed through a combination of these five methods of member-to-member or interest-to-member persuasion. While workplace conditions and member preconditions have decreased the number of purely personal appeals, this technique is still in evidence, with members inclined to offer quid pro quo incentives in soliciting help from their colleagues whenever possible. The examples in which personal friendships helped to facilitate legislative success at critical junctures are noted throughout the case histories. Relationships such as the close working and personal relationships among the members on Otto Passman's foreign operations subcommittee, and the similarly important relationship between David Obey and Bob Livingston in the 1993 subcommittee enabled those willful agents to realize legislative success.

The solid working relationship forged between Obey and Livingston on a trip to Russia is reminiscent of numerous anecdotes related by respondents from the early 1960s. These respondents often referred to social events and fact-finding trips to Vietnam, Europe, Central America, and other places that not only provided opportunities to conduct business but also facilitated the critical member relationships that make personal appeals all the more feasible. One respondent related a story in which a presidential phone call on the member's birthday afforded him the opportunity to arrange a meeting with a key advisor that eventually resulted in the passage of a project he had been pursuing for years. The respondent added, "I'd done the spadework years before, and you had to have it all ready to go, with the facts straight and your reasoning sound. But sometimes it took an opportunity like that call to get the foot in the door."

Edith Green took her subcommittee members to Russia, and John Brademas routinely had members over to his office to discuss policy and other topics. Prayer breakfasts were a popular activity for some subcommittee members, too. A member from the 1960s said, "It's hard to comprehend now the esprit de corps that we had in the House in the '60s. . . . [W]e were all World War II veterans, and ideology and party didn't matter after adjournment. We enjoyed each other's fellowship, and you didn't have the sneering that I saw in the '70s and later." Regardless of changes in the number of opportunities to build member-to-member relationships, the methods of persuasion employed by members seeking to realize legislative success remained constant over the two periods.

PACKAGING

Since much has been made of the heightened use of the omnibus packaging strategy, my goal here was to look at the cases and the committees to see if there were significant differences in the impact of omnibus packaging on the pursuit of legislative success over the period. Specifically, I was interested in the prevalence of the omnibus packaging technique as a strategy and the perceptions of the actors regarding the importance of this and other legislative packaging strategies. As Charles Tiefer notes, "Since the 1970s, the increasing use of continuing resolutions which wrap many appropriations bills together in one package has, at times, altered the very nature of legislating, from a piecemeal exercise . . . to an exercise in backstage creation of an omnibus measure impervious to floor tampering and too massive for presidential impact."[20]

The Banking and Currency Committee and Education and Labor Committee calendars from the Eighty-eighth Congress show that the omnibus packaging of legislative proposals was a common practice on both committees in the early 1960s. For example, Albert Rains's Housing Subcommittee had 246 bills referred to it during the Eighty-eighth Congress.[21] Of those bills, there were thirty-two packages of bills eventually considered by the committee, ranging in size from paired bills to a package of twelve. Omnibus strategies were prominent in the passage of the Higher Education Facilities Act of 1963, with the Kennedy administration trying individual bills, then an omnibus approach, and then abandoning the strategy as congressional support ebbed and waned before passage.

Omnibus packaging empowers the chamber leadership at the expense of the committee leadership, and it makes those major packages inaccessible to most members seeking to influence or understand the legislation. Efforts at influence are hampered by the commonly restrictive rules in the modern case, and any legislator is hard pressed to wade through the big bills coming in at one thousand statute pages apiece. The whole bill usually rides on one up or down vote. One respondent noted, "The leadership loves omnibus packages because they're up or down votes that are hard to say no to because everybody has something in it. And the staff loves them because they can write them up in the dark of night under manufactured deadlines."

There are other innovative packaging strategies used by the actors, however. David Obey innovated in packaging the foreign aid bill, especially important given foreign aid's traditional political unpopularity made even worse by a deficit-focused election year. He constructed the package in such a way that any member voting for the package at any point in the process could claim truthfully to have voted for cuts in foreign aid funding. Otto Passman also utilized the strategy of including a number of "bogus" provisions that he could use as trade bait on the floor or in conference. Stephen Neal considered, then abandoned, a time-tested packaging strategy of dropping the RTC funding's SAIF provisions when the measure was about to go to the floor with the intention of resurrecting the provision in conference, since conference reports are traditionally (though not always) given easier passage than original bills. In sum, the evidence indicated the following key changes and continuities.

Change: Appropriations riders are authorized now, but they were not allowed in the early 1960s. There are a number of advantages to appropriations rider strategies, particularly given the decline of the authorizing process and the advantages offered by the annual appropriations deadlines. Members know that the Appropriations Committee leaders and chamber leaders want to meet those deadlines, and the Congress is generally less friendly to stand-alone legislative initiatives in the modern era.

Change: Constraints on new spending authority limit new stand-alone initiatives and encourage members to focus their legislative efforts on the existing big-ticket money bills. Table 8.1 offers an interesting perspective on this assertion. For all of the heightened partisan bluster of the 1990s, when this period is compared to the 1960s, the average significant program of the 1990s is much smaller in real money terms than its counterpart of the 1960s. Without overstating this trend given the small sample size, the foreign aid program offers an excellent example of this phenomenon. The fiscal 1994 foreign aid program was less than half of the fiscal 1963 program when both funding levels are adjusted for inflation. Similarly, while the major education initiative of the early 1990s, Goals 2000, cost only $90 million, the Kennedy/Johnson startup programs in 1964 cost $1.9 billion, or fourteen times more! Furthermore, the 1964 startup program represented only a fraction of the entire program sought by Kennedy. All of the increased rancor in the modern era occurs over far less in the way of new discretionary spending authority.

One key continuity emerged as well.

TABLE 8.1
Program Money, in Nominal and Adjusted Dollars, for the Six Cases

Case/Year Passed	Authorized/ Appropriated Then-current Dollars	Authorized/ Appropriated 1967 Dollars
Foreign Aid/1962	$6.3 billion	$7.0 billion
College Aid/1963	$1.2 billion	$1.3 billion
Urban Mass Transit/1964	$0.38 billion	$0.43 billion
Foreign Aid/1993	$14.6 billion	$3.4 billion
Goals 2000/1994	$0.40 billion	$0.09 billion
RTC Closeout/1993	$18.3 billion	$4.2 billion

Continuity: Omnibus packaging may be more prevalent and used in "blockbuster" fashion now, but the legislative strategy is not a new one. With incumbents concerned about the far greater constituent and challenger scrutiny resulting from increased recorded voting and other phenomena, omnibus packaging offers attractive room for negotiation, compromise, and political cover in an era of heightened electoral sensitivity. Ask a member these days, on the record, what he or she thinks of a recent legislative vote cast, and the likely response is, "We didn't get everything we wanted, and the bill wasn't perfect, but there was a lot to like, and we had to take what we could get." In an era of heightened reelectoral sensitivity, omnibus strategies offer political cover for the increased exposure caused by increases in recorded voting.

USE OF THE MEDIA

In examining the strategy of going public and the actors' perspectives on the use and utility of the media in the legislative process, key indications of change, if present, would be found in the number of references to media contacts, the perceptions of the actors regarding the public strategy's effectiveness, and the relative impact of media accounts on the eventual legislative outcome. The following change and continuity emerged from the evidence.

Change: The House leadership is increasingly concerned with managing the legislative policy message in the 1990s, but primarily for reelectoral reasons rather than policy ones. Most respondents with House experience in both periods of interest in the study identified an increased desire on the part of the chambers' party leadership to go public in seeking to manage the terms of the debate. Most ascribed electoral motives to this trend, and many pointed to Speaker Jim Wright as the original modern proponent of this House strategy. In any event, this increased role of the party leadership in the committee's treatment of legislative initiatives became a source of some friction within the parties themselves in the 105th Congress, a subject addressed briefly in the epilogue.

Continuity: All of the actors seek to influence media perception of policy change, though most members retain a dim view of the media's ability to "get it right." Most respondents in both periods acknowledged the necessity of attempting to manage the media in pursuing legislative success. As the media shape public perception of any legislative initiative, particularly given the prevalence of issue polling today, the respondents recognized the necessity of seeking to shape the media message, even as they denounced the media for their inability to get the story right with any consistency.

PARLIAMENTARY PROCEDURAL INNOVATION

The case histories offer several examples of innovative uses of parliamentary procedure as legislator strategies. One example of an effective attempt in this direction was the push by a group of House conservatives opposed to federal aid to the schools to support an unintentional "killer amendment" proposed by Adam Clayton Powell Jr. in a principled though perhaps legislatively unwise bid to end school segregation. Later in the consideration of the same measure, the Kennedy administration was unable to overcome procedural blockage of its initiative in the Rules Committee in spite of parliamentary maneuvers of its own. Likewise, the mass transit bill suffered the same fate when an attempt to use the Calendar Wednesday procedure to bring that bill to the floor was defeated, with both of these attempts at parliamentary maneuver stymied by none other than Judge Smith of the Rules Committee himself.

In the 1990s cases, first-term Representative Herb Klein (D-NJ) overcame a committee stalemate by suggesting a means through which the committee could appropriate the full amount needed to close out the thrift funding without technically authorizing any more money. Obey applied a similar maneuver in "re-appropriating" unused funds from the year before for the fiscal 1994 foreign operations bill. Senator Alphonse D'Amato (R-NY), with support of like-minded colleagues, used an innovative parliamentary strategy of denying the appointment of conferees on the Senate side in order to extract preconference concessions from the

House negotiators. He was able to influence the first-tier issues around which the conference debate would center, including the bill's statute of limitations and its minority-contracting provisions. The following continuity emerged from the analysis of the evidence.

Continuity: Procedural innovation is often instrumental in facilitating legislative progress, and parliamentary procedural strategies are also often successful in slowing or halting the progress of legislative initiatives. As the Klein and Obey examples above illustrate, timely parliamentary innovation can go a long way in moving a legislative initiative past an obstacle. At the same time, as the House's conservatives demonstrated frequently during the early 1960s, procedural strategies can be equally effective at halting legislative initiatives either temporarily or in some cases, permanently. Procedural innovation is a commonly applied strategy.

HOUSE NORMS AS STRATEGIC CONSIDERATIONS

The evidence suggested some key strategic and normative changes and continuities.

Change: Members now campaign in opposition to one another within their colleagues' districts. One longtime staffer noted, "Parties are much more antagonistic now. In the 1960s, members never talked directly about one another, and they didn't go to each other's districts without notifying each other. They wouldn't contribute to their neighbor's opponent. Today it's all different." As has been the case with most changes over the periods, this obviously makes it more difficult to realize legislative success, as members are more prone to refuse to support initiatives across party lines when electoral politics have taken this turn.

Change: "Bomb throwing" is viewed as an acceptable practice by many more legislators now. One respondent with service in the early 1960s described Pat Robertson's father, Senator A. Willis Robertson (D-VA), as the "original conservative." "However," he noted, "unlike the 'rightist elements' you see today that refuse to work with anybody, he was a 'superconservative' but highly respected and generally just left alone. He was limited in his criticism, well liked, and very gentlemanly." Another Democratic respondent from the 1960s added, "There was no question about it . . . some of my best friends were Republicans, and we could sit down and work through problems without getting mean about it." Gerald Ford (R-MI) had a tremendous reputation and was often the first Republican mentioned when members talked about national focus and the placement of public-interest considerations above personal political ones. The respondents with service in the 1960s often fondly remembered leaders from the other side of the aisle, unlike the respondents from the 1990s. As another member with service through the early 1980s described this phenomenon, "The House became anti-intellectual, anti-evidence, and pure ideology. The member today comes into the House thinking, I know what is right, and I don't need to listen." John Boehner (R-OH), Dick Armey (R-TX), and Sonny Callahan (R-AL), among others, were identified as bomb throwers at several points in the case histories from the 1990s.

Change: The spending constraints of the early- and mid-1990s made omnibus and appropriation rider strategies more attractive. The Obey/Passman difference is again particularly illustrative of this idea. In spite of the fact that Obey worked to support foreign aid while Passman was a committed, energetic opponent of that aid, Passman presided over twice as much aid as Obey in real terms. A staffer with House experience in both periods noted, "In the 1960s, we had money. In the 1990s, it's just not available. Today, the question is, what to force, what to do, and what can we make it without. In the 1960s, we could make a model for it, get organizational support, and fund it. You don't shop ideas or programs now . . . times make quite a difference." With this in mind, the yearly appropriations are viewed as the only game in town. While recent budget surpluses certainly have mitigated this situation, the reliance on those strategies remains.

Change: The power of the California delegation has created a new regional imbalance. While this trend, identified by several respondents, appears to be somewhat diffused at the committee level, at least for the committees represented in this study, the fifty-two (and soon to be fifty-three) House representatives from that state can wield tremendous influence at the chamber level whenever they are so inclined. One byproduct of this clout, according to one respondent, has been the shortening of the congressional workweek, a trend aimed at accommodating the great number of representatives from the West as they make the lengthy, weekly trek home. Once again, the net effect has been to make it somewhat more difficult to build policy coalitions, unless of course the legislative objective pleases all of California!

Change: Misinformation or disingenuousness as a strategy is commonplace in the 1990s. Intentional misinformation was evident in the 1990s cases but not the 1960s ones. Furthermore, respondents noted that the use of this strategy is now at least tacitly accepted by members, even those who do not employ disingenuousness as a strategy themselves. To put this another way, the outrage is gone. However, as several members noted, in order to realize legislative success, a reputation for honesty is crucial. "People who aren't trustworthy don't last past maybe one forgiven mistake. A reputation for integrity is critical . . . otherwise people won't bother with you." A number of respondents from the 1990s cases asserted that members had outright lied in their portrayals of the legislative initiatives, while no respondent from the 1960s made any such allegation. An Education and Labor Committee member reported, "In the debate, [the identified congressman] made a statement that was entirely false, about an issue that didn't exist." This characteristic extends to the external actors as well. Religious activist groups, in energizing grassroots activism against supposed but nonexistent provisions in Goals 2000 banning home schooling, did so, according to respondents, just to demonstrate their power in the process even though they were alleged to have known that no such provisions existed. Without question, this trend has made it more difficult to achieve legislative success.

Change: At some point between the 1960s and the 1990s, "pressure" groups became "interest" groups. Many respondents from the 1960s persisted in using the more pejorative term *pressure group* when describing organized interests, and several of those member respondents went out of their way to distance themselves from them. Respondents from the 1990s, however, in addition to using the friendlier term *interest group*, generally accepted the groups as vital actors in the process. As one member from the 1990s put it, "You need their information, and the door is always open."

Two key normative continuities emerged from the evidence.

Continuity: Even if the full committee chairs still do not know all of the early termers on their committees, the stereotype of casual disregard for junior members by senior members is a false one, regardless of the period. Gibbons, Brademas, and Sickles, though early termers on Powell's Education and Labor Committee, were often selected over more conservative senior members of the committee to chair important legislative task forces and analyses for Chairman Powell. One example of this included Brademas's selection by Powell to chair his newly created Advisory Group on Higher Education as a second termer.[23] That nomination irritated the more senior and increasingly conservative Edith Green. In all three sets of hearings from the early 1960s, junior members were offered and took advantage of opportunities to ask questions and participate in the proceedings. Sam Gibbons (D-FL) was given significant responsibilities on the Education and Labor Committee as a first termer in the early 1960s, primarily due to his lengthy service on the analogous committee in the Florida legislature. Likewise, Karan English (D-AZ) received similar responsibilities for the same reasons as a first termer in the 1990s.

Continuity: "Real" bipartisanship is often an effective strategy.   Just as Obey and Livingston were able to stand together to advance the unpopular foreign aid bill in an election year, other respondents, such as John Brademas (D-IN) and Albert Quie (R-MN), were able to forge working bipartisan subcommittee coalitions on many issues to greatly enhance their own prospects for success. Sincere bipartisan agreements at the subcommittee level have credibility. In the case of Goals 2000, it was a privately negotiated bipartisan compromise that salvaged the initiative.

SUMMARIZING THE RESULTS

In sum, substantial changes in the House actors' norms and strategic techniques, like the great majority of other consequential changes identified in this book, have had the net effect of making the construction of ad hoc issue coalitions more difficult in recent times. The magnitude of the legislative task grew even as the major ingredients of that policy success remained constant over the decades. At the same time, however, the conventional portrayal of the chairmen of the 1960s as gruff, poor-listening, and arbitrary autocrats is in need of revision. Regardless of their public personas, the chairmen represented in the cases from the 1960s in fact were either regularly inclusive in executive sessions, hearings, and other subcommittee and committee activities, or casually indifferent in giving autonomy down the chain of command. Likewise, the evidence shows that the commonly lamented decline in the policymaking power of the parties is overstated at best. But given that the net effect of the consequential changes in the House actor strategies has been to make the realization of legislative success more difficult, it is not surprising that legislators have adopted a variety of less personal strategies to cope with these new challenges.

CHAPTER 9

Legislative Products

The legislation we passed still had gaping holes in it—but it was the best we were going to get.

—House member from the 1990s

The leadership today sees governing as campaigning.

—House member with service
in both the 1960s and the 1990s

The law itself is only one of a variety of legislative products that can emerge from the consideration of any bill. The fourth and final broad category of plausible change in the legislative process certainly includes possible consequential changes in the thickness, scope, number, or language of the laws produced by the Congresses in the different periods. However, consequential changes and essential continuities in the legislative product might also involve changes in other products ranging from the published hearings to committee and conference committee reports to conferee statements to the *Congressional Record*. Significant changes in the various legislative products that might have an impact upon the pursuit of legislative success include increases in the enacted laws' level of "technicality" or the increased use of complex, interest-specific jargon, as well as possible changes in a recurring national or local focus. Another plausibly consequential change, one cited in the congressional literature, might include an increase in the House's propensity toward legislating bureaucratic oversight and authority instead of enacting more specific terms of policy implementation.

More specifically, significant product change could refer to systematic variations over time in the *nature* of the legislative products, their *thickness*, the products' level of *complexity*, the laws' national or local *focus*, or the *mass* of legislation and other products created in the cases or by a particular Congress. Other plausible sorts of meaningful change could arise from changes in the *vehicles* used by the committees, as well as the conference committee *reports*.

As was the case in the other categories of change, scholars have identified a variety of these changes, ascribing serious consequences to the legislative process as a result. In the first category of product change, change in the *nature* of the legislation enacted, scholars have asserted that two major product changes have come about since the 1960s. These include an increasing propensity on the part of Congress to oversee rather than to legislate, as well as a recent inclination of the institution to grant broad, categorical powers rather than more constrained grants of authority with specific, detailed terms of implementation. Huntington foreshadowed these trends in 1965, noting that one of three dominant evolutionary tendencies of the Congress in the twentieth century was toward the oversight function.[1] He wrote, "In discharging this function, congressmen uncover waste and abuse, push particular projects and innovations, highlight inconsistencies, correct injustices, and compel exposition and defense of bureaucratic decisions."[2] Sundquist (1981) added, "Both houses devoted more effort to oversight, spurred by the reforms of 1974 . . . [making] twice as many reports on executive branch activities in 1976–80 as in 1966–70."[3] More recent scholarly accounts have depicted a continuation of the trend, with Heclo (1989), Aberbach (1990), and Rieselbach all noting increased oversight, though Rieselbach blames the Legislative Reorganization Act of 1946, rather than 1970s reforms, for the phenomenon.

While Davidson (1988 and 1992) and Browne and Paik (1993) note an increased recent legislative *thickness*, findings they attribute at least in part to a recent reliance on omnibus packaging, Heclo (1978) and Aberbach (1990) note the increased product *complexity* predicted by Bailey in 1950. Bailey wrote, "The growing complexity of government as a result of the economic and political changes of the past sixty years [has] made it impossible for the lay congressional mind to deal adequately with the myriad technical problems of modern practical law."[4] Heclo found evidence of this predicted growth in complexity, writing that the emerging regime was shaped, in part, by the "layering and specialization that have overtaken the government work force . . . [and] the development of specialized subcultures composed of highly knowledgeable policy-watchers."[5] Consistent with this view, Aberbach (1990) blames increases in issue and product complexity for the growth of the administrative sector as well as the growth in the power held by top bureaucrats.[6]

In terms of the change in product *focus*, Huntington (1965) spoke of a general "provincialism" of congressmen in the early 1960s. He argued that this provincialism led to a focus on "local needs and small-town ways of thought" at the expense of national questions, such as foreign policy concerns and broader economic issues.[7] More recently, however, Quirk (1992), writing of the modern postreform Congress, argues that the institution "provides less advantage to randomly selected groups or localities; it gives less deference to narrow group or local interests and more to diffuse, unorganized interests."[8] At the same time, Browne and Paik (1993) argue that a shift to local focus has occurred, with members seeking voting information from local stakeholders."[9] The literature regarding the question of shifts in focus, if even one exists, is inconclusive.

Last, in terms of the *mass* of legislation enacted, Heclo (1978) described a fundamental change in the "growth in the sheer mass of government activity and associated expectations" and the "mushrooming of federal regulations."[10] Picking up the theme more recently, Sinclair (1989) notes "a major change in the issue agenda; a variety of new and highly contentious issues ranging from environmental protection to abortion came to the fore."[11] Interestingly, Cameron, et al (1996) demonstrate remarkable similarities between the amount of significant legislation enacted by Congresses of the early 1960s and those of the early 1990s.[12]

THE LEGISLATIVE PRODUCTS IN THE CONGRESSES

Table 9.1 summarizes the changes in the legislative products of the Congresses from the early 1960s to the 1990s. The evidence indicates the following three key changes and one important continuity.

Change: The average statute thickness has increased dramatically.   The average thickness of statute for laws passed in the early 1960s was 2.3 pages per statute in the 87th Congress and 3.0 pages in the 88th

TABLE 9.1
The Legislative Product from the 1960s to the 1990s

Period/ Congress	Public and Private Bills Introduced	Public Bills Passed	Public Laws Enacted	Pages of Statute Enacted	Average No Pages Per Statute	Private Bills Enacted
1960s						
87th	14,328	1,927	885	2,078	2.3	684
88th	14,022	1,267	666	1,975	3.0	360
1990s						
103rd	6,647	749	465	7,542	16.2	8

Congress, but this average thickness exploded to 16.2 pages per statute by the 103rd Congress. Even accounting for the decreased number of laws passed by the later Congress, there were still 2,078 and 1,975 pages of statute enacted in the 87th and 88th Congresses, but 7,542 pages enacted in the 103rd. One way of viewing the effect of this change on the construction of supportive voting majorities is this: there are roughly four times as many potential controversies for members to seize upon in seeking to deny the passage of legislation.

Change: The depth, breadth, and range of the federal policy scope have increased enormously since the early 1960s.   As one respondent with experience in both periods noted, "The congressional agenda has expanded greatly from the early 1960s . . . medical ethics, computers, privacy, environmental policy, it's all new." There are still only 435 members attempting to vote on a vastly increased range of policy issues. The depth and breadth of each of those issue areas has grown a great deal as well.

Change: Fewer laws are produced in each session, but the laws are generally much larger, with very few of them being private bills.   As noted above, the number of statute pages produced by each Congress has increased by about four times since the early 1960s. With most of the secondary issues being negotiated by House and Senate staffs and the executive agencies, and given the extreme time crunch under which members operate today, there is no reason to believe that the average member is four times more aware of the laws being enacted.

Continuity: The complexity and technicality of the federal legalese is dependent upon the maturity of the policy area.   As table 9.5 illustrates for the cases, the primary determinant of the level of technicality or comprehensibility of the modern statutes is the maturity of the policy area being legislated. In considering issue complexity, the number of years that the federal government has been involved in the issue area appears to be directly correlated with that issue area's level of technicality.

THE HEARINGS

Congressional hearings are legislative products as well, both in terms of the public record of the proceedings and of the political theater offered during the process. In evaluating change and continuities in the congressional hearings, I was interested in the number of hearings held in the consideration and passage of the cases as well as the number and type of participants in the hearings. Furthermore, I examined the tone of

TABLE 9.2
The Hearings on the Cases

Case/ Year Passed	Number/ Over[13] How Many Months	Pages	Number[14] of Witnesses	Admin Officials	Interest Group Leaders	State/ Local Officials	Other	General Tone[15]
For Aid/ '62	15/ 6	1,018	67	67	0	0	0	Adversarial
Col Aid/ '63	8/ 27	313	59	12	34	1	12[16]	Cordial
UMT/ '64	7/ 2	487	49	10	22	16	11[17]	Cordial
For Aid/ '93	2/ 1	2,830	74	12	58	0	4[18]	Mixed
Goals/ '94	3/ 3	254	14	5	8	0	1[19]	Cordial
RTC/ '93	4/ 3	1,474	12	9	2	1	0	Mixed

the proceedings and the relative importance of the hearings as noted by the respondents and indicated by the cases.

The total number of hearing pages is misleading as a measure of the length of the hearing process. For example, while Otto Passman's 1,018 pages of hearings reflected the grueling hundreds of hours of subcommittee deliberation, analysis, and challenges to the administration plan, David Obey's 2,830 pages were long on "statements for the record" and extremely short on actual testimony. As a rough comparison, fewer than 50 percent of Passman's hearing pages were charts, tables, or reports, but more than 90 percent of Obey's were in the form of submitted reports, letters, and analysis. The following trends and continuities emerged.

Change: There are fewer hearings per bill, and the hearings are generally pro forma, with groups electing to insert major studies into the record after brief statements.   The action that used to take place in the committee and subcommittee hearings is taking place somewhere else in the Congress of the 1990s. But, as one respondent put it, "The interest groups think *somebody* is reading those reports." That somebody is usually a member of the staff in the modern Congress.

Change: Some of the most influential interest groups do not even bother to testify in the hearings process anymore.   In the hearings on Goals 2000, the National Education Association (NEA) and the Christian Coalition, the two interest groups most energized on the legislative initiative in the view of the respondents, did not testify before the House Education and Labor Committee, electing to lobby in other ways instead.

Change: Field hearings and other member fact-gathering trips are far less popular with most members, since members fear being labeled a "junketeer."   As one member respondent with service in both periods put it, "If you travel these days, you better be headed to Haiti, Somalia, or Bosnia . . . anywhere else, and it's a campaign issue." Field hearings, which used to be the norm, are now viewed by many members as fairly risky propositions. This trend is unfortunate for a number of reasons, among them the fact that field hearings were identified by the respondents from the 1960s as an excellent means of forging personal relationships across party lines and among committee members.

Continuity: Hearings are still part of the process and "expected," and they occasionally influence the process.   As was noted above, the groups certainly expect someone to read their submissions. And as one lobbyist respondent put it, "It's still expected that we'll testify. . . . [I]t's part of dotting the i's and crossing the t's." As desultory as they may have become, hearings are still scheduled, witnesses still (briefly) testify, and the process moves forward in this way as it did in the 1960s.

Continuity: The tone of the hearings depends primarily upon the chairman's style.   The key predictor of the tone of the hearings for each of the six cases was the style and preference of the relevant committee or subcommittee chair, rather than the issue or its general contentiousness.

THE REPORTS AND CONFERENCE STATEMENTS

Congressional reporting has been described as a "dark science." Meaningful change and continuity in this legislative product could be indicated by changes in the length, complexity, or technicality, purposes, and relative importance of the committee and conference committee reports. Passman's subcommittee report, adopted as the full committee's report as well, consists of a series of scathing attacks on both the president's foreign aid plan and the administration's inability to justify the numbers they had submitted. The report is a thirty-nine-page indictment of alleged administration mismanagement, with examples of testimony and the subcommittee's analysis liberally sprinkled throughout. The college aid bill's committee report was a carefully documented justification of the need for the program and cited private college, interest group, and administration views on the college construction aid proposal. More generally, the following continutity emerged.

Continuity: The committee and conference committee reports are primarily intended to report the legislation agreed upon by the committee and to offer the opportunity for formal dissent.   Consistent with the members' view that the conference represented the time at which the chambers got down to business "to legislate," the conferences were generally characterized by serious policy discussions. Furthermore, the complexity of the various reports generally mirrored the complexity of the bill being reported, rather than varying systematically over time. Some committee reports merely consisted of the amended bill itself, without further comment from the conferees. Tables 9.3 and 9.4 support these assertions.

THE CONGRESSIONAL RECORD

Examining the *Congressional Record*, I expected that there might be changes in both the member use of the *Record* and their perspectives on it. The evidence indicated one change.

TABLE 9.3
The Committee Reports

Case/ Year	Length in Pages	Objectives	Other Views
For Aid/ '62	39	Denounce agency mismanagement/ unpreparedness, report bill	0
Col Aid/ '63	27	Advocate bill, report bill	3
UMT/ '64	30	Advocate bill, report bill	1
For Aid/ '93	123	Detailed analysis fy country with aid objectives, advocate and report bill	1
Goals/ '94	68	Describe bill, justify budget, report bill	2
RTC/ '93	125	Explain bill, report bill	6

TABLE 9.4
The Conference Committee Reports and Conferee Statements

Case/ Year	Length in Pages	Objectives	Other Views
For Aid/ '62	6	Explain amendment compromises, House conferee statement	0
Col Aid/ '63	17	Explain amendment compromises	0
UMT/ '64	—	Williams and Rains avoided conference	—
For Aid/ '93	42	Explain amendment compromises	0
Goals/ '94	57	Explain amendment compromises	0
RTC/ '93	231	Explain amendment compromises, joint conferee statement	0

Change: There are more insertions and revisions in the Congressional Record *in the 1990s.* This trend can be attributed, at least in part, to two factors. First, members now operate under the constraints of severely limited floor time for each measure, and they therefore use these insertions as a means to "do something" and to get on the public record. Also, the members are far more concerned about the electoral implications of each vote in the modern case, and they work to ensure that the public record reflects the policy stances that they want it to reflect.

THE LAWS

Last, in terms of the analysis of change and continuity in the legislative product, I looked closely at the thickness, complexity, level of technicality, comprehensibility, and nature of the case laws. Occasionally, as was the case of the passage of Goals 2000, the only real consensus on a piece of legislation was that the policy goals were wholly unrealistic. One member of those remarking on the infeasibility of the goals exclaimed, "Everyone read by the year 2000? No way!" Table 9.5 summarizes some of the key features of the six laws. One consequential change and four essential continuities resulted:

TABLE 9.5
The Case Laws

Case/ Year Passed	Length in Statute Pages	Nature: General Oversight vs Specificity in Implementation	General Comprehensibility/ Technicality
For Aid/ '62	7	General oversight	Comprehensible
Col Aid/ '63	16	Specific terms of implementation	Comprehensible
UMT/ '64	6	General oversight	Comprehensible
For Aid/ '93	5	Specific terms of implementation	Comprehensible
Goals/ '94	165	Specific terms of implementation	Comprehensible
'RTC/ '93	48	Specific terms of implementation	High level of technicality

Change: Arithmetic complexity alone explains a great deal of the increased statute length and general increase in the scope of federal regulation.   Since the government more often adds to the body of existing law than it subtracts from it, or regulates more often than deregulates, the nature of the legislative process tends toward increasing, rather than decreasing, statute length and scope.

Continuity: Legislation is still written primarily by staff, the legislative counsel, and the administration.   In all three of the 1960s cases, and in the 1990s cases as well, it was not members who authored the legislative initiatives, but rather the various supporting actors instead. Respondents in both periods agreed that this was the case generally, although some respondents from the 1960s recalled members who were adept at the improvisational drafting of provisions and amendments. Members from the 1990s were more willing to acknowledge the periodic role of interest groups in the authoring of legislation.

Continuity: Policy changes are still likely to be incremental in nature, with success coming in discrete chunks.   In each case, the net effect of the legislative process was to moderate more radical attempts at policy changes. The very nature of the legislative process, demanding the construction of policy majorities in sequential steps, tends to draw legislative proposals to an acceptable center, rather than promote radical change.

Continuity: Successful policy initiatives still usually come from prior debates and proposals floated in previous Congresses.   Goals 2000 was a repackaged and tweaked version of Bush's circumstantially doomed America 2000, itself having a history dating back to education program debates of the 1960s and before. Foreign aid programs in times of fiscal tightening are usually the last year's bills with the furniture rearranged, as was the case in 1993. The college construction aid package was a refurbished dormitory construction program. The RTC closeout funding was necessitated by the actions of some of the same committee members who had contributed to the trouble in the first place in the 1980s. All of the initiatives were debated, if not pursued, in Congresses prior to the one in which they passed.

Continuity: The level of technicality in the legislation depends primarily on the maturity of an industry, policy history, or existing body of law. As table 9.5 indicates, no policy area got less complex as the decades passed, but the represented policy areas did not uniformly increase in incomprehensibilty to the average citizen either. Instead, the level of complexity for a particular initiative or body of policy seemed to depend most on the amount of debate and body of previously existing legislation or the policy or industry maturity of previously considered initiatives. In areas of public policy in which the federal government had been involved for a long time, the new initiatives were fairly complex and marked by more "legalese."

MIXED CONSEQUENCES

Consequential changes in legislative products have also had a negative net effect for legislators seeking to pull together policy coalitions, though the exact effects of these changes are less clear than the others mentioned in this book. For example, it is true that arithmetic complexity alone has created more difficulty for the average legislator seeking to understand the legislative initiatives he or she is voting upon. However, there is no definitive evidence to indicate that this trend has made the construction of policy majorities more difficult, as these larger legislative packages can hold more in the way of the individual legislators' district-specific provisions. As in the past, the successful legislative initiatives came from earlier attempts at legislating or came about as extensions of earlier debates, and again the legislation was written primarily by staffers, legislative counsel, and the administration actors. Perhaps most important, however, the committee hearing products reflect the generally pro forma, uninformative, and sparsely attended nature of the hearing process in the modern period. This lost opportunity to bring members together and the challenges posed by the prodigious change in the size and scope of federal legislating were identified by the respondents as the most significant changes in the legislative products to have emerged over the decades.

CHAPTER 10

Continuities in Context:
A Model of Legislative Success

Congressman X was very conservative . . . maybe the original ultra-conservative. But he was very gentlemanly, and he was respected, even though not much went his way.

—House member from the 1960s

Y was a self-described expert on that issue—but he was really just a "bomb-thrower."

—House member from the 1990s

Combining all of the elements of the analysis, two distinct portraits of the legislative process in the 1960s and the 1990s emerge. In some ways, the two portraits fit snugly with the literature's common assertions of wholesale changes in the way the nation does its legislative business. But in many important respects, the basic message that the cases and the respondents offer is that the more things have changed, the more they have stayed the same. The difference between the two portraits is best described in terms of context and essence. That is, it is undeniable that a number of featuristic changes in the actors, procedures, strategies, and products have had major consequences for the process viewed as a whole. At the same time, however, the underlying ingredients that lead to the realization of legislative success have remained essentially the same over the decades. The congressional context presents new challenges to potential policymakers, but the basic blueprint for that success is still recognizable to the actors who came before.

These contextual challenges are consistent with both comprehensive and featuristic accounts of consequential change in the literature, but from the actors' perspective the continuities overshadow those changes. In any event, the respondents viewed these essential continuities as enduring features of the process that still matter the most. To put it another way, respondents viewed the new contextual challenges standing in the way of success as significant hurdles, but they also noted that these challenges had changed before and might change again. Nevertheless, to construct a relevant model of legislative success in the modern era, both a snapshot view of the context and an understanding of the more enduring essential qualities are necessary to capture the whole story. Both context and essence combine to define the problem for actors seeking to realize legislative success in the contemporary Congress.

MODERN CONTEXTUAL CONSIDERATIONS

Without question, the United States Congress is a far less civil and less collegial institution in the 1990s than it was in the early 1960s. The institution is less well suited to the construction of supportive voting majorities needed to realize legislative success in American government. A legislative actor seeking to realize legislative success in the modern era faces a number of high hurdles that never challenged his predecessors in past decades, consequential changes in the actors, procedures, strategies, and products that shape this process. Of the changes held to have been consequential by the participants in the process, nearly all of those changes have pointed toward making the pursuit of legislative success more difficult in the modern Congress.

Beginning with the internal House actors, the period since the early 1960s has seen an important demographic change take place, with far greater racial, gender, and social diversity existing among the House membership in the 1990s. Respondents noted that while this phenomenon has increased the representativeness of the body, it has also increased the likelihood that racial- and gender-specific considerations (among others) are given extra attention during any debate over pending legislative initiatives. The consequences of this change, setting aside its positive normative aspects, have been to increase the likelihood that would-be legislative champions must negotiate at least two additional sets of issues before achieving any policy success. The case evidence clearly bears out this respondent perspective. Concurrent with this change, and adding to its effects, members of all demographics have been given greatly expanded issue opportunities or the ability to involve themselves in many more issues at many more junctures than the average member once could hope to do. This trend has developed primarily as a result of the proliferation of committee and subcommittee assignments arising from the expansion of the various committees. With increased diversity and numerous points of entry into the process, these changes have combined to give the average member far more opportunities to seek to shape or to stop any initiative, thus creating more obstacles to success for members trying to push a legislative initiative forward.

In the view of respondents from both periods of interest to the study, the propensity of the average member to form significant interpersonal relationships is much less in the modern era, and members come to the chamber with stronger policy predispositions and "less willingness to listen." At the same time, a major consequence of the "money chase" and an otherwise greatly increased member workload has been to limit those opportunities to forge solid interpersonal relationships even as the members are less inclined to do so. Likewise, the 1960s-era norm against member-to-member criticism has seriously weakened, leading to the practice of bomb throwing becoming more widespread and accepted than it was in the 1960s, as evidenced in the cases and respondent accounts. Also, as the House staffs have grown explosively in the period since the early 1960s (even if one factors in the across-the-board staff cuts implemented by the Republicans in 1994), staffers aiming to justify their jobs at the same time they seek to influence the process have added more players to the legislative mix while reducing staff accountability. These changes, coupled with an increase in strident partisanship, have combined to help cause a net decrease in the trust and cohesion among the congressional membership, adding serious handicaps to those aiming to realize policy goals.

Simultaneously, the influential actors external to the House have gone through a number of profound changes as well. Although interest group lobbying techniques in the 1990s are similar in type to those of the 1960s, the applications of those techniques have become far more sophisticated today, a finding consistent with several scholarly accounts. Furthermore, these interest groups have been aided in their efforts to shape public policy by an increase in the number of congressional insiders who have turned to lobbying after relatively brief introductory stints as staffers in the modern era. While this phenomenon is difficult to quantify, House member respondents felt that this trend had created a strategic disadvantage for the legislators themselves.

Other key external actors have changed in important ways, as well. Electorally independent and electorally sensitive members seeking media attention in support of reelectoral goals today find media very much willing to highlight partisan and personal strife among the members, even as those media increasingly offer their own perspectives, interpretations, and policy judgments away from the editorial pages. The case evidence and respondent accounts show that the media cover politics differently today, in terms of both quantity and objective, and they focus more on partisan strife than policy in the 1990s. Added to this mix of energized actors external to the House are far more constituents, constituents inclined to contact their legislators in the 1990s at a far greater rate with far more sophistication than those of the 1960s. This trend, in part, has come about because there are half again as many constituents per House member in the 1990s at the same time the means of communicating with one's member have become more numerous, easier to access, and less expensive. Constituents therefore have far more contact with their House member now, and this development and others have added to the already heightened electoral sensitivity and increased workloads of incumbents in the 1990s.

Consistent with this increase in electoral sensitivity, polling has become faster and more efficient, and the practice influences the legislative process more now than ever before in the view of the respondents. The simple measure of this trend in the cases is the lack of reference to polling by the respondents from the 1960s juxtaposed against the frequent references among respondents from the 1990s. In concert with these changes, innovations in electronic voting in the House and a concurrent increase in recorded votes have combined to help fundamentally shift the average member's primary voting accountability concerns from his colleagues to his constituents. Moreover, this change has meant that far less "wiggle room" is available to legislators desiring to make a deal. Last, to add to the rising crescendo of interests and advocates, once-objective think tanks, academics, and other actors are perceived to have become more advocacy oriented and less objective over the period since the 1960s, in the view of the process participants.

In terms of the significant procedural changes in the House since the early 1960s, the average legislator aiming to accomplish a policy success must contend with greatly increased demands for campaign funds. The "money chase" now absorbs a tremendous amount of the legislators' time that it did not consume before, time a member could have used to improve his or her network of interpersonal relationships or to seek out the member-to-member contacts vital to the pursuit of legislative success. Exacerbating this time crunch is the fact that the majority of members are now "ITOT," or "in Tuesday and out Thursday," a phenomenon that has caused another corresponding decline in member contact and interpersonal opportunities. There are far fewer legislative days in the modern era with more meetings and requirements packed into them, and as such there is again less time for the social activities that often yielded legislative advantages. Furthermore, the larger workload and the widespread substitution of C-Span for time spent on the floor add to the members' tendency to spend far less time with their colleagues than they did in the 1960s, thus allowing for even fewer professional and personal member-to-member contacts. Members sponsor fewer bills and cosponsor more, wanting to be able to claim to have "done something," but they lack the opportunity for the personal contacts instrumental to the construction of the ad hoc issue coalitions needed to pass stand-alone initiatives.

At the same time, there have been other consequential changes to legislative procedures that also constrain members in their pursuit of success in the modern case. While the legislative action has shifted in large part to the budget process and the appropriations bills, the rise of multiple jurisdiction and multiple referral has allowed more decision makers to provide input into policymaking. The net effect of this trend has been to increase the ability of a variety of legislators to slow down the process. Concurrent with this change, the increasing breadth, depth, and diversity of federal regulations have (at least partly) created more jurisdictional overlap in the significantly larger committees and subcommittees of the 1990s, causing both members and staffers to spend precious time in multicommittee negotiations and jurisdictional squabbles. With so much else going on, committee activities in the 1990s have become generally pro forma affairs that are poorly attended by the committee and subcommittee members. Likewise, while the authorizing committees have generally broken down, no longer performing their own gatekeeping function, the Rules Committee has become less independent in the 1990s, with structured, restrictive rules now the norm.

Adding to this host of new challenges facing those seeking to realize their policy goals, none of the members spends significant time on the floor anymore, except when the membership is called to vote. Once proud floor debate has devolved into "getting your licks in on C-Span" in the 1990s, as rancorous partisan and personal attacks happen more often than serious discussions of the issues. To make matters worse for those aiming to build consensus, there is less floor debate, due in part to the fact that there is less time allotted for floor debate on each issue and also partly as a result of the now commonly restrictive rules. Conferences now have many more conferees assigned than was the case in the early 1960s, and the net result of this increased size and the sunshine laws has been to force the legislative action to other venues, but there are fewer naturally occurring venues in the 1990s.

In terms of the meaningful strategic changes identified within the cases and by respondents, the fact that appropriations riders are authorized now, but were not allowed in the early 1960s, has had significant consequences for legislator strategizing. Similarly, constraints on new spending authority have limited new stand-alone initiatives and have encouraged members to focus their legislative efforts on the existing big-ticket money bills. The House leadership has become increasingly concerned with managing the legislative policy message in the 1990s, but primarily for reelectoral reasons rather than policy ones, in the eyes of the respondents. With little new money available (until recent budget surpluses and the attendant partisan debates about their uses), omnibus and appropriation rider strategies have become more attractive than past independent packaging strategies. Bomb throwing, once viewed as a mark of a lack of seriousness in a legislator, is now viewed as an acceptable (or unstoppable) strategy by many more legislators. Members now campaign in opposition to one another within their colleagues' districts, further eroding both the trust among the members and the prospects for the construction of supportive House voting majorities. To add to the modern challenges, the power of the huge California delegation has created a regional imbalance, one with serious strategic consequences as legislative champions must factor this contingent into their strategic calculus. If all of this were not enough of a challenge to the average legislator pursuing policy goals, misinformation and disingenuousness are increasingly common political strategies employed in the 1990s, as noted by the respondents and indicated by the cases.

In terms of significant product changes, the average statute thickness has increased dramatically in the period since the early 1960s. Similarly, the depth, breadth, and range of federal policy have increased greatly since the 1960s. Fewer laws are produced in each session in the modern era, but the laws are generally much larger today. There are fewer hearings per bill, and the hearings are regularly pro forma, with groups electing to insert major studies into the record after brief statements during the actual hearings. Some of the most influential interest groups do not even bother to testify in the hearing process anymore. Field hearings and other member fact-finding trips are far less popular with most members, since members fear being labeled as junketeers in these more electorally sensitive times. For reelectoral reasons in part, there are more insertions and revisions in the *Congressional Record* in the 1990s. The legislators view these consequential changes in the legislative products as both good news and bad news, as there are fewer legislative horses to hitch one's policy wagon to in the modern case, but there is also a better chance that district-sized projects can get lost inside the massive statutes. All things considered, the Congress is rife with contextual challenges for the would-be legislative champion of the 1990s.

ESSENTIAL CONTINUITIES:
THE BASIC INGREDIENTS OF LEGISLATIVE SUCCESS

In spite of the consequential and generally success-averse changes facing the modern actor in his or her pursuit of legislative success in the modern Congress, members from both the 1960s and the 1990s pointed to the same necessary ingredients for policy success in both periods. The respondents highlighted these durable and essential continuities as the most important features of the process when the legislative act was viewed as a whole. Considered collectively, these continuities constitute a practical model of legislative success. When considered in concert with the consequential changes noted in the preceding section, they yield a framework for legislative success specific to the modern era.

Beginning again with the House's internal actors, every initiative continues to need a champion, or one or a few key actors willing to demonstrate the persistence, patience, hustle, and willingness to compromise that are essential to the realization of legislative success. While the average House legislator's qualifications did not change significantly over the period from the early 1960s to the early 1990s, neither did the relative importance of seniority within the legislative process. To put this more directly, legislative success was not dependent upon or a function of legislator qualifications, and it was not limited to the senior members of the Congress, in either period. The more important considerations that facilitated success were the personal qualities of the various legislative champions. In the view of the respondents, legislative success depends upon the reputation, interpersonal skills, issue competence, integrity, and perseverance of the legislators who seek to build consensus on an issue. Those traits are crucial in building the ad hoc coalition of interests and ideology that can eventually bring about a policy success. Respondents in both periods were unanimous in their assertions that these traits were and remain critical to the realization of legislative success.

Likewise, the evidence indicated that the legislators who make up those issue coalitions pursued the same four kinds of self-determined goals in both periods, goals that must be kept in mind by those who aim to construct a policy coalition. Three of the goals in evidence, effectively highlighted by Mayhew, Kingdon, and Fenno in their writings, included the legislators' desires for policy, influence, and reelection identified by those authors. The fourth goal, indicated by the case evidence and respondent accounts, was the inclination of many members to support or oppose the efforts of other legislative actors for strictly personal reasons, whether those reasons were principled or merely petty.

In terms of other internal actor considerations, the support or (at minimum) casual disinterest of the majority party leaders of the chamber and the policy committees remains a critically important element of legislative success. Similarly, the power of position was clearly evident in both periods, and it was also true of the leaders in those positions of power that their leadership styles were highly individualized and primarily dependent on the leader's personality. These personalities greatly influenced the eventual shape and the likelihood of legislative success in all six cases, and those seeking to realize success would do well to understand the personal attributes of the leaders at the outset of their efforts. Regarding the staffers, members alone still deal in the first-tier issues, but the staff, the legislative counsel, and the administration's agents dominate the other negotiations and compromises involved in reaching a broad agreement. Actors pursuing legislative success are well served to involve the administration and staff actors early, thoroughly, and often.

In terms of the external House actors, presidential direction is critical in setting the legislative agenda. Respondents emphasized the crucial importance of presidential support, and simple math tells us that this support is equivalent to about seventy-three votes on the House floor, aside from the other major benefits to the determined actors. Legislative champions can expect the administration's agents to carry out the general policy objectives of the president and his cabinet, as carefully selected representatives charged with doing so. Involving the administration personnel early and often in the policy-drafting process was critical to legislative success in all six cases examined, and the respondents indicated that this was a critical step toward legislative success in general. In mediating legislation, or legislation within a policy area dominated by well-organized interest groups, a similar strategy of involving the groups in the process up front was critical to the eventual success. Would-be legislative champions must understand that information still is power, and interest groups with leverage nearly always use it.

The average member had a dim view of the media's accuracy, influence, and grasp of events in both periods. However, actors can expect that the chamber leadership, the president, and administration personnel will still make concerted efforts to inform the media as part of every national legislative initiative, seeking the support of the media given their ability to sway public opinion. Additionally, on the issues that generate the most mail, constituent desires matter, and they must be taken into consideration by the coalition builders. Other considerations include the fact that there is very often a disconnect between a legislator's national policy interests (or committee work) and local constituent concerns, a situation that offers some opportunities. Finally, in spite of the actors' best efforts, external and arbitrary events can combine to prevent legislative success, though those events can have the opposite effect as well. Legislators interviewed as part of this study emphasized the importance of persistence, and several respondents noted that they usually had a number of legislative initiatives working all the time, as they never knew which idea would suddenly emerge as the flavor of the moment. This process, such as was the case for several of the laws in this study, can take years if not decades to come to fruition.

In terms of procedural continuities, members still sponsor bills as a credit-claiming activity, but respondents felt that bills based on administration drafts have the highest probability of legislative success. The case evidence supports this contention. Moreover, since the underlying details of any bill are rarely debated, the actor who controls the drafting process generally gets about 95 percent of what he or she wants in the final legislative outcome. Prospective legislative champions can expect to spend less time on the referral process, given stated jurisdictions in the committee rules and the usual Speaker's almost automatic approval of the parliamentarian's assignment to committee. They would instead do well to spend their time on research, as all of the respondents indicated that this aspect of the legislative push still matters to all of the participants, and a mastery of the issue at hand provides clear leverage for the actors involved.

Likewise, the actor seeking policy success can also expect that any and all information shared with colleagues during the process may turn up in media accounts, as even the details of the closed sessions of the 1960s were usually promptly leaked. While the Rules Committee still serves as the majority leadership's traffic cop, and a less independent one at that, chairman-to-chairman contact and the personal relationships between the committee heads are still critical in realizing that step toward legislative success. Similarly, the real heavy lifting at conference time gets done in preconference meetings between the key insiders. At the actual conference committee, members expect to deal in the top-tier "hot-button" issues while the staff negotiates the rest. Last, most success comes on its own schedule, and there are few specific legislative timelines except for the cyclical money bills. The respondents' message was to seek and ride a deadline if possible, as they attract both legislative business and potential support.

In considering the category of strategic continuities over the two periods, the evidence indicates that legislative success really depends on the construction of ad hoc issue coalitions because parties and single-issue interests alone cannot deliver policy change. The methods of persuasion have not changed over the decades, and they still include threats, bribes, personal appeals, public policy logic, and public service appeals. Omnibus packaging may be more prevalent now and is used increasingly in "blockbuster" fashion, but the legislative strategy is not a new one. Packaging changes in the face of focused opposition has worked well in the past, and procedural innovation is also often instrumental in facilitating legislative progress, though parliamentary procedural strategies are used successfully just as often to slow or halt legislative initiatives. Even if the full committee chairs still do not know the early termers on their committees, the stereotype of casual disregard for junior members by senior members was a false one in both periods. As such, the cases show that real bipartisanship, particularly sincere bipartisanship forged at the subcommittee level, is one of the most effective strategies employed by members seeking to advance a legislative initiative.

In terms of the essential continuities among the legislative products, members pursuing success should expect to tailor their efforts to the maturity of the policy area in question. Hearings are still part of the process and "expected," and they occasionally influence the process, but the tone of the hearings will depend primarily upon the chairman's personal style, interest, and energy. The committee and conference committee reports are primarily intended to report the legislation agreed upon by the committee and to offer the opportunity for formal dissent. Legislation is still most often written by staff, the legislative counsel, and the administration, and policy changes are likely to be incremental in nature, with success coming in discrete chunks. Successful policy initiatives still usually come from prior debates and the initiatives begun in previous sessions, so potential policymakers should be familiar with the relevant policy history.

In sum, the legislative participants represented in this study agreed upon these elements as the critical concerns, requirements, and guiding principles that give the would-be legislative champion the best probability of enacting desired public policy changes.

THE IMPLICATIONS

These consequential changes and the essential continuities viewed from the actors' perspective combine to affect the way we should understand the legislative process and the significance of documented and argued changes within it. To begin with, *the United States House of Representatives is a much less civil and less collegial institution in the modern era than it was in the 1960s.* In a very real sense, consensus building has given way to a war of attrition. The unquestionable net effect of the contextual changes identified in this book has been to make the construction of supportive voting majorities, the fundamental precondition of legislative success, far more difficult in the 1990s than in the 1960s. The consequential changes in the actors, procedures, strategies, and products detailed in the book were identified by the respondents as the most significant differences in the Congress since the early 1960s, and the great majority of these key changes made coalition building more difficult over the last several decades. The case evidence confirmed the respondents' assertions of a clear pattern of increasing impediments to the realization of legislative success in the Congress over the years. Chief among these increased impediments to success is the weakening of the interpersonal glue among members that once routinely counterbalanced the too often negative forces of personality and personal agenda.

Furthermore, while parties play an important role in coalition building, the parties never delivered on policy changes by themselves, and the increased "party unity" scores of the 1990s are misleading. Another important story to emerge from this analysis is that political parties never really "went away" because they were never really there in the first place from a policy perspective. While the majority of respondents from the early 1960s were quick to give credit to their parties for electoral assistance, none discussed the parties in terms of serious legislative voting commitments. Similarly, respondents from the 1990s generally discussed their own policy concerns rather than offering any party-based rationales for their legislative decisions. Willful agents, rationally pursuing self-determined and sometimes personal goals, are much in evidence in both periods of the study, and the ad hoc issue coalitions of actors are not described accurately by party or interest group simplifications even in the early 1960s. Those who lament the loss of party organizational strength might have a case from an electoral standpoint, but their case is much less compelling from the perspective of the parties' delivery of policy change.

Similarly, the case and respondent evidence here offer a response to those who point to increased party unity scores as a sign of party resurgence, as this evidence indicates that "party unity" is not the same as "policy unity." This characteristic holds true even in these cases in which one party controls the executive branch and both chambers of the Congress. Party-centered explanations miss far too much of the relevant legislative stories to adequately explain any one of the six episodes of legislative success described in this book. While the majority party's powers of agenda setting and chamber organization remained intact over the years studied, and while parties served as one source of raw material for consensus building, in none of the six cases was a party or the party leadership able to routinely deliver legislative victories.

At the same time, the evidence shows that persistence in making member-to-member contact and gaining the support of the leadership has been and remains among the most critical elements of legislative success. With the power of the membership being a "positive" one and the power of the leadership often being "negative," or vetolike, these two elements of legislative success were two elements quickly identified by nearly every respondent to the study as being critical to the eventual policy success. Unfortunately, it is also the case that member-to-member contact opportunities, both social and professional, are clearly limited in the modern Congress when compared to years past. Personal relationships and trust may serve as the glue that binds the members together, but members are hard-pressed to realize either one in an environment as demanding as the current congressional context. As one respondent from the early 1960s summarized, "The personalities are the critical element of success . . . person-to-person contact, a leader with legislative know-how, willing to use every energy and knowing how to time things." Another member added, "People who aren't trustworthy don't last past maybe one forgiven mistake. A reputation for integrity is critical . . . otherwise people won't bother with you." Finally, one respondent with service in both periods startled me by putting it much more bluntly, and in the vernacular, loudly asserting, "Pricks don't get shit." Clearly, interpersonal skills are critical, and decreased opportunities and negative member predispositions have made this a waning art.

Likewise, members operate today in an era of greatly heightened electoral sensitivity, and this change has come with many adverse consequences for those who hope to shape public policy. Chief among the consequences of this change is the fact that there is a systemic incentive for the average lawmaker to avoid taking positions on all but the most noncontroversial measures, since every vote is intensely scrutinized by someone with a mind to do him electoral harm. The party and committee leaders charged with conducting the nation's legislative business have responded to the members' desires for stance anonymity for this and other reasons with adaptive strategies that allow legislators to obscure their true legislative preferences. Blockbuster omnibus packaging, sequentially layered fund-cutting votes, and other strategies allow the legislators to act upon their personal policy preferences while maintaining wide latitude in justifying their votes to their constituents. Given the usual emphasis on big-ticket money bills common today, the ordinary response from a legislator asked to comment on his or her vote on a bill is, "This bill wasn't everything we wanted, but we took the best deal we could get." The member has the flexibility to change his explanation of "what the bill was missing" from venue to venue.

Moreover, any realized policy changes are likely to be incremental in nature. While this trend might please the Founders, the nature of the American legislative process is such that the actions necessary to construct supportive majorities attenuate the possibility of radical change at every step. Unlike the possibility (or even probability) of more radical policy changes predicted by Schattschneider (1960) and others, the most likely policy outcomes in American policymaking will tend toward a moderate center. Similarly, current conditions of declining discretionary spending authority and party-led squabbles over the uses of surpluses favor omnibus packaging as a reactive strategy to declining dollars, less civil member relationships, and other factors. Omnibus packaging is not a new legislative strategy, but fiscal constraints and appropriations riders make it a far more attractive and effective one today. Today's average legislator seeking a district benefit or even national policy change goes straight to the relevant appropriating subcommittee now, since the authorization process is generally defunct, and legislators are unlikely to secure enough money for new stand-alone projects.

As another key trend, the information revolution and explosive technological advances have fundamentally altered the average legislator's relationships with the external actors. Technological changes that have affected the average member in performance of his or her various duties have included everything from C-Span to e-mail to fax machines to letter chains to the Internet and other innovations. Furthermore, cheap airline fares and the relatively inexpensive cost of telephone calls today mean that the demands upon the legislators' scarce time have increased dramatically in the modern era. While one effect of these changes has been to enhance the incumbents' reelectoral prospects, though that enhancement does not come cheaply, the dominant impact of technology has been to make the average member's job all the more difficult. Technological and information age changes have created nearly overwhelming and greatly sophisticated constituency requirements that did not exist before.

As a result, the actor seeking legislative success now competes on a playing field with interest groups and government agencies that have used those technological innovations to dramatically increase the sophistication of their own efforts. To continue a trend begun elsewhere, these technological changes have further limited the time and effort available to legislators interested in forming interpersonal relationships with other members, relationships that generally serve as a primary foundation for stand-alone legislative successes. Last, these technological transformations have combined to shift the average legislator's primary accountability relationship to his constituents, a clear shift from the legislator of the 1960s, who felt more directly accountable to his colleagues in general.

It is also the case that the participants in the process view individuals, rather than institutional procedures, aggregated interests, or parties, as the most effective unit of analysis in the explanation and prediction of individual legislative outcomes. The shape of the eventual legislative outcome, in each of the six cases, can be traced to the persistent intentions and actions of a handful of willful actors. In the view of the respondents, and as indicated by the cases, analysis of a legislative outcome or predictions of future legislative prospects should incorporate assessments of the actions and capabilities of the core legislative actors, as well as those actors' positions of authority and available resources. While the legislators' available tools, support, and procedural mechanisms have changed notably since the 1960s, the most fundamental and important aspects of the legislative process have remained the same. In order to understand legislative outcomes, one must first focus attention on the legislators and their motives.

In this vein, the finer resolutions of legislator motive posited by Fenno, Mayhew, and Kingdon are similarly well supported by this analysis. However, the closer one gets to the legislative outcome, the larger personal motives loom, clouding the waters of the motives identified by those authors. *While actors are not quick to admit to the influence of personal motives in their own choices and actions in the process, they are uniformly willing to speculate about purely personal motives on the part of the other actors. It is clear that they operate on the assumption that personalities, personal relationships, and private agendas are important factors that shape the pursuit of legislative success.* Looking at both periods in his book *The Politics of Education* (1987), former House member John Brademas notes that in the determination of legislative outcomes, "the force of individual personality still looms large."[1] Personal motives and interpersonal relations, when legislative outcomes are explained individually, take on a proportionally greater importance to the individual actors. At the individual outcome level, the legislative actors demonstrate routinely changing inclinations that challenge the assumptions of stable, ordered, and transitive preferences assumed by most proponents of rational choice perspectives.

Finally, leadership emerges out of the field of all variables as a crucial one. As powerful as the various models of Mayhew, Kingdon, and Fenno are in attributing correct motives to legislator behaviors, one must still probe the particulars of the vaguely defined individual legislator's leadership abilities and personal preferences in order to understand and predict legislative outcomes. In the modern congressional context, it takes more effort for the average legislator just to maintain his or her place within the system. As these new requirements are consuming in of themselves, they hardly afford that legislator any opportunity to engage in casual or professional efforts at building the interpersonal relationships that could serve as a foundation for future legislative endeavors. While the staff and the other increasingly savvy external actors all play an important role in the formulation of American public policy, it is still the individual legislator who stands at the center of all of this policy activity. To echo Kingdon, sometimes the civics textbooks are right.

Last, while it is a seemingly random variable, there is no question that leadership styles serve as key outcome determinants in the complex mix of actors, interests, and external events that dictate legislative success. The human element of the legislative process is one that can be easily overshadowed given our discipline's modern methodological focus, but the respondents are convinced that people trump the process in importance. In sum, regardless of the consequential changes in procedures, strategies, and product, the legislative process remains intact in the ways that matter most. At root, in spite of the chill in the modern House, the actors themselves believe that the essential continuities define the legislative process more than any changes over the last few decades. Legislating remains primarily a people business, rather than a procedural one, and the roots of success lie in the characteristics of the key actors. Leadership matters.

A BRIEF EPILOGUE

Future Prospects

Given that my primary objective in this study was to compare the pursuit of legislative success in the early 1960s with that same pursuit in the 1990s, I necessarily focused my interviewing efforts on the legislative process in those two periods. However, speaking at length to current and former members, staffers, long-time observers, and others keenly interested in American politics, most could not help but comment on their perceptions of contemporary events and the actors in the contemporary Congresses. Republican and Democratic respondents alike frequently offered their views on the current politics and policymaking in the House. These veteran legislators were almost uniformly pessimistic, or at least concerned, about several trends that they believed would exacerbate the difficulties that have developed over the years for those seeking to build policy coalitions in the 1990s. While I did not investigate these assertions with any rigor, the identified concerns are interesting in their own right, and they tend to reinforce the notion that the findings identified in this book will hold up over time. I have highlighted some of those thoughts here.

The centralization of power in the Speaker's office, once viewed by many as a necessity for purposes of coherence and efficiency, went too far. Now, in the eyes of many of these interested observers, committee chairs lack any semblance of autonomy. One respondent described his House committee as having a "lawyer tasked by Gingrich to instruct the chairman on how to run the committee. This lawyer would stand behind him and monitor his activities." In the view of many respondents, the pendulum had swung too far. The subsequent turmoil caused by Speaker-designate Livingston's hasty retirement and Speaker Hastert's difficulties has not seemed to make anyone feel better about the future of this critical office.

The Republican Party leadership's tendency to alter committee-reported legislation prior to floor consideration and its occasional bypass of the committees altogether disturbs many members of both parties. Sinclair found six examples of committee bypass in the House of the 103rd Congress, eleven examples in the 104th, and only two examples in the 91st Congress (1969–70).[1] Similarly, she found no examples of legislation subjected to a postcommittee adjustment in the 91st, but twenty-nine were subjected to this treatment in the House of the 103rd and forty-seven in the House of the 104th Congress.[2] House actors identified this trend as a particularly disturbing extension of the general trend on the part of the House leaders of both parties to seek to centralize the "message" at the chamber level.

The use of party task forces to circumvent the committees adds to the partisan rancor. Again, this trend reinforced the observed decline in civility, collegiality, and bipartisan initiatives, as Republican party leaders increasingly have turned to Republican Party task forces to work out legislative solutions without consulting with Democratic Party committee and subcommittee members or the party's chamber leadership. It is interesting to note that members of both parties mentioned this trend as a concern.

Additional legislated limits on member travel have reduced relationship-building opportunities even further. There was a clear sense on the part of respondents that while ethics initiatives had achieved their desired effects, they had gone too far and were poised to go even further, to the detriment of House collegiality. Members are highly sensitized to the risks of funded travel. Also, *strengthened ethics reforms have further limited social opportunities and opportunities for the routine exchange of important information.* As a broader case of the effects engendered by the travel restrictions noted above, many respondents felt that the previous reforms had pushed past the meat into the bone.

Many members view term limits as a particularly bad idea in light of the additional difficulties in constructing supportive majorities in the 1990s. As one member put it succinctly, "It takes a while to cultivate the friendships and relationships that grease the system. . . . [Y]ou have to know someone awhile before you can expect to get help." An additional consideration is the relationship between staff and members, and as one member noted, "The staff will do more and more until you rein them in. They are vital, but you have to be careful."

"Payback time" after the Republican takeover made things worse in terms of the problem of incivility and is viewed by most as having exacerbated the trend toward excessive partisanship. One former senior leader in the House remarked, "Everybody said Newt was more conservative than me. Check the voting records, and you'll find my record was much more conservative than his. The difference is that I was willing to talk to people across the aisle. They confuse ideology with a willingness to work with people." Similarly, *the impeachment of President Clinton contributed new grounds for divisiveness within the Congress.*

The demise of the JFK school week was viewed as an unfortunate occurrence, as it was described as a tremendous opportunity to meet and get to know your new colleagues. In the view of some respondents, the demise of the week-long orientation held at the John F. Kennedy School at Harvard was seen as unfortunate because it had been an effective means of facilitating the working and personal relationships critical to the construction of supportive majorities in the House.

The respondents identified only a few slim causes for hope against this dreary backdrop. Among them, they noted the member and family outing to Hershey Park sponsored by the leadership of the 105th Congress, which was viewed by many as a potential harbinger of a return of civility. Similarly, a few respondents viewed *the congressional compliance law* as a small but concerted step aimed at restoring respect for institution among the public, and we know that the Congress's approval ratings have improved somewhat. Furthermore, the *Republican staff reductions and the efforts to streamline the executive agencies* were viewed positively by many, as they hoped that these changes would increase member responsibility over and control in the legislative process. *The recently balanced budget and budget surpluses,* in spite of the attendant rancor over what to do with them, were identified by some as a plausible agent of both increased civility and policy latitude. Last, a few respondents pointed to the Republicans' *marginal House majority* as a positive, as it was expected that the parties' leadership would have to learn to work together in order to get anything done—though this has not necessarily been the case to date. While these identified key trends certainly represent at best only a partial list of potentially consequential recent changes, it is also apparent that few if any of these changes will improve the chill in the House identified by the respondents. At the same time, it is also true that the first step in solving a problem is defining it. Only time will tell.

APPENDIX 1

Case Selection Criteria
and the Case Selection

THE GOALS AND SIGNIFICANCE OF CASE SELECTION

The fundamental goal of the case selection process was to identify three pairs of significant and representative laws near the beginning and end of the period of interest to this research. That is, the cases selected had to be representative of significant legislation passed by that Congress yet also be representative of routine legislating, in order to allow for valid inferences regarding the presence and significance of any changes in the legislative process. Given the broader objective of looking at a few cases of legislating in serious detail, careful case selection was of paramount importance to the study's validity. I needed to control for a number of extraneous variables that were theorized to likely sources of unwanted random and nonrandom background noise.

A random selection of cases was inappropriate here given the small n and the resulting biases that random selection might therefore introduce. While random selection in some instances "provides a selection procedure that is automatically uncorrelated with all variables," I viewed this technique as inappropriate to the study given the likely effects of several correlated but extraneous variables.[1] Those variables are detailed below. Furthermore, random selection could introduce its own biases, including the possibility of inadvertent selection on the dependent variable.[2] The goal of the research design was to achieve efficient parameter estimates of the variables, while minimizing bias. Efficiency was the most desirable design characteristic here, given that the primary goal of the data collection was to achieve estimates close to the true parameter values with limited observations. Any systematic (nonrandom) measurement error will bias descriptive inference.[3] However, systematic measurement errors affecting all units by the same constant amount cause no bias in causal inference. In short, I aimed for efficiency through the imposition of several case selection criteria.

KEY "CASE" DEFINITIONS
AND THE CASE SELECTION CRITERIA

This study defines its case as the set of all events leading to the passage of a particular piece of legislation, and in this sense the number n of cases examined equals six. However, as King, Keohane, and Verba (1994) argue, the more relevant measure of case breadth is the observation.[4] I observed the implications of each variable, including the actors, products, procedures, and strategies, at multiple levels of analysis. These levels of analysis included the respective bills' movements from hopper through to Senate conference and all of the steps in between. Furthermore, to observe the four categories of potential changes fully and efficiently at each level, I interviewed respondents until the observations were confirmed by at least three consistent responses between interviews and background accounts of the events leading to passage. This standard of triangulation and the observation of variable implications at numerous levels of analysis meant that while six "cases" were examined, the number of observations on the variables was much greater.

As noted, the goal of the case selection was to choose three pairs of enacted laws that are, as much as possible, "mean" significant laws relative to the times in which they were passed. At the same time, I needed to maximize the likelihood that the three pairs of laws were broadly representative of the environment from which they came. Additionally, it was desirable to control for other likely correlated, though extraneous, variables. To accomplish these goals, the case selection involved three stages. The three sets of selection criteria are categorized as the *preconditions*, the *pairing criteria*, and the *issue variance criteria*.

The first of these, the *preconditions* for selection, consisted of three criteria corresponding to a control for conditions of party control in the legislative and executive branches, a measure of legislative significance, and measures that compare levels of media scrutiny. I first controlled for differing conditions of party control of the executive and legislative branches of government by considering only laws passed under conditions of a unified, Democratic Party control of government. The thought here was that the comparison of laws passed under differing conditions of party control of the Congress might reflect some unwanted, random variation in the types of laws passed or the legislative procedures involved in passage. Random or nonrandom variation of this type might reflect differing party legislative priorities, party ideologies, or other party conflicts.

By imposing this criterion, I avoided these random or nonrandom variations by requiring candidate laws to have been passed under similar conditions of party control of government. This criterion did not mean that the bills were necessarily put into the hopper for the first time under unified party conditions. Given the usual condition of Democratic Party control of the Congress during the period of interest to this study, the logical choice of party control conditions was the condition of unified Democratic control of Congress and the executive. Similarly, the choice of this condition of party control supported the goal of identifying changes likely to have resulted from several of the plausible agents of change. These included changes that might have occurred due to the increasing importance of the media in member electoral and legislative activities or the influence of the Watergate reforms of the early seventies, among others. This condition meant that I considered for inclusion only candidate laws that had been passed during the 87th or 88th (1961–64) and 103rd (1993–94) Congresses.

One might expect some issue bias to result from the sole use of laws passed under conditions of Democratic Party control of both the executive and legislative branches of the federal government. For example, it might be expected that the use of this criterion might result in an over-representation of social or domestic issues in the six case studies or even a subtle but systematic shift in the nature of executive-legislative relations. In fact, the evidence shows that the largest proportion of viable cases in both the early 1960s and the early 1990s turned out to be laws related to foreign aid or foreign affairs, which would not lend themselves intuitively to bias of this sort. Table A1.2 supports this assertion.

The second precondition involved a measure of legislative significance. Seeking a consistent and relevant measure of significance over time, I used the *Congressional Quarterly Weekly Report*'s yearly listings of House and Senate key votes as an indicator of legislative significance. Using the key votes as a starting point, I included for consideration all laws that were passed during the 87th, 88th, or 103rd Congresses and had resulted directly from the listed votes.[5] The *Congressional Quarterly Weekly Report* defines a key vote as such: "An issue is judged by the extent to which it represents: a matter of major controversy; a matter of presidential or political power; or a matter of potentially great impact on the nation and lives of Americans."[6] In some cases, the key votes did not lead to enacted legislation and were not considered any further. Additionally, to qualify as a candidate law, the law arising from the key vote had to have been considered by the House in the form of an original House version, rather than merely reflecting passage of an intact Senate version.[7] This precondition ensured that the analysis examined a fuller version of House legislating rather than a "rubber stamp" passage of a bill.

The final precondition involved assessing the level of media scrutiny to which a bill was subjected during passage. I used two measures of media scrutiny to eliminate those public laws subjected to either too much or too little media attention during passage. The first, hits in the *New York Times*, as measured using the *New York Times Index*, involved coding and counting the number of mentions each law received in the period from one month prior to passage until one week after. Specifically, with the goal of measuring media scrutiny "outside of the Beltway" around the time of passage, I counted articles, editorials, cartoons, and other related items.[8] The goal of this measure was to assess the relative scrutiny accorded each candidate law by a national medium targeting an informed, but "generalist," audience outside of the Beltway around the time of passage. Another potential bias in case selection might arise from the use of the *New York Times* as a measure of media scrutiny. For example, the *New York Times* is sometimes described, perhaps with some justification, as a "liberal, northeastern paper." One might expect these alleged traits to lead to a disproportionate coverage of social legislation or the like, leading to an unwarranted and disproportionate exclusion from the study of related laws. Similarly, these purported ideological and regional motives might also lead to a shortage of coverage (and corresponding exclusion from the study) of legislation not of interest to the northeastern readership. However, as the goal of the case selection was the identification of six representative laws, rather than the six *most* representative laws, these potential biases are not that significant in their impact upon the case selection. Furthermore, a quick examination of the laws excluded from consideration by the *New York Times* measure shows no evidence of systematic social program or regional biases. Last, any bias of this sort was attenuated by the use of the key vote measure and a second coverage measure, the *Congressional Quarterly Weekly Report*.

The second measure of the precondition of media scrutiny I used was the coverage in the *Congressional Quarterly Weekly Report* during the session of Congress in which the legislation was passed, up until the time of passage. This medium offers a Beltway view specifically targeted at observers of Congress.[9] After tallying each of these measures of media scrutiny, I excluded from consideration those laws that fell outside of one standard deviation from the mean level of media scrutiny, comparing laws by medium and treating those passed in the early 1960s and those passed in the 1990s as a set. The effects of these measures and the other precondition criteria on the case selection are detailed in the accompanying data tables.

Having established the preconditions for inclusion in the study, the next criteria used were *pairing criteria*. To keep random committee idiosyncrasies from affecting the variable values from one case to the next, I first paired the viable candidate laws from the 1960s with viable candidate laws from the 1990s that originated in the same House committee. I felt that the committee "personalities" identified by Fenno (1973) could be a significant source of systematic measurement error. That is, it was possible that since the observations of the legislative process were to be drawn exclusively from three House committees, the resulting inferences might be biased to reflect the particular styles, personalities, or motives of the members of those committees and their relevant subcommittees. The application of this criterion eliminated a number of candidate laws. Additionally, wherever possible, I deemed it advantageous to have pairs of laws that pertained to the same broad policy area. While the first of these two pairing criteria was mandatory, the second was preferred but not necessary.

The third and final category of case selection criteria was that of *issue variance*. Issue variance refers to the desirability of looking at different major policy areas among the three pairs of laws rather than at one kind of policy alone. Consistent with Fenno's findings regarding the differences and similarities among committees, this final criterion meant seeking three pairs of cases looking at legislation from three distinct major policy areas.[10] Along the same lines, I viewed it as advantageous to select laws, as much as possible, from different Congresses or, at minimum, different sessions of the 87th, 88th, and 103rd Congresses. All in all, while no single criterion, standing alone, ensured the selection of mean cases by itself, the criteria combined to give the study the best chance of efficient parameter estimates. The case selection criteria, applied collectively, greatly diminished the unwanted random and nonrandom variation in the categories of change and the broader process itself, thus enhancing the validity of the study.

THE CASE SELECTION RESULTS

Applying the first of the preconditions, I considered only laws having been passed under conditions of unified, Democratic Party control at the beginning and toward the end of the period of interest to this study. Applying the second precondition regarding legislative significance then, I listed in order the key votes from the *Congressional Quarterly* House and Senate key vote lists from 1961 through 1964 and 1993 and 1994, or the 87th, 88th, and 103rd Congresses. This listing resulted in 155 key votes. Since the study is concerned with successful legislating, or legislative efforts that resulted in the passage of laws, I then traced the key votes forward to identify the law that resulted from the key vote, if any. This sweep eliminated 48 key votes from further consideration, as they did not lead directly to the passage of a law. Similarly, many of the key votes in the House and Senate in a given year overlapped or led to the same law. This sorting resulted in an initial pool of 61 candidate laws, with 39 of these having been passed by the 87th or 88th Congresses and 22 having been passed by the 103rd Congress. Applying the third precondition, that of the requirement that the candidate law having had an original House version, eliminated no candidates.

The fourth and final precondition involved determining the level of media scrutiny using the *New York Times* and *Congressional Quarterly Weekly Report* measures. Thirteen candidate laws were eliminated from consideration by these media measures. The analysis of this measure is set forth in table A1.1.

Applying the pairing criteria next, 15 laws were eliminated because there were no companion laws that originated in the same House committee. The resultant viable candidate cases, with committee of origin and respective major policy areas, are listed in table A1.2. The application of the pairing criteria left 16 viable candidate cases from the 87th and 88th Congresses and 13 viable candidate cases from the 103rd Congress. Additionally, the choice of committees of origin had been pared down to five: Education and Labor, Ways and Means, Foreign Affairs, Appropriations, and Banking.

The final selection, then, depended upon the third set of criteria, the issue variance criteria. The primary goals of these criteria were to achieve a variance of issues and Congresses or sessions of those Congresses, and I also wanted to achieve the desired goal of a commonality of major policy area within each pair of laws.[11] I first selected a pair of laws originating in the Education and Labor Committee, including PL 88–204 of 1963, which provided for general college construction aid, and Goals 2000, the education reform legislation PL 103–227 of 1994. Pursuing issue variance, I then selected a pair of laws similar in committee of origin and major policy area that dealt with foreign policy issues, PL 87–872 (the foreign aid appropriations law for 1962) and PL 103–87 (the foreign aid appropriations law for 1993). These initial choices fit into the Fenno model of committee differences well.

These initial choices constrained my choice of a third pair. Given my criterion of issue variance and the fact that I had already included a "money" committee and a foreign policy issue, the logical third choice of a committee was the Banking Committee. Having already selected laws from 1962 and 1963 in the first two pairs, this alternative was also desirable in that the available Banking Committee law from the early 1960s was the urban mass transportation law of 1964, PL 88–352. This law would offer variance in the sessions of the Congresses from the early 1960s. I paired the law with the Resolution Trust Corporation funding closeout legislation (PL 103–204), passed in 1993. Case selection had satisfied my established case selection criteria, and two of the three pairs of laws fit neatly into the Fenno model, thus enabling me to identify some of the committee "personality" at the outset.

In sum, I had to take into consideration both potential random measurement error and nonrandom measurement error in the case selection. The careful case selection described above was a particularly critical means through which I minimized the uncertainty in the design. In conjunction with careful interview design and the imposition of the standard of triangulation in evaluating responses and background accounts, the case selection criteria gave me the best possible chance of efficient parameter estimates.

TABLE A1.1
Congressional Quarterly and *New York Times* "Hits"

60s CQW	60s NYT	90s CQW	90s NYT	
21	26	1	45	
10	12	18	125	
18	25	8	8	
17	29	35	8	
13	30	12	9	
16	5	7	5	
24	88	28	11	
18	14	29	88	
8	16	14	96	
5	1	8	45	
28	15	17	176	
20	28	4	17	
24	18	14	7	
25	43	8	1	
10	10	7	21	
23	8	6	6	
52	64	8	16	
23	36	7	19	
10	47	22	33	
13	12	9	1	
8	18	13	5	
24	39	17	61	
8	12			
27	48	13.27272	36.5	Means
10	9	8.735160	46.25267	Std Dev
5	12			

(continued on next page)

TABLE A1.1 *(continued)*

60s CQW	60s NYT	90s CQW	90s NYT	
14	20		Low	High
14	9	60s CQW Range=	8.3	27.7
9	11	60s NYT Range=	0.0	75.0
9	62	90s CQW Range=	4.6	22.0
21	97	90s NYT Range=	0.0	82.8
21	17			
44	251			
24	67			
15	27			
23	16			
10	12			
13	10			
18	9		60s CQW	60s NYT
17.971428	32.64103	Means Std. Dev.	9.6678299	42.42919

TABLE A1.2
Viable Candidate Cases, with Committee of Origin and Policy Area

PL Number	Committee of Origin	Major Policy Area
Passed in 1961:		
87–6 (Jobless pay)	Ways and Means	Social/labor
87–30 (Minimum wage)	Education and Labor	Social/labor
Passed in 1962:		
87–565(Foreign aid auth.)	Foreign Affairs	Foreign aid
87–543 (Welfare reform)	Ways and Means	Social/welfare
87–616 (War damages)	Foreign Affairs	Foreign affairs
87–731 (UN bonds)	Foreign Affairs	Foreign affairs
87–794 (Foreign trade)	Ways and Means	Foreign trade
*87–872 (Foreign aid)	Appropriations	Foreign aid
Passed in 1963:		
88–30 (Public debt limit)	Ways and Means	Fiscal policy
88–205 (Aid loans)	Foreign Affairs	Foreign aid
*88–204 (College aid)	Education and Labor	Education
88–210 (Vocational educ)	Education and Labor	Education/civil rights
88–258 (Wheat sales)	Appropriations	Foreign policy and trade

(continued on next page)

PL Number	Committee of Origin	Major Policy Area
Passed in 1964:		
88–482 (Meat imports)	Ways and Means	Foreign trade
88–633 (Aid loans)	Foreign Affairs	Foreign aid
88–310 (Devel Assoc)	Appropriations	Foreign aid
*88–365 (Mass transit)	Banking and Currency	Urban mass transit
88–452 (Antipoverty)	Education and Labor	Social programs
Passed in 1993:		
103–82 (National service)	Education and Labor	Social/education
103–160 (Defense—gay ban)	Appropriations	Defense
103–138 (Interior—grazing)	Appropriations	Interior
*103–87 (Foreign aid)	Appropriations	Foreign aid
103–112 (Agencies—abortion)	Appropriations	Fiscal/social
103–126 (Energy—water)	Appropriations	Energy/water
*103–204 (Thrift bailout)	Banking, Finance, Urban	Fiscal policy
103–211 (Spending cuts)	Appropriations	Fiscal policy
Passed in 1994:		
103–236 (Vietnam trade)	Foreign Affairs	Foreign affairs
*103–227 (Goals 2000)	Education and Labor	Education
103–259 (Clinic access)	Judiciary	Abortion/social
103–335 (Bosnia arms)	Appropriations	Foreign affairs
103–327 (Ethanol use)	Appropriations	Agency funding
103–465 (GATT)	Ways and Means	Foreign trade

*Law eventually selected for case study.

APPENDIX 2

Interview Methodology and Design

GOALS OF THE INTERVIEW METHODOLOGY

Like the case selection process, the primary goal of the interview methodology was to provide unbiased and efficient estimates of the variables of interest to allow valid inferences. Again, the limited number of observations meant that the most desired trait was efficiency. Prudent interview design offered the primary means of reducing estimate bias, and I accordingly included correctives for expected biases in the interview questions and in the procedures for the conduct of the interviews. Finally, the interviews were intended to fill in seen and unseen gaps in the background research on each case, enabling the book to achieve its secondary objective of providing a rich, detailed description of lawmaking in both the 1960s and the 1990s.

THE GUIDING FEATURES OF THE
INTERVIEW DESIGN AND METHODOLOGY

The objective of the research design, then, was to provide for a "structured, focused comparison" of cases, including a disciplined collection of data.[1] To achieve this resolution, and to minimize the potential measurement errors in estimating the variable values, I applied the standard of triangulation in including data in the case legislative histories. Triangulation refers to "the practice of using more than one form [of data collection] to test a hypothesis."[2] I achieved triangulation through thorough background research, or secondary data analysis, prior to the interview process and through the conduct of multiple interviews of key actors at numerous levels of analysis. The interviews were conducted both personally and telephonically. To qualify as "fact," data had to be confirmed through at least two independent forms (background research and a confirming independent interviewee) or by multiple confirming accounts within one form (three consistent accounts from three interviewees, for example). In the cases where respondents directly contradicted one another, this standard increased to a majority of confirmations and the conflicting information was noted.

While a structured, focused comparison was the ultimate goal of the interview process, and while triangulation was the standard applied, it was also of critical importance to the interview process that I interviewed the respondents while already possessing a thorough prior knowledge of the legislative history of each case. This prior knowledge was gained through an analysis of relevant contextual, historical, and personal accounts of the passage of the six laws. At the same time, I avoided creating artifacts, or products of the data analysis methods, by my own actions during the interviews or through bias in the structure of the interview format itself. Another key guiding feature of the interview design and interview methodology was the incorporation of a "funnel sequence" of questions for each category of change.[3] *Funnel sequence* refers to a sequencing of questions such that each question is related to the previous one, with each question getting progressively narrower in scope.[4] This technique is particularly useful in assisting respondents in recalling specific events when interviewing about events from the relatively distant past.

Additionally, I incorporated into the interview design both direct and indirect measures of the observable implications in the question structure to provide an internal gauge of response accuracy within the structure of the interview itself.[5] The interview design also included a standardized flow and structure designed to result in consistent measurement of the variables of interest, although I did not follow the format slavishly. Prior background preparation, data triangulation, and an interview format that helps the respondents recollect past events without introducing bias and creating artifacts served as critical components of the interview process.

POTENTIAL BIASES AND CORRECTIVES

There are a number of potential respondent and interviewer biases that I identified beforehand and took into account in order to avoid systematic skew in the parameter estimates. Specifically, there were seven respondent biases and two interviewer biases that the interview design and interview procedures aimed to prevent. Respondent biases included the natural tendency to exaggerate one's role in events and the related bias that results from a respondent's desire to protect his or her personal reputation. The correctives intended to prevent biases of this sort included thorough background research prior to the interview, triangulation of observations, and a "separation from the credit." That is, in addition to the thorough preparation and the confirming independent accounts I required for observation inclusion, I announced to the respondent prior to the interview my intention not to attribute specific comments to any particular respondent. Furthermore, I did not respond to any questions from the respondent regarding comments made by other respondents in any other interview. The announcement regarding attribution was intended to take away much though not all of the incentive on the part of the respondents to inflate his or her own importance in the passage of the legislation of interest. The confidentiality openly accorded previous respondents and the statement of nonattribution were intended to help reassure the current interviewee of the "off-the-record" nature of the proceedings. The thorough background preparation and the standard of triangulation ensured that interviewee "outliers" were identified in the course of the interview process.

Two other related interviewee biases I anticipated included unbalanced perspectives and what I call the "rosy glow/dark days" bias. Triangulation, the funnel sequence of questions, and the interview evaluation were used to correct for these possible biases. *Unbalanced perspective* refers to an exaggeration not of one's own role in events, but an exaggeration of the role of the respondent's organization in events. For example, a respondent affiliated with a particular interest group might make the claim that his particular organization "drove" the passage of a law or that his organization "owned" a key legislator. The rosy glow/dark days bias refers to the human inclination toward broadly favorable or broadly unfavorable recollection of past events. For both biases, the funnel sequence of questions helped to reduce the exaggeration of role or "glow" by facilitating without further biasing the respondents' memories of past events. Additionally, I annotated any likely incidence of these biases after each interview for subsequent reference.

Two other possible obstacles to the respondents' accurate recollection of past events were oversimplification and memory lapses. Triangulation, the funnel sequence, thorough background preparation, careful probing questions, and a postinterview evaluation also helped with these potential problems. While these two potential sources of error are by their nature more likely to result in random measurement errors rather than systematic, nonrandom error, the correctives noted helped to avoid these uncertainties while assisting the respondents in the recollection of long-ago events. A postinterview assessment aided in the aggregate ordering of the data by allowing for greater emphasis on the accounts of those respondents offering more detailed information without losing information of value contributed by the less precise respondents. These postinterview evaluations brought some quality assurance to the data collection.

The final anticipated respondent bias was any systematic denial of interviews on the part of some particular category of interviewee. This problem would be bias resulting from interest group representatives refusing to be interviewed, legislators being unwilling to address certain aspects of the legislative process, or the like. The only correctives used for this potential problem were thorough background preparation and a clear and convincing statement of nonattribution of comments. The respondents' names are listed in a section of this appendix, but they do not show up anywhere in the text of the cases themselves.

Conversely, there were two potential sources of interviewer bias that I was concerned about and guarded against in the conduct of the interviews. The first of these potential biases was accusatory phrasing of questions and corresponding leading body language. It was important that I not influence the respondents by the phrasing of probing questions indicating any preconceived notions on my part, either verbally or non-verbally. Utilizing the standard format for each interview helped in avoiding this potentially biasing behavior, and I guarded against this potential problem in the probing portion of the interview as well. The second potential interviewer bias is related, in a sense, to the first. "Pre-disposition" bias involves not hearing an answer because of preconceived notions about expected "right" answers. The corrective for this potential bias is active listening, something that actually got easier as I became more familiar with the case histories and respondent accounts. There were no correctives for this potential problem other than inter-viewer vigilance and the postinterview evaluation.

THE INTERVIEW PROCESS AND FORMAT

The intent of the interview methodology was to allow for the freest exchange possible between interviewer and respondent, eliciting responses to like questions from each respondent without introducing biases into the interview. With this goal in mind, I used no recording devices other than a pen, tablet, and the interview sheets during the interviews.[6] While this approach necessitated summarized, rather than verbatim, accounts of the interview, the benefit was that the technique increased response validity. A second key feature of the interview pro-cess was the standard tone I established prior to each interview. The goal here was to establish the ground rules prior to commencing the interview to emphasize the confidential nature of the respondent's comments, again promoting response validity. The introductory com-ments included defining the planned uses of the information gathered, stating that the comments are off the record (with attribution only by general job title), and stating that any deviation from the above will only occur after explicit permission is given by the interviewee.

In conducting the interviews, I followed a specified format, but not slavishly so. The intent in this regard was to ask the standard format questions identically prior to probing to enhance the validity of measure. After the funneling sequence of questions relating to the variables of interest, the interviews proceeded to more open-ended questions in which the respondents had the freedom to take the interview in the direction they desired. After this portion of the interview, which also involved probing any areas of particular interest, the interviews concluded with questions that asked the respondent to "quantify" the relative significance of the actors and to place the account offered into its proper context within that Congress.

To summarize, the goal of the interview process was to provide a standard structure to each interview while simultaneously allowing for free exchange of the information the respondents felt to be most significant. The interview design included direct and indirect measures of the variables of interest, and I utilized the funnel sequence of questions intended to help the respondents recollect events from some time ago. As I progressed through the interview process, I noted several potential biases that I had not planned for emerge in the process, though none of them was fatal. First, I noted a "current player" bias. Those respondents currently active in the legislative process kept their views closer to the vest than those who were no longer actively participating in government. Another bias involved the fact that active members have less time available to talk, particularly since I was not a constituent. Also, the "nice guy/gal" bias arose from the fact that few people like or are comfortable with speaking poorly of someone else. This bias in the data meant that I often had to read between the lines of the respondents' comments or probe to glean exact assessments. There was also a bit of "thinker bias" in the interviews; that is, I suspected that the individuals who agreed to be interviewed were those who were interested in the legislative process in general or intrigued by the topic of the research. Last, there was a slight "performance evaluation" bias to the interviews, in that like inflated performance evaluations, everyone said positive things about the other players. The key in "reading" the interview respondents was to carefully construct what the respondents were similarly carefully avoiding saying. Many respondents were blunt; others, however, chose their words carefully, with the goal being to impart the information without actually having spoken poorly of a colleague.

As noted, I did not have any reason to believe that these biases skewed the results in any way. Table A2.1 lists the formal respondents and other contributors to the study separately.

TABLE A2.1
Interview Respondents and Other Contributors

Interview Respondents:

Name/Title/St-Party (if app)	Position in '60	Position in '90	Present Status
Ashley, Thomas Ludlow D-OH	MC, Banking Cmtee	N/A	Retired
Brademas, John D-IN	MC, Educ Labor	N/A	Retired
Broder, David Journalist	Wash Star Journalist	Wash Post	Wash Post
Chamberlain, Charles R-MI	MC	N/A	Retired
Crawford, George Prof Staff	N/A	Staff dir, Rules Cmtee	Min St dir, Rules
English, Karan D-AZ	N/A	MC, Educ Labor	College prof
Ford, Gerald President	MC, Approps	N/A	Retired
Friedman, John Profess Staff	N/A	Staff dir, Hamilton	St Dir, Hamilton
Gibbons, Sam D-FL	MC, Educ Labor	MC	Retired
Hamilton, Lee D-IN	MC	MC	MC
Jennings, Jack Leg Counsel	Subc staff, EL ('67)	Leg counsel, EL	Retired
Klein, Herb D-NJ	N/A	MC, BFU	Retired
LaRocco, Larry D-ID	N/A	MC, BFU	Private business
McMurray, Gerry	Staff, Banking Cmtee	N/A	Fannie Mae
McNamara, Dan Lobbyist	N/A	Lobbyist	Lobbyist, Cassidy
Meek, Kelsay Prof Staff	Staff, Banking Cmtee	Maj staff dir, BFU	Min Stf dir, BFS
Michel, Robert R-IL	MC, App	Minority leader	Retired
Monagan, John D-CT	MC, For Aff	N/A	Retired
Murphy, Austin D-PA	N/A	MC, EL subc chair	Retired
Murray, Mark Prof Staff	N/A	For Aid subc staff	Min Stf dir, App

(continued on next page)

TABLE A2.1 (continued)

Name/Title/St-Party (if app)	Position in '60	Position in '90	Present Status
Neal, Stephen D-NC	N/A	MC, subc chr App	Retired
Nelson, Kenneth Prof Staff	N/A	LA, Cm Hamilton	LA, Cm Hamilton
Nelson, Paul (aide to Patman)	Staff, Banking Cmtee	N/A	Retired
Price, David D-NC	Aide to Sen Bartlett	MC, App	MC
Quie, Albert R-MN (gov MN)	MC, EL	N/A	Retired
Reed, Jack D-RI	N/A	MC, Educ Labor	Senator
Rogers, Walter D-TX	MC	N/A	Retired
Schnee, Alexander State Liais	A/Sec, Cong Aff	N/A	Retired
Skocki, Stan Prof Staff	N/A	LA, Cm Livingston	Prof Staff
Stedman, Jim CRS Staff	N/A	Educ/ Labor staff	CRS, Educ issues
Stephens, Robert G., Jr. D-GA	MC, BC	N/A	Retired
Unsoeld, Jolene D-WA	N/A	MC, EL	Retired

Other Discussants:

Borden, Rob Min stf, Educ/Wkf	N/A	Maj staff, EL	Min staff, EW
Broder, David Journalist	*Wash Star*	*Wash Post*	*Wash Post*
Christman, Daniel General	N/A	A-Nat Sec Adv	College Pres
Christopher, Warren Secretary	N/A	Sec of State	Retired
Clark, Wesley General	N/A	Southcom Cdr	SACEUR
Cushman, Charles Prof Staff	N/A	Staff, MC Price	Think tank
Czarnecki, Marian For Af staff	Maj St Dir, For Aff	N/A	Retired
DesRoche, David Prof Staff	N/A	O/Nat'l D.C.P.	O/Nat'l D.C.P.

(continued on next page)

TABLE A2.1 (continued)

Name/Title/St-Party (if app)	Position in '60	Position in '90	Present Status
Downie, Leonard Exec Editor	*Wash Post*	*Wash Post*	*Wash Post*
Fulgham, Matt Nat'l Archives	N/A	Archivist	Archivist
Herman, Alexis Secretary	N/A	WH Public Liais	Sec Labor
Jennings, Peter Journalist	N/A	ABC anchor	ABC anchor
Joulwan, George General	N/A	SACEUR	Retired
Lelyveld, Joseph Exec Editor	*NY Times*	*NY Times*	*NY Times*
Lignelli, Louis Prof Staff	N/A	N/A	Dist staff, Masc
Lowrey, Bonnie Prof Staff	N/A	N/A	Press sec, Masc
Lugar, Richard Senator	N/A	Senator	Senator
Manthos, Chris Leg Liais, NRA	N/A	Leg Liais, NRA	Leg Liais, NRA
Mascara, Frank D-PA	N/A	N/A	MC
McCaffrey, Barry General	N/A	Cabinet	Cabinet
Mizusuwa, Bert Prof Staff	N/A	Sen Arm Service	Sen Arm Service
Mullin, Betsy Press Sec	N/A	Staff, DCCC	Press, Sen Reed
Painter, Will Prof Staff	N/A	LA, Cm Obey	LA, Cm Obey
Peck, Vincent Commissioner	N/A	GSA	GSA
Reed, Jack D-RI Senator	N/A	MC, EL	U.S. Senator
Runkel, David Maj Staff, BFU	N/A	Min staff, BFU	Maj St, Banking
Scott, Bruce General	N/A	Exec, VCS Army	O/Cong Leg Liais
Sember, William Prof Staff	N/A	N/A	AA Mascara
Shimkus, John R-IL	N/A	N/A	MC
Souter, David Justice	N/A	Supreme Court	Supreme Court
Thurmond, Strom R-SC	Senator	Senator	Senator

NOTES

CHAPTER 1

1. See also Lewis G. Irwin, "Dancing the Foreign Aid Appropriations Dance," *Public Budgeting & Finance* 20 (Summer 2000), 30–48. Portions of this chapter are reprinted by permission.

2. Richard E. Cohen, *Washington at Work* (New York: McMillan, 1992).

3. See David R. Mayhew, *Divided We Govern* (New Haven: Yale, 1991).

4. Chava Frankfort-Nachmias and David Nachmias, *Research Methods in the Social Sciences*, 5th ed. (New York: St. Martin's, 1996), 243.

5. Gary King, Robert O. Keohane, and Sidney Verba, *Designing Social Inquiry* (Princeton: Princeton, 1994), 44.

6. See David Collier, "The Comparative Method," ch. 2 in Rustow and Erickson, eds., *Comparative Political Dynamics* (New York: HarperCollins, 1991); Stanley Lieberson, "Small N's and Big Conclusions," *Social Forces* 70 (December 1991); and King, Keohane, and Verba, *Designing Social Inquiry*.

7. Lieberson, 307.

8. Charles Tiefer, *Congressional Practice and Procedure* (New York: Greenwood, 1989), 17.

CHAPTER 2

1. "Kennedy Legislative Boxscore for 1963," *Congressional Quarterly Almanac* (Washington: Congressional Quarterly, 1963), 102.

2. Norman J. Ornstein, Thomas E. Mann, and Michael J. Malbin, *Vital Statistics on Congress, 1995–1996* (Washington: Congressional Quarterly, 1996), 40–41.

3. John W. Baker, ed., *Member of the House: Letters of a Congressman*, by Clem Miller (New York: Scribners, 1962), 116.

4. Ornstein, Mann, and Malbin, *Vital Statistics*, 40–41.

5. Ibid., 121.

6. Ibid., 158–59.

7. Ibid., 22–23.

8. Ibid.

9. Ibid., 19.

10. Ibid., 62.

11. Unpublished speech by Congressman Lee Hamilton (D-IN) regarding changes in the House since 1965 that served as basis for remarks delivered at American University on June 17, 1997.

12. All entries are from Ornstein, Mann, and Malbin, *Vital Statistics* except as noted.

13. In the 1960, 1962, and 1992 elections, respectively.

14. Of those incumbents seeking reelection.

15. Defined as 60 percent of the major party vote.

16. The 1960 election.

17. These numbers are from the Eighty-fourth and Ninetieth Congresses, for this category and the joint, special, and related subcommittee entries as well.

18. After 1975, only those meetings requiring secrecy for national security reasons were closed. Numbers after 1975 are not available, but they are believed to be negligible.

19. Numbers are from 1957 and 1967, respectively.

20. Number in 1970.

21. Number in 1993. Increased to 3,335 in 1994.

22. This is a very rough estimate, using the highest anecdotal figure cited by the respondents. Lee Hamilton cites this figure in his speech on changes in the House since 1965. I use it here to give a general sense of the increased magnitude of campaign spending. Other respondents cited lower numbers, ranging from "a couple of thousand" to $10,000. The figures are not adjusted for inflation. The earliest good data on campaign spending are from 1978. The average for all serious (greater than $5,000 spent) House candidates for that year was $109,440.

23. These numbers are for the first session of each Congress in the 87th, 88th, and 103rd.

24. Ornstein, Mann, and Malbin, *Vital Statistics*, 81.

25. Ibid., 204.

26. Compiled from the *Congressional Directory, 103rd Congress, 1993–1994* (Washington: GPO, 1993). I counted National Guard and Reserve service as well as active duty service in a medical or legal specialty. I did not count Congressman Jay Kim (service in the Korean army) or others' listed service in the Civil Air Patrol.

CHAPTER 3

1. See also Lewis G. Irwin, "Dancing the Foreign Aid Appropriations Dance." Portions of sections 3.1 and 4.1 are reprinted by permission.

2. "Foreign Aid Funds," *The 1962 Congressional Quarterly Almanac* (Washington: Congressional Quarterly, 1963), 314.

3. Russell Porter, "President Signs 9 Billion in Bills," *New York Times*, October 1, 1961, A1; "Foreign Aid Funds," *Congressional Quarterly Weekly Report* (September 29, 1961): 1653–54.

4. Felix Belair Jr., "President Urges 4.1 Billion in Aid; Cites Red Threat," *New York Times*, February 19, 1960, A1 and A11.

5. Ibid., A11; and "House of Illusion," *Wall Street Journal*, February 17, 1960, 12.

6. "President Signs Foreign Aid Bill," *New York Times*, May 17, 1960, A1.

7. Appropriation amounts and presidential requests are taken from *Congressional Quarterly Weekly Report*. The budget totals are from the federal government's budget report.

8. This sum was a continuing resolution finally adopted as "emergency stopgap" funding.

9. This sum was the foreign aid portion of a supplemental omnibus appropriation.

10. "Committee Roundup," *Congressional Quarterly Weekly Report*, May 27, 1960, 943.

11. "Mutual Security Funds," *Congressional Quarterly Weekly Report*, September 2, 1960, 1512.

12. "Message on Aid," *Congressional Quarterly Weekly Report*, September 9, 1960, 1560–61.

13. "President Signs Foreign Aid Bill," *New York Times*, September 3, 1960, 1.

14. Felix Belair Jr., "President Urges U.S. Aid to East European Nations," *New York Times*, January 31, 1961, 1.

15. "Washington at Work," *Wall Street Journal*, May 29, 1961, 9.

16. "The Presidential Report," *Congressional Quarterly Weekly Report*, July 21, 1961, 1294.

17. Felix Belair Jr., "Aid Measure Sent to Senate Floor," *New York Times*, July 25, 1961, 1, 4; and Belair Jr., "House Unit Backs Aid Bill," *New York Times*, July 28, 1961, 1, 3.

18. "House Votes $3.6 Billion New Foreign Aid Canceling $300 Million of Committee's Cuts," *Wall Street Journal*, September 6, 1961, 4.

19. Felix Belair Jr., "Senate Restores Most of Aid Cuts; Passes Bill 62–17," *New York Times*, September 16, 1961, 1, 8.

20. "Floor Action," *Congressional Quarterly Weekly Report*, September 29, 1961, 1653–54.

21. Russell Porter, "President Signs 9 Billion in Bills," *New York Times*, October 1, 1961, A1.

22. Felix Belair Jr., "Foreign Aid Plan Is Near 5 Billion," *New York Times*, January 19, 1962, 19.

23. Felix Belair Jr., "Kennedy Chides Critics Who Seek Foreign Aid Cuts," *New York Times*, March 15, 1962, 1,18.

24. Ibid.

25. "Senate Democrats Act to Reverse Defeats On India Aid, Philippine War Claims Bills," *Wall Street Journal*, May 14, 1962, 6.

26. Felix Belair Jr., "4.6 Billion Voted by Senate Panel for Foreign Aid," *New York Times*, May 23, 1962, 1, 16.

27. "Battle Ahead on Foreign Aid," *New York Times*, August 2, 1962, 24.

28. Felix Belair Jr., "President Warns against Aid Slash," *New York Times*, August 30, 1962, 1, 10.

29. Ibid.

30. "Kennedy's Foreign Aid Request Is Slashed Almost $1.5 Billion by House Subcommittee," *Wall Street Journal*, September 18, 1962, 7.

31. Ibid.

32. Congress, House, Representative Otto Passman, speaking on the Foreign Operations Appropriation for fiscal 1963 in the 87th Congress, *Congressional Record*, v. 108, 19743.

33. "Foreign Aid Funds," *The 1962 Congressional Quarterly Almanac*, 314–22.

34. Ibid.

35. "College Aid," *The 1963 Congressional Quarterly Almanac*, 1964, 194.

36. Ibid., 195.

37. John Brademas, *The Politics of Education* (Norman: Oklahoma University, 1987), 7.

38. "President Voices Peace and Optimism," *New York Times*, January 8, 1960, 1, 11.

39. "College and VA Housing," *Congressional Quarterly Weekly Report*, January 15, 1960, 71.

40. "Powell Chairmanship," *Congressional Quarterly Weekly Report*, January 29, 1960, 169.

41. "College Construction Aid," *Congressional Quarterly Weekly Report*, March 25, 1960, 499.

42. Paul Duke, "Nixon Apparently Gets President to Accept Democrat's School Aid Bill, If It's Modified," *Wall Street Journal*, May 26, 1960, 30.

43. Tom Wicker, "House Approves School-Aid Bill with Ban on Bias," *New York Times*, May 27, 1960, 1, 14.

44. "House Rules Unit Rejects School Compromise," *Wall Street Journal*, June 23, 1960, 26.

45. Fred M. Hechinger, "School Bill's Defeat," *New York Times*, September 4, 1960, IV, 10.

46. "Text of Republican Planks on Civil Rights, Defense, and Education," *New York Times*, July 27, 1960, 18.

47. Anthony Lewis, "Plank-by-Plank Comparison of the Platforms of Democratic and Republican Parties," *New York Times*, July 28, 1960, 15.

48. "The Myth That Won't Die," *Wall Street Journal*, August 4, 1960, 8.

49. John D. Morris, "Kennedy Will Press School Aid and Wage Bills," *New York Times*, December 1, 1960, 23.

50. "Administration to Change School Aid Plan to Meet Liberal Democrats' Objections," *Wall Street Journal*, January 31, 1960, 26.

51. "Kennedy Offers $5.6 Billion, 5–Year Plan for Federal Aid to Education," *Wall Street Journal*, February 21, 1961, 28.

52. "Kennedy Ties Federal School Aid Bill to Cut in Help for Areas of Big U.S. Installations," *Wall Street Journal*, February 28, 1961, 4.

53. Cabell Phillips, "School-Aid Fight Arouses Lobbies," *New York Times*, April 17, 1961, 1.

54. Robert D. Novak, "White House Seeks to Unite 3 Education Aid Bills in One; Some Democrats Oppose Plan," *Wall Street Journal*, April 28, 1961, 2.

55. See former House member and occasional Green adversary John Brademas, *The Politics of Education*, ch. 3.

56. Lawrence E. Gladieux and Thomas R. Wolanin, *Congress and the Colleges* (Lexington, Mass.: Lexington, 1976), 83.

57. "House Unit Votes Additional $200 Million for President's Aid-to-Education Program," *Wall Street Journal*, May 9, 1961, 2.

58. "Senate Unit Votes School Aid Above Kennedy Request," *Wall Street Journal*, May 12, 1961, 2.

59. "House Backers of Parochial School Loans, Foes of All Education Aid Stall Kennedy Bill," *Wall Street Journal*, June 12, 1961, 3.

60. John Morris, "2 Key Democrats Stall School Aid," *New York Times*, June 16, 1961, 17.

61. Tom Wicker, "Eisenhower Hits School-Aid Plan," *New York Times*, June 29, 1961, 18.

62. "President Asks Congress to Rescue His Education Bill with Parliamentary Devices," *Wall Street Journal*, July 20, 1961, 2.

63. "Ribicoff's Woes," *Wall Street Journal*, September 5, 1961, 14.

64. "Kennedy Maps Tariff-Cut Bills," *New York Times*, January 13, 1962, 1, 3.

65. "College Construction," *Congressional Quarterly Weekly Report*, January 26, 1962, 110.

66. "Senate Approves Scholarships, Passes College Aid Bill," *Congressional Quarterly Weekly Report*, February 9, 1962, 198.

67. Paul Duke, "Chances for Kennedy's College Aid Bill Fade Further over New Religious Issue," *Wall Street Journal*, June 19, 1962, 8.

68. "College Aid Recommitted," *Congressional Quarterly Weekly Report*, September 21, 1962, 1574.

69. Jonathan Spivak, "Kennedy's New Education Aid Plan Drops across-the-Board Approach," *Wall Street Journal*, January 28, 1963, 30.

70. See Marjorie Hunter, "President Asks Broad Program to Aid Education," *New York Times*, January 30, 1963, 1, 4; and "President Asks $5 Billion Omnibus Education Program," *Congressional Quarterly Weekly Report*, February 1, 1963, 110–12.

71. "Omnibus School Aid," *Congressional Quarterly Weekly Report*, February 15, 1963, 199–200.

72. Ibid.

73. Ibid.

74. Marjorie Hunter, "School Aid Plan Split into 4 Bills," *New York Times*, May 23, 1963, 1.

75. "College Aid," *Congressional Quarterly Weekly Report*, August 16, 1963, 1436–37.

76. "Senate Passes College Aid Bill, 60–19," *Congressional Quarterly Weekly Report*, October 25, 1963, 1842–43.

77. "House Adopts College Aid Conference Report, 258–92," *Congressional Quarterly Weekly Report*, November 8, 1963, 1897–98.

78. "$375 Million Authorized for Urban Transit Grants," *The 1964 Congressional Quarterly Almanac*, 1965, 556–60.

79. "Budget Message Text," *New York Times*, January 19, 1960, 22.

80. Richard E. Mooney, "Overhaul Asked in U.S. Transport," *New York Times*, March 15, 1960, 1, 77.

81. Richard E. Mooney, "Mayors Ask Congress to Vote 100 Million in Commuter Aid," *New York Times*, May 24, 1960, 1, 59.

82. "Omnibus Housing Bills," *Congressional Quarterly Weekly Report*, June 10, 1960, 1025.

83. "The Democratic Platform," *New York Times*, July 13, 1960, 13–14.

84. "Texts of the Planks Approved by the Republican Convention," *New York Times*, July 25, 1960, 14–15.

85. "Senate Study Backs Vast Transportation Overhaul, Single Agency to Control Field," *Wall Street Journal*, January 5, 1961, 28.

86. "Housing Task Force," *Congressional Quarterly Weekly Report*, January 20, 1961, 73.

87. "Congress Pushing Transit-Aid Plan," *New York Times*, March 20, 1961, 24.

88. "Mass Transportation," *Congressional Quarterly Weekly Report*, March 31, 1961, 530.

89. Clayton Knowles, "Good Chance Seen for Transit Bill," *New York Times*, June 9, 1961, 41.

90. "Kennedy Submits Token Plan to Aid Transit Systems," *Wall Street Journal*, June 20, 1961, 4.

91. "Presidential Report," *Congressional Quarterly Weekly Report*, June 23, 1961, 1047; and Peter Braestrup, "Housing Bill Sent to the President," *New York Times*, June 29, 1961, 19.

92. Louis M. Kohlmeier, "Kennedy's Transit Policy Message Could Goad Revision of Key Laws," *Wall Street Journal*, March 16, 1962, 22.

93. "B&O May Request Authority to Abandon All Passenger Service," *Wall Street Journal*, March 16, 1962, 22.

94. Richard P. Hunt, "Kennedy Transport Plan" *New York Times*, April 6, 1962, 1, 19.

95. Ibid.

96. Peter Braestrup, "Urban Transit Law Giving 500 Million in Aid Is Predicted," *New York Times*, April 20, 1962, 1, 11.

97. "Urban Aid Wins Senate Test," *New York Times*, June 14, 1962, 35.

98. "Traffic Jam Costs Placed at 5 Billion," *New York Times*, July 4, 1962, 22.

99. "22 Bills Held Up in House Rules Committee," *Congressional Quarterly Weekly Report*, September 14, 1962, 1528.

100. "Youth Corps, Transit," *Congressional Quarterly Weekly Report*, September 21, 1962, 1562.

101. "Issues Facing Congress," *Congressional Quarterly Weekly Report*, January 4, 1963, 6.

102. See "New Bills Appear among Hardy Perennials," *Congressional Quarterly Weekly Report*, January 18, 1963, 44; and "President's Transportation Program Heads for Clashes," *Congressional Quarterly Weekly Report*, February 14, 1963, 184.

103. "Mass Transit Bill, Losing Favor in Senate," *Wall Street Journal*, March 27, 1963, 3.

104. "House Panel Approves Kennedy's $500 Million Mass Transit Proposal," *Wall Street Journal*, March 29, 1963, 15.

105. "Senate Votes Modified Mass-Transit Bill after Supporters Calm Labor's Fears," *Wall Street Journal*, April 5, 1963, 2.

106. "Strictly on Merit," *Wall Street Journal*, April 8, 1963, 16.

107. "Transit Proposals Provoke Bitter Rail-Highway Battle," *Congressional Quarterly Weekly Report*, October 4, 1963, 1727–37.

108. Ibid., 1727.

109. "Johnson Presses for Transit Help," *New York Times*, January 9, 1964, 18.

110. "Weaver Asks Expanded Transit and Better Suburban Planning," *New York Times*, January 10, 1964, 40.

111. "Text of President Johnson's Economic Report on the Nation," *New York Times*, January 21, 1964, 16–18.

112. Ibid.

113. "House Unit Votes $500 Million Aid to Mass Transit," *Wall Street Journal*, May 21, 1964, 8.

114. Warren Weaver Jr., "$375 Million Transit Bill Passed by House, 212–189," *New York Times*, June 26, 1964, 1, 61.

115. "Mass Transit Bill Cleared by House," *Wall Street Journal*, June 26, 1964, 3.

116. "Congress Clears $375 Million Mass Transportation Bill," *Congressional Quarterly Weekly Report*, July 3, 1964, 1338–41.

CHAPTER 4

1. "$2.5 Billion Approved for Ex-Soviet States," *The 1993 Congressional Quarterly Almanac*, 1994, 603–17. Portions of section 4.1 are reprinted by permission from Irwin, "Dancing the Foreign Aid Dance."

2. Gerald F. Seib, "U.S. Foreign Aid, Unpopular at Home, Is Slow to Adjust to a Changing World," *Wall Street Journal*, January 6, 1992, A11.

3. Robert S. Greenberger, "Hard Line on Israeli Loan Guarantees Reflects Public's Election-Year Mood," *Wall Street Journal*, March 11, 1992, A16.

4. "Congress' Clock Winds Down on Stopgap Funding," *Congressional Quarterly Weekly Review*, March 28, 1992, 814.

5. John Harwood, "Bush to Propose Aid for Former Soviet Union," *Wall Street Journal*, March 30, 1992, A3.

6. Gerald F. Seib and John Harwood, "Bush, Allies Pledge $24 Billion to Russia," *Wall Street Journal*, April 2, 1992, 2.

7. "Stopgap Bill Becomes Law after Deadline Threat," *Congressional Quarterly Weekly Report*, April 4, 1992, 890–92.

8. Gerald F. Seib, "Foreign-Aid Bill for Former U.S.S.R. Encounters Election-Year Opposition," *Wall Street Journal*, April 30, 1992, A14.

9. "Baker Seeks to Avoid Link on Jobs, Russian Aid," *Wall Street Journal*, May 1, 1992, A2.

10. Adam Clymer, "House Approves Foreign Aid at Lowest Level Since 1977," *New York Times*, June 26, 1992, A2.

11. "Foreign Aid Is Backed; Guarantees for Israel," *New York Times*, October 7, 1992, A13.

12. David Wessel and Carla Anne Robbins, "Clinton Weighs $1 Billion More in Russian Aid," *Wall Street Journal*, March 29, 1993, A8.

13. Ann Devroy, "Clinton Said to Be Considering Boost in Level of Aid to Russia," *Washington Post*, March 30, 1993, A17.

14. Carla Ann Robbins and Jacob M. Schlesinger, "G-7 Nations Unveil $28.4 Billion Plan to Aid Ex-Soviet Union, Back Yeltsin," *Wall Street Journal*, April 16, 1993, A3.

15. "The Wall Street Journal/NBC News Poll," *Wall Street Journal*, April 23, 1993, A1.

16. David S. Broder, "Panetta: President in Trouble on the Hill," *Washington Post*, April 27, 1993, A1, A6.

17. Eric Pianin and Ruth Marcus, "White House, Hill Democrats Consider Linking Jobs Bill to Russian Aid," *Washington Post*, April 30, 1993, A11.

18. Carroll J. Doherty, "Economic Aid for Ex-Soviets Takes Big Step Forward," *Congressional Quarterly Weekly Report*, May 29, 1993, 1370–71.

19. Ibid.

20. "$2.5 Billion Approved for Ex-Soviet States," *The 1993 Congressional Quarterly Almanac*, 1994, 603–17.

21. Ibid.

22. David Rogers, "House Approves Aid for Russia," *Wall Street Journal*, June 18, 1993, A14.

23. Ibid.

24. "$2.5 Billion Approved for Ex-Soviet States," *The 1993 Congressional Quarterly Almanac*, 1994, 603–17.

25. "Hill Votes More Funds for Thrift Bailout," *The 1993 Congressional Quarterly Almanac*, 1994, 150–7.

26. John R. Cranford, "House Panel Heeds RTC Head, Adds $25 Billion to Bailout," *Congressional Quarterly Weekly Report*, February 29, 1992, 461.

27. John R. Cranford, "More Funds Being Routed toward RTC Pipeline," *Congressional Quarterly Weekly Report*, March 14, 1992, 609–10.

28. Ibid.

29. Susan Schmidt, "House Votes against S&L Funding Bill," *Washington Post*, April 2, 1992, A1, A11.

30. Paulette Thomas, "Additional Spending for Thrift Bailout Is Unexpectedly Rejected in the House," *Wall Street Journal*, April 2, 1992, A16.

31. Susan Schmidt, "House Votes against S&L Funding Bill," *Washington Post*, April 2, 1992, A1, A11.

32. "RTC Expects to Fall Short of Goal for Asset Sales," *Wall Street Journal*, April 16, 1992.

33. Susan Schmidt, "Bush Renews Push for $42 Billion to Maintain Funding of S&L Cleanup," *Washington Post*, July 30, 1992, D14.

34. See also Andrew Taylor, "Freshmen Shift the Balance on House Banking Panel," *Congressional Quarterly Weekly Report*, January 30, 1993, 209–12.

35. "Top Treasury Official Will Serve as Chief of RTC Temporarily," *Wall Street Journal*, March 16, 1993, B10.

36. Andrew Taylor, "Bentsen Requests $45 Billion to Finish Thrift Bailout," *Congressional Quarterly Weekly Report*, March 20, 1993, 659–60.

37. "Senate Panel Approves Funding for S & L Bailout," *Wall Street Journal*, March 26, 1993, A2.

38. "RTC Gets Ready for Toughest Sell," *Wall Street Journal*, April 1, 1993, A4.

39. "Clinton Expected to Trim Bailout Request," *Wall Street Journal*, April 21, 1993, A16.

40. Andrew Taylor, "Reduced Bailout Bill Headed for First Round in House," *Congressional Quarterly Weekly Report*, April 24, 1993, 1010.

41. See Jerry Knight, "House Panel Finds Dollars in a Deadline," *Washington Post*, April 30, 1993, F2; and Andrew Taylor, "House Panel Chops $12 Billion from Bailout Request," *Congressional Quarterly Weekly Report*, May 1, 1993, 1070–71.

42. Andrew Taylor, "House Panel Chops $12 Billion from Bailout Request," *Congressional Quarterly Weekly Report*, May 1, 1993, 1070–71.

43. Ibid.

44. Richard L. Vernaci, "House Panel Approves 'Final' RTC Funding," *Washington Post*, May 7, 1993, F2.

45. Andrew Taylor, "Judiciary, Banking at Odds over Thrift Bailout Bill," *Congressional Quarterly Weekly Report*, June 12, 1993, 1468.

46. Andrew Taylor, "Democrats Vow to Return to RTC in September," *Congressional Quarterly Weekly Report*, August 7, 1993, 2147.

47. Andrew Taylor, "Bailout Heads to Conference after Squeaker in House," *Congressional Quarterly Weekly Report*, September 18, 1993, 2440.

48. Ibid.

49. Andrew Taylor, "Minority Contract Provision Stalls Bailout Measure," *Congressional Quarterly Weekly Report*, November 13, 1993, 3110.

50. Albert R. Karr, "Conferees Clear Compromise Bill for RTC Funds," *Wall Street Journal*, November 19, 1993, A2.

51. "National Education Goals Set," *The 1994 Congressional Quarterly Almanac*, 1995, 397–99.

52. See Gene Currivan, "National Agency on Schools Urged," *New York Times*, July 7, 1960, 1. In the article, Dr. John H. Fischer, dean of the Teacher's College, Columbia University, calls for an organization similar to the American Red Cross that "would not make or execute educational policies, but would define programs to relate education to the national goals."

53. Jill Zuckman, "Senate Rejects Demonstration of Bush's 'School Choice' Plan," *Congressional Quarterly Weekly Report*, January 25, 1992, 176.

54. Hilary Stout, "Bipartisan Panel on Education Urges National Standards, Voluntary Exams," *Wall Street Journal*, January 27, 1992, B4.

55. Ibid.

56. Jill Zuckman, "New Bill Kills Federal Money for Private School 'Choice,'" *Congressional Quarterly Weekly Report*, February 29, 1992, 471–72.

57. Chester E. Finn, "Fear of Standards Threatens Education Reform," *Wall Street Journal*, March 23, 1992, A10.

58. Jill Zuckman, "Panel Gives Listless Approval to Scorned Reform Bill," *Congressional Quarterly Weekly Report*, May 23, 1992, 1451.

59. Ibid.

60. See the NEA letter, entitled "Let's Reinvest in America" in the *Washington Post*, September 20, 1992, C4, for an example of an advertisement from this television, radio, and print campaign.

61. Hilary Stout and Alan Murray, "Real Differences on Education Between Clinton and Bush Come Down to Commitment, Money," *Wall Street Journal*, August 6, 1992, A14.

62. "Choosing a School for Chelsea," *New York Times*, January 7, 1993, A22.

63. Mary Jordan, "Top Educators Look Back," *Washington Post*, January 12, 1993, A15.

64. Karen DeWitt, "U.S. Students Advance in Math," *New York Times*, January 13, 1993, B6.

65. Jill Zuckman, "Riley Explains Reform Ideas," *Congressional Quarterly Weekly Report*, February 27, 1993, 466.

66. Jill Zuckman, "The Next Education Crisis: Equalizing School Funds," *Congressional Quarterly Weekly Report*, March 27, 1993, 749–54.

67. Rochelle Sharp, "Clinton Package For Schools Has Chance to Pass," *Wall Street Journal*, April 16, 1993, B1, B6.

68. Jill Zuckman, "Reform Bill Moves Forward, but Partisanship Recurs," *Congressional Quarterly Weekly Report*, May 8, 1153.

69. "Clinton's Education Plan Clears Senate Hurdle," *Wall Street Journal*, May 20, 1993, A18.

70. Jill Zuckman, "School Improvement Bill Snagged by Standards," *Congressional Quarterly Weekly Report*, May 22, 1993, 1297.

71. See Diane Ravitch, "Clinton's Math: More Gets Less," *New York Times*, May 26, 1993, A21; Linda Gottsfredson, "Clinton's New Form of Race-Norming," *Wall Street Journal*, June 3, 1993, 17; and Clifford Adelman, "Turn Diplomas into Report Card," *New York Times*, June 19, 1993, 21.

72. Adam Clymer, "Clinton Bill on Educational Standards Advances," *New York Times*, June 24, 1993, A19.

73. Jill Zuckman, "School Standards Approved along Party-Line Vote," *Congressional Quarterly Weekly Report*, June 26, 1993, 1663.

74. Mary Jordan, "Riley Assails Lack of Progress on Improving U.S. Schools," *Washington Post*, October 1, 1993, A2.

75. "House Advances Education Reform Bill," *The 1993 Congressional Quarterly Almanac*, 1994, 404–07.

76. Jeffrey L. Katz, "School Prayer, Choice Part of Senate 'Goals' Debate," *Congressional Quarterly Weekly Report*, February 5, 1994, 248.

CHAPTER 5

1. Samuel Huntington, "Congressional Responses to the Twentieth Century," ch. 1 in David B. Truman, ed., *The Congress and America's Future* (Englewood Cliffs, New Jersey: Prentice-Hall, 1965).

2. James L. Sundquist, *The Decline and Resurgence of Congress* (Washington: Brookings, 1981), 369.

3. Ibid., 371–72.

4. John W. Kingdon, *Congressmen's Voting Decisions*, 2d ed. (New York: Harper, 1981), iv.

5. John R. Hibbing, *Choosing to Leave* (Washington: University Press of America, 1982), 131–36.

6. Steven S. Smith, *Call to Order* (Washington: Brookings, 1989), 8.

7. Ibid.

8. Burdett Loomis, *The New American Politician* (New York: Basic, 1988), 3–51; and Heclo, "The Emerging Regime," ch. 11 in Richard A. Harris and Sidney Milkis, eds., *Remaking American Politics* (Boulder, Colorado: Westview, 1989), 316.

9. John R. Hibbing, "Contours of the Modern Congressional Career," *American Political Science Review* 85 (June 1991), 405–28.

10. Morris Fiorina, *Congress: Keystone of the Washington Establishment*, 2d ed. (New Haven: Yale, 1989), see chs. 1, 3, and 6 in particular.

11. Alan Ehrenhalt, *The United States of Ambition* (New York: Times, 1992), 55.

12. William P. Browne and Won K. Paik, "Beyond the Domains: Recasting Network Politics in the Postreform Congress," *American Journal of Political Science* 37 (November 1993), 1054–78.

13. Eric M. Uslaner, *The Decline of Comity in Congress* (Ann Arbor: University of Michigan, 1997), ch. 2; and Anthony King, *Running Scared* (New York: Free Press, 1997), 1–5 and 29–51.

14. Heclo, "Issue Networks and the Executive Establishment," ch. 3 in Anthony King, ed., *The New American Political System* (Washington: American Enterprise), 100.

15. Sundquist, *The Decline and Resurgence of Congress*, 402–14.

16. Kingdon, *Congressmen's Voting Decisions*, 206–09.

17. Huntington, "Congressional Responses to the Twentieth Century," 21–23.

18. See Roger H. Davidson, "The New Centralization on Capitol Hill," *Review of Politics* 50 (Summer 1988), 345–63; and Roger H. Davidson, ed., *The Postreform Congress* (New York: St. Martin's, 1992). See also Richard L. Hall's *Participation in Congress* (New Haven: Yale, 1996).

19. Gary W. Cox and Mathew D. McCubbins, *Legislative Leviathan* (Berkeley: University of California, 1993).

20. All the statistics here were calculated or taken from table 2.1.

21. "Percentage of Members with Bachelors' Degrees." The qualifications listed in tables 5.1 and 5.2 were coded from the *Congressional Directory*. In the three instances the legislators did not include biographies in the *Directory* for these sessions, I used previous or subsequent entries.

22. "Percentage of Members with Professional Degrees" includes all law degrees, masters' in business administration (MBA), and medical or dental degrees.

23. "Percentage of Legislators with Graduate Degrees" includes M.A. or Ph.D. of any kind.

24. "Percentage with Relevant Graduate Degrees" includes advanced non-professional degrees relevant to the policy areas dealt with by the committee. For

example, a master's in education or a Ph.D. in economics are relevant on the Education and Labor Committee.

25. There were two Democratic vacancies on the Appropriations Committee at the time of passage.

26. Numbers do not include full committee chairs and ranking minority members if ex oficio only.

27. Number does not include the resident commissioner or delegates on the committee.

28. There was also one independent on the committee, Bernie Sanders (I-VT).

29. "Percentage Who Served in the American Military" includes all American military service, including active duty, Reserve, combat service or peacetime. This treatment likely biases the 103rd's "percent military experience" upward, since most of the 87th/88th's veterans served during World War II while about half of the 103rd veterans served part-time in the Guard and Reserve.

30. "Percentage of Members with Prior Public Service" includes community service and/or appointed or elected public office. This is a "yes/no" category.

31. "Average Number of Terms of Service for Committee Members" is general service, not committee service, in the House, and includes the current term in which the law was passed.

32. "Percentage of Members with Prior Policy Service." This is a "yes/no" count of the percentage of members listing relevant prior policy service in their biographies that would assist them in understanding the issues put before the committee. This includes service as a legislative aide in the policy area, relevant job experiences, or relevant interest group activism.

33. "Percentage of Members Listing Party Activities as Significant Activities" includes a "yes/no" percentage of members listing party and partisan interest group activities and awards, such as "Republican Party county chairman" or the like, prior to their service in the House.

34. "Percentage of Carpetbaggers on the Committee" is a measure of the number of carpetbaggers, defined as members born and schooled in a state other than the one represented.

35. "Percentage of Members with Bachelors' Degrees." The qualifications listed in tables 5.1 and 5.2 were coded from the *Congressional Directory*.

36. "Percentage of Members with Professional Degree." includes all law degrees, masters' in business administration (MBA), and medical or dental degrees.

37. "Percentage of Legislators with Graduate Degrees" includes M.A. or Ph.D. of any kind.

38. "Percentage with Relevant Graduate Degrees" includes advanced non-professional degrees relevant to the policy areas dealt with by the committee. For example, a master's in education is relevant on the education and labor committee.

39. A few (less than five for each period) members who served on more than one of the three sample committees are counted twice for both sets of cases.

40. "Percentage Who Served in the American Military" includes all American military service, including active duty, Reserve, combat service, or peace-

time. This treatment likely biases the 103rd's "percent military experience" upward, since most of the 87th and 88th's veterans served during World War II, while about half of the 103rd veterans served part-time in the Guard and Reserve.

41. "Percentage of Members with Prior Public Service." Community service and/or appointed or elected public office. This category is a "yes/no" category.

42. "Percentage of Members with Prior Policy Service" is a "yes/no" count of the percentage of members listing relevant prior policy service in their biographies that would assist them in understanding the issues put before the committee.

43. "Percentage of Members Listing Party Activities as Significant Activities" is a "yes/no" percentage of members listing party and partisan interest group activities and awards, such as "Republican Party county chairman," prior to their service in the House.

44. "Percentage of Carpetbaggers on the Committee" is a measure of the number of carpetbaggers, defined as members born and schooled in a state other than the one represented. In-state carpetbagging is not counted, likely biasing the count downward for both periods.

45. A few (less than five for each period) members who served on more than one of the three sample committees are counted twice for both sets of cases.

46. "Number of Sponsors/Average Seniority" includes sponsor plus all cosponsors at time of passage and gives the mean term of service for all sponsors at the time of passage.

47. "Number of Committee and Subcommittee Amendments Offered/Average Seniority" includes all committee and subcommittee amendments identified by name. Amendments are not included where there are no transcripts or summaries of the executive sessions, or amendments are not identified by the legislator.

48. "Number of Floor Motions and Amendments Offered/Average Seniority": these amendments and motions were identified in the *Congressional Record* and the *Congressional Quarterly Almanac* articles. The number includes amendments and motions to recommit. Other parliamentary motions, such as quorum calls, are not included. Each member counts once for average seniority.

49. "Number of Different Floor Speakers/Average Seniority." Each speaking member is counted once for the purpose of average seniority, including the duration of consideration within the Committee of the Whole and general debate but excluding consideration of the rule (if any).

50. This category includes the number of House conferees in House-Senate conference and average seniority.

51. This category includes multiple committee jurisdiction and additional committee members with jurisdiction.

52. The subcommittee met in executive session to mark up the bill, and there are no published records of the proceedings. The subcommittee reported the bill with no dissent. The full committee reported the bill with only one amendment (restoring $300 million in aid), but the amendment was described as a "committee amendment" and not attributed to any one person.

53. These amendments were described in the minutes of the executive sessions of Green's Special Education Subcommittee and Powell's full committee, during which the measures were negotiated. The records were located at the National Archives in Washington, D.C. The minutes, when compared to the reported legislation, show that a good deal of negotiating was going on outside of the executive sessions as well.

54. Similar to the foreign aid case, the archival records do not include minutes or summaries of the executive sessions for either the housing subcommittee or the full committee. These records are extremely limited and generally only offer already published materials.

55. Of the thirty-nine sponsors (thirty-eight co-sponsors), seventeen came from outside of the committee, and all thirty-nine were Democrats. For the sake of comparison, the sponsor (Kildee) was in his ninth term.

56. Payne and Matchley offered a joint amendment. Both were counted for average seniority.

57. This number includes nine members from the Energy and Commerce and Foreign Affairs committees.

58. This number does not take into consideration any possible overlap and is intended as a general measure of the effects of multiple jurisdiction.

59. All eight sponsors (seven co-sponsors) were members of the committee. Two co-sponsors were Republicans, and the sponsor (Chairman Gonzalez) was in his seventeenth term.

60. Ten additional conferees were designated from the Government Operations Committee and the Judiciary Committee, but only four of them actually attended.

61. Unpublished draft of a speech Hamilton gave regarding changes in Congress. He summarized these remarks in a conference at American University on June 17, 1997.

62. Ibid.

63. Leadership styles (centralized, decentralized, or mixed) are defined in terms of committee leader autonomy and control of the chamber processes for the Speakers and inclusiveness in committee decision-making for the committee and subcommittee chairs, gleaned from respondent accounts.

64. The main purpose of this chart is to examine the significant actions, goals, and levels of influence over the outcome that the key leaders had in the passage of the six case laws, in the view of the respondents. I have also inserted into the table several other key House actors from the cases to give a sense of the diverse nature of the "willful agents" identified by the respondents.

65. This is a general assessment of the actor's influence in the process as noted by the respondents.

66. All entries are from Ornstein, Mann, and Malbin, *Vital Statistics on Congress*, except as noted. Committee staff numbers are for 1960 for the 1960s cases, and 1993 for the 1990s cases.

67. This is from 1957, the closest year available.

68. Remaining table numbers are from 1960 for the early 1960s cases.

69. The Congressional Budget and Technology Assessment offices were created in the 1970s.

70. The entries for this row are the 1993 data, the last available.

CHAPTER 6

1. Bertram M. Gross, *The Legislative Struggle* (New York: McGraw-Hill, 1953), 450.

2. Raymond A. Bauer, Ithiel De Sola Pool, and Lewis Anthony Dexter, *American Business and Public Policy*, 2d ed., (Chicago: Aldine Atherton, 1972), 327.

3. Samuel P. Huntington, "Congressional Responses to the Twentieth Century," ch. 1 in David B. Truman, ed., *The Congress and America's Future*, 6–7.

4. Hugh Heclo, "Issue Networks and the Executive Establishment," ch. 3 in King, ed., *The New American Political System*, 96–97.

5. Sundquist, *The Decline and Resurgence of Congress*, 369–70.

6. Jack L. Walker, "The Origins and Maintenance of Interest Groups in America," *American Political Science Review* 77 (1983), 394.

7. Ibid., 401–04.

8. Hugh Heclo, "The Emerging Regime," ch. 11 in Harris and Milkis, eds., *Remaking American Politics*, 292–93, 310.

9. Mark A. Peterson, *Legislating Together* (Cambridge: Harvard, 1990), 277.

10. Ibid.

11. Ronald J. Hrebenar and Ruth K. Scott, *Interest Group Politics in America*, 2d ed. (Englewood Cliffs: Prentice-Hall, 1990), 10, 207.

12. Ibid., viii, and ch. 5.

13. Richard L. Hall and Frank W. Wayman, "Buying Time," *American Political Science Review* 84 (September 1990), 797–819.

14. Gross, *The Legislative Struggle*, 450.

15. Huntington, "Congressional Responses to the Twentieth Century," 8.

16. Ibid., 22–3.

17. Paul E. Peterson and Jay P. Greene, "Why Executive-Legislative Conflict in the United States Is Dwindling," *British Journal of Political Science* 24 (1993), 33–55.

18. Edward V. Schneier and Bertram Gross, *Congress Today* (New York: St. Martin's, 1993), 1–9.

19. Barbara Sinclair, *The Transformation of the U.S. Senate* (Baltimore: Johns Hopkins, 1989), 5.

20. Heclo, "The Emerging Regime," 317.

21. A term he used to describe the increasing democratization and increased influence of interest groups in the governing process in a speech at West Point, New York.

22. From the text of remarks made at American University in June 1997.

23. Sources checked for mention of the groups and group activities included the relevant congressional hearings, the *Wall Street Journal*, the *New York Times*, the *Congressional Record*, *Congressional Quarterly Weekly Report*, the *Congressional Quarterly Almanac*, archival records at the National Archives, and respondent accounts.

24. Baker, ed., *Member of the House*, 55.

25. Ibid., 58.

26. These are the articles directly addressing the passage of the law or the central policy issues of the legislative initiative with reference to the legislative process, not including editorials.

27. These are the articles primarily describing the events leading to passage of the law or policy area.

28. These are the articles primarily concerned with analysis of the legislators' or other actors' motives in seeking to pass or prevent passage of the case or the personal politics of passage.

29. A "balanced" article both addressed actor motives and described events to a similar degree.

30. These and other statistics are from Ornstein, Mann, and Malbin, *Vital Statistics*. See also table 2.1.

31. Brademas, *The Politics of Education*, 47.

32. Ibid., 47–48.

33. Support is assessed as "yes," "no," or "mixed," based on references to public opinion by various legislative actors. "Unknown" refers to cases where public opinion data were not mentioned.

34. Both leadership categories refer to the majority of opinions among the party's ranking leaders in chamber, committee, and subcommittee.

35. While ranking committee and subcommittee member Bill Goodling (R-PA) was initially vehemently opposed to the measure reported by the committee, he acquiesced once his "non-State-encroaching" amendment was accepted by near-unanimous vote during House floor debate.

36. All of the noted banking and savings and loan industry officials, and depositors, were in favor of the legislation. The only identified dissent came from advocacy groups such as Congress Watch and the Center for Public Responsiveness.

CHAPTER 7

1. Four books were particularly helpful for their analysis of changes in legislative procedure over the period from the 1960s to the present, including Sundquist, (1981) *The Decline and Resurgence*; Smith, (1989) *Call to Order*; Tiefer, (1989) *Congressional Practice and Procedure*; and Rieselbach, (1994) *Congressional Reform: The Changing Modern Congress*.

2. Richard F. Fenno Jr., *Congressmen in Committees* (Boston: Little, Brown, 1973), 280–91, and Tiefer, *Congressional Practice and Procedure*, 59–60.

3. Tiefer, *Congressional Practice and Procedure*, 111 and 120.

4. Barbara Sinclair, "From Monopoly to Management," ch. 7 in Davidson, ed., *The Postreform Congress*, 141.

5. Huntington, "Congressional Responses to the Twentieth Century," 8.

6. Ibid., 21.

7. Ibid.

8. Nelson W. Polsby, Miriam Gallagher, and Barry Spencer Rundquist, "The Growth of the Seniority System in the U.S. House of Representatives," *American Political Science Review* 63 (1969), 790.

9. Sundquist, *The Decline and Resurgence of Congress*, 368.

10. Ibid., 375 and 378.

11. Rieselbach, *Congressional Reform*, 205–09.

12. Smith, *Call to Order*, 16; and Tiefer, *Congressional Practice and Procedure*, 380–89.

13. See Smith, *Call to Order*, 40–45, on special rules, and 253–55, for the House calendars; and Tiefer, *Congressional Practice and Procedure*, ch. 5, for a thorough treatment of all House rules.

14. Sundquist, *The Decline and Resurgence of Congress*, 401.

15. Quoted in Smith, *Call to Order*, 26.

16. Sundquist, *The Decline and Resurgence of Congress*, 368–69.

17. Heclo, "The Emerging Regime," 305.

18. Davidson, *The Postreform Congress*, 12; and Rieselbach, *Congressional Reform*, 133–35.

19. See table 2.1.

20. Representative Lee Hamilton cites this figure as his 1964 campaign expenses in his unpublished speech on changes in Congress. His figure is the highest of the respondent figures for that period, with most ranging from "a couple thousand" to "about ten thousand."

21. Baker, ed., *Member of the House*, 143.

22. Barbara Sinclair, *Unorthodox Legislating* (Washington: Congressional Quarterly, 1997), 84.

23. Tiefer, *Congressional Practice and Procedure*, 59.

24. Baker, ed., *Member of the House*, 13.

25. Previously, executive session records were sealed for thirty years, and investigatory records were sealed for fifty years. These records from the 1960s are spotty at best anyway.

26. Baker, ed., *Member of the House*, 17.

27. Ibid., 38.

28. Tiefer, *Congressional Practice and Procedure*, 2.

29. *Congressional Record*, September 14, 1993, H6685.

30. Barbara Sinclair, *Unorthodox Legislating*, 90.

31. Includes bloc or committee mass amendments as a package (one amendment).

32. Tiefer, *Congressional Practice and Procedure*, 10.

33. Baker, ed., *Member of the House*, 113.

CHAPTER 8

1. Tiefer, *Congressional Practice and Procedure*, 405–11.

2. Barry R. Weingast, "Fighting Fire with Fire: Amending Activity and Institutional Change in the Postreform Congress," ch. 8 in Davidson, ed., *The Postreform Congress*, 142–53.

3. Smith, *Call to Order*, 52–53.

4. Tiefer, *Congressional Practice and Procedure*, 53.

5. R. Douglas Arnold, *The Logic of Congressional Action* (New Haven:

Yale, 1990), 100–02. Chapter 5 effectively analyzes three categories of legislator (or "coalition leader") strategies, including strategies of persuasion, procedure, and modification.

6. Ibid.

7. Ibid., 101.

8. Davidson, *The Postreform Congress*, viii and ch. 1.

9. Donald R. Matthews, *U.S. Senators and Their World*, 2d ed. (New York: Norton, 1973), 92–93.

10. Charles L. Clapp, *The Congressman: His Work as He Sees It* (Washington: Brookings, 1963), 10–12. See chapter 1 for a good overview of congressional norms in the early 1960s.

11. Huntington, "Congressional Responses to the Twentieth Century," 16.

12. Smith, *Call to Order*, 20–24.

13. Heclo, "The Emerging Regime," 309.

14. Sundquist, *The Decline and Resurgence of Congress*, 400–01.

15. Samuel Kernell, *Going Public*, 2d ed. (Washington: Congressional Quarterly, 1993).

16. Baker, ed., *Member of the House*, 131.

17. David E. Price, *The Congressional Experience: A View from the Hill* (Boulder: Westview, 1992), 56.

18. Ibid., 73.

19. Baker, ed., *Member of the House*, 104.

20. Tiefer, *Congressional Practice and Procedure*, 11.

21. See the full committee's *Legislative Calendar* from the Eighty-eighth Congress.

22. This amount represents the entire funding authorized by the law, rounded off.

23. Brademas, *The Politics of Education*, 18.

CHAPTER 9

1. Huntington, "Congressional Responses in the Twentieth Century," 8.

2. Ibid., 25.

3. Sundquist, *The Decline and Resurgence of Congress*, 326–28.

4. Bailey, *Congress Makes a Law*, 61.

5. Heclo, "The Emerging Regime," 88–94.

6. Joel D. Aberbach, *Keeping a Watchful Eye* (Washington: Brookings, 1990), 4.

7. Huntington, "Congressional Responses in the Twentieth Century," 15.

8. Paul J. Quirk, "Structures and Performance: An Evaluation," in Davidson, ed., *The Postreform Congress*, 321–22.

9. Browne and Paik, "Beyond the Domain," 1066–71.

10. Heclo, "Issue Networks and the Executive Establishment," 88–93.

11. Sinclair, *The Transformation of the U.S. Senate*, 5.

12. Charles Cameron and others, "Measuring the Institutional Performance of Congress in the Post-War Era," unpublished APSA manuscript, May 10, 1996, 20–35.

13. Includes all relevant subcommittee and committee hearings.

14. This category includes the number of witnesses who testified. The prepared and submitted statements of other groups and individuals who did not actually testify are included in the "Pages" in table 9.1, and the interest groups are counted in table 6.1: "Interest Groups Active in the Passage of the Cases."

15. I settled on three general descriptors of the hearings viewed in the aggregate. Adversarial: witnesses generally challenged for justifications and accuracy; cordial: members did not challenge witnesses; mixed: a mixture of challenges and "friendly" treatment.

16. These were college professors not representing an interest group or association.

17. These witnesses were all House members from interested districts.

18. Two were House members, and two were UNICEF officials.

19. This was a university professor with no listed interest group affiliation.

CHAPTER 10

1. Brademas, *The Politics of Education*, 38.

EPILOGUE

1. Sinclair, *Unorthodox Legislating*, 86.

2. Ibid. See also Gregory Wawro, *Legislative Entrepreneurship in the U.S. House of Representatives* (Ann Arbor: University of Michigan, 2000).

APPENDIX 1

1. See King, Keohane, and Verba, *Designing Social Inquiry*, 124.

2. Ibid., 128–29.

3. Ibid., 156.

4. Ibid., 52.

5. The details regarding the application of these criteria are described in appendix 1.

6. *Congressional Quarterly Weekly Report*, December 31, 1994, 3632.

7. I used the *Congressional Quarterly Almanac* and the Congressional Information Service (CIS) database to verify this criterion. The minimum was an HR bill number during consideration.

8. Front-page articles, editorials, and cartoons counted as two "hits," while other articles and letters to the editor counted as one. I did not count corrections, but I did count accompanying "texts" and transcripts as one hit each. For both media measures, I counted articles dealing directly with the passage of the law as well as articles dealing with the key vote issue. The *New York Times Index* generally lists related articles in chronological order under subheadings.

9. The *Congressional Quarterly Weekly Report* offers a measure of "inside the beltway" media attention, and it also offers a true second type of medium, which is advantageous to the study. For the evaluation of media scrutiny in the

years 1961 through 1964, I used the year-end *Congressional Quarterly Weekly Report* indices. For the years 1993 and 1994, I used the *Congressional Quarterly Weekly Report* year-end "Issue Report" indices.

10. Richard F. Fenno, *Congressmen in Committees* (Boston: Little Brown, 1973).

11. Though not essential, I also desired to fit my cases into the Fenno paradigm when possible.

APPENDIX 2

1. King, Keohane, and Verba, *Designing Social Inquiry*, 45, and Frankfort-Nachmias, *Research Methods*, 235–42.

2. Frankfort-Nachmias, *Research Methods*, 204.

3. Ibid., 260.

4. Ibid.

5. Ibid., 205.

6. See Richard F. Fenno Jr., *Homestyle: House Members in Their Districts* (New York: Harper, 1978), 279–82. This technique is borrowed from his analysis. See also John W. Kingdon's *Agendas, Alternatives, and Public Policies* (New York: Harper Collins, 1995), 231–44.

BIBLIOGRAPHY

Aberbach, Joel D. *Keeping a Watchful Eye.* Washington: Brookings, 1990.

Adelman, Clifford. "Turn Diplomas into Report Card." *New York Times*, June 19, 1993, 21.

"Administration to Change School Aid Plan." *Wall Street Journal*, January 31, 1960, 26.

"Aid to Education." *Congressional Quarterly Weekly Report*, March 24, 1961, 486.

"Aid to Higher Education." *Hearings before a Subcommittee of the Committee on Education and Labor, House of Representatives, 87th Congress.* Washington:GPO, 1961.

Annual Report of the U.S. Dept. of Health, Education, and Welfare. Washington: GPO, 1962.

Arnold, R. Douglas. *The Logic of Congressional Action.* New Haven: Yale, 1990.

"B&O May Request Authority to Abandon All Passenger Service." *Wall Street Journal*, March 16, 1962, 22.

Bailey, Stephen Kemp. *Congress Makes a Law.* New York: Columbia, 1950.

Baker, John W., ed. *Member of the House: Letters of a Congressman, by Clem Miller.* New York: Scribners, 1962.

Baker, Russell. "Nixon and Kennedy Clash in TV Debate on Spending, Farms, and Social Issues." *New York Times*, September 27, 1960, 1, 28–29.

"Baker Seeks to Avoid Link on Jobs, Russian Aid." *Wall Street Journal*, May 1, 1992, A2.

Barone, Michael, and Grant Ujifusa. *The Almanac of American Politics, 1994.* Washington: National Journal, 1993.

"Battle Ahead on Foreign Aid." *New York Times*, August 2, 1962, 24.

Bauer, Raymond A., Ithiel De Sola Pool, and Lewis Anthony Dexter. *American Business and Public Policy.* 2d ed. Chicago: Aldine Atherton, 1972.

Belair, Jr., Felix. "Aid Measure Sent to Senate Floor." *New York Times*, July 25, 1961, 1, 4.

———. "Foreign Aid Plan Is Near 5 Billion." *New York Times*, January 19, 1962,19.

———. "4.6 Billion Aid Bill Voted by House Unit." *New York Times*, May 25, 1962, 1, 5.

———. "4.6 Billion Voted bv Senate Panel for Foreign Aid." *New York Times*, May 23, 1962, 1, 16.

———. "House Unit Backs Aid Bill, 19 to 10." *New York Times*, July 28, 1961, 1, 3.

———. "Kennedy Chides Critics Who Seek Foreign Aid Cuts." *New York Times*, March 15, 1962, 1, 18.

———. "President Urges 4.1 Billion in Aid; Cites Red Threat." *New York Times*, February 19, 1960, A1 and A11.

———. "President Urges U.S. Aid to East European Nations." *New York Times*, January 31, 1961, 1, 17.

———. "President Warns against Aid Slash," *New York Times*, August 30, 1962, 1, 10.

———. "Rusk and Dillon Send Plea on Aid to Both Houses." *New York Times*, July 20, 1961, 1, 4.

———. "Senate Restores Most of Aid Cuts; Passes Bill 62–17." *New York Times*, September 16, 1961, 1, 8.

Bradburne, Norman M., and Seymour Sudman. *Improving Interview Method and Questionnaire Design.* San Francisco: Jossey-Bass, 1981.

Brademas, John. *The Politics of Education.* Norman: Oklahoma University, 1987.

Braestrup, Peter. "Housing Bill Sent to the President." *New York Times*, June 29, 1961, 19.

———. "Urban Transit Law Giving 500 Million in Aid Is Predicted." *New York Times*, April 20, 1962, 1, 11.

Broder, David S. "Panetta: President In Trouble on the Hill. *Washington Post*, April 27, 1993, A1, A6.

Browne, William P. and Won K. Paik. "Beyond the Domains: Recasting Network Politics in the Postreform Congress." *American Journal of Political Science* 37 (November 1993): 1054.

"Budget Message Text." *New York Times*, January 19, 1960, 22.

Cameron, Charles. "Measuring the Institutional Performance of Congress in the Post-War Era." Unpublished APSA manuscript. May 10, 1996.

Chamberlin, William Henry. "Incipient Welfarers." *Wall Street Journal*, May 26, 960, 16.

"Choosing a School for Chelsea." *New York Times*, January 7, 1993, A22.

Clapp, Charles L. *The Congressman: His Work as He Sees It.* Washington: Brookings, 1963.

"Clinton Expected to Trim Bailout Request." *Wall Street Journal*, April 21, 1993, A16.

"Clinton's Education Plan Clears Hurdle in Senate." *Wall Street Journal*, May 20, 1993, A18.

Clymer, Adam. "Clinton Bill on Educational Standards Advances." *New York Times*, June 24, 1993, A19.

———. "House Approves Foreign Aid at Lowest Level Since 1977." *New York Times*, June 26, 1992, A2.

Cohen, Richard E. *Washington at Work.* New York: McMillan, 1992.

"College Aid." *Congressional Quarterly Weekly Report*, August 16, 1963, 1436–37.

"College Aid." *The 1963 Congressional Quarterly Almanac*, 1964, 194–201

"College Aid Recommitted." *Congressional Quarterly Weekly Report*, September 21, 1962, 1574.

"College and VA Housing." *Congressional Quarterly Weekly Report*, January 15, 1960, 71.

"College Construction." *Congressional Quarterly Weekly Report*, January 26, 1962, 110.

"College Construction Aid." *Congressional Quarterly Weekly Report*, March 25, 1960, 499.

Collier, David. "The Comparative Method: Two Decades of Change." Ch. 2 in D. A. Rustow and K.P. Erickson, eds. *Comparative Political Dynamics: Global Research Perspectives.* New York: HarperCollins, 1991.

"Committee Roundup: Mutual Security." *Congressional Quarterly Weekly Report*, May 27, 1960, 943.

"Commuter Plan Revised in House." *New York Times*, June 20, 1962, 14.

"Congress Clears $375 Million Mass Transportation Bill." *Congressional Quarterly Weekly Report*, July 3, 1964, 1338–41.

"Congress' Clock Winds Down on Stopgap Funding." *Congressional Quarterly Weekly Review*, March 28, 1992, 814.

Congress, House, Representative Otto Passman, speaking on the Foreign Operations

Appropriation for Fiscal 1963. *Congressional Record*, v. 108, 19743.

"Congress Pushing Transit-Aid Plan." *New York Times*, March 20, 1961, 24.

Congressional Directory, 87th Congress, 1st Session. Washington: GPO, 1961.

Congressional Directory, 87th Congress, 2d Session. Washington: GPO, 1962.

Congressional Directory, 88th Congress, 1st Session. Washington: GPO, 1963.

Congressional Directory, 88th Congress, 2d Session. Washington: GPO, 1964.

Congressional Directory, 103rd Congress, 1993–1994. Washington: GPO, 1993.

The Congressional Record. The United States Congress, Volumes 108–110 and 139–140. Washington: GPO, 1962–64 and 1993–94.

Cox, Gary W., and Mathew D. McCubbins. *Legislative Leviathan: Party Government in the House.* Berkely: University of California, 1993.

Cranford, John R. "House Panel Heeds RTC Head, Adds $25 Billion to Bailout." *Congressional Quarterly Weekly Report*, February 29, 1992, 461.

———. "More Funds Being Routed toward RTC Pipeline." *Congressional Quarterly Weekly Report*, March 14, 1992, 609–10.

Currivan, Gene. "National Agency on Schools Urged." *New York Times*, July 7, 1960, 1.

Davidson, Roger H. "The New Centralization on Capitol Hill." *Review of Politics* 50 (Summer 1988): 345–63.

———, ed. *The Postreform Congress.* New York: St. Martin's, 1992.

"The Democratic Platform, Giving Highlights of Democrats' Declaration of Policy." *New York Times*, July 13, 1960, 13–14.

Devroy, Ann. "Clinton Said to Be Considering Boost in Level of Aid to Russia." *Washington Post*, March 30, 1993, A17.

Dewhirst, Robert E. *Rites of Passage: Congress Makes Laws.* Upper Saddle River, New Jersey: Prentice Hall, 1997.

DeWitt, Karen. "Riley Led Charge to Improve His State's Schools." *New York Times*, December 22, 1992, B9.

———. "U.S. Students Advance in Math." *New York Times*, January 13, 1993, B6.

Doherty, Carroll J. "Economic Aid for Ex-Soviets Takes Big Step Forward." *Congressional Quarterly Weekly Report*, May 29, 1993, 1370–71.

Duke, Paul. "Chances for Kennedy's College Aid Bill Fade Further over New Religious Issue." *Wall Street Journal*, June 19, 1962, 8.

———. "Nixon Apparently Gets President to Accept Democrat's School Aid Bill, If It's Modified." *Wall Street Journal*, May 26, 1960, 30.

Ehrenhalt, Alan. *The United States of Ambition*. New York: Times, 1992.

Fenno, Jr., Richard F. *Congressmen in Committees*. Boston: Little, Brown, 1973.

———. *Homestyle: House Members in Their Districts*. New York: Harper-Collins, 1978.

———. *The Power of the Purse*. Boston: Little, Brown, 1966.

Final Report of the Commission on Administrative Review, U.S. House of Representatives. Washington: GPO, 1977.

Finn, Chester E. "Fear of Standards Threatens Education Reform." *Wall Street Journal*, March 23, 1992, A10.

Fiorina, Morris. *Congress: Keystone of the Washington Establishment*. 2d ed. New Haven: Yale, 1989.

"Floor Action." *Congressional Quarterly Weekly Report* (September 29, 1961), 1653–54.

"Foreign Aid Funds." *Congressional Quarterly Weekly Report* (September 29, 1961): 1653–55.

"Foreign Aid Funds." *The 1962 Congressional Quarterly Almanac*. Washington: Congressional Quarterly, 1963, 314–322.

"Foreign Aid Is Backed; Guarantees for Israel." *New York Times*, October 7, 1992, A13.

"Foreign Operations Appropriations for 1963." *Hearings before a Subcommittee of the Committee on Appropriations, House, 87th Congress, Parts I/II*. Washington: GPO, 1962.

"Foreign Operations, Export Financing, and Related Programs Appropriations for 1994." *Hearings before a Subcommittee of the Appropriations Committee, House, 103rd Congress, Parts I-IV*. Washington: GPO, 1993.

Frankfort-Nachmias, Chava, and David Nachmias. *Research Methods in the Social Sciences*, 5th ed. New York: St. Martin's, 1996.

"Funding Needs of the Resolution Trust Corporation and the Savings Association Insurance Fund." *Hearing before the Subcommittee on Financial Institutions Supervision, Regulation, and Deposit Insurance of the Committee on Banking, Finance, and Urban Affairs, House of Representatives, 103rd Congress*. Washington: GPO, 1993.

Gladieux, Lawrence E., and Thomas R. Wolanin. *Congress and the Colleges*. Lexington, Mass.: Lexington, 1976.

Gottsfredson, Linda. "Clinton's New Form of Race-Norming." *Wall Street Journal*, June 3, 1993, 17.

Greenberger, Robert S. "Hard Line on Israeli Loan Guarantees Reflects Public's Election-Year Mood." *Wall Street Journal*, March 11, 1992, A16.

Gross, Bertram M. *The Legislative Struggle.* New York: McGraw-Hill, 1953.

Hall, Richard L. *Participation in Congress.* New Haven: Yale, 1996.

Hall, Richard L., and Frank W. Wayman. "Buying Time: Moneyed Interests and the Mobilization of Bias in Congressional Committees." *American Political Science Review* 84 (September 1990): 797–819.

"Hard-to-Sell Assets Plan of the Resolution Trust Corporation." *Hearing before the General Oversight, Investigations, and the Resolution of Failed Financial Institutions of the Committee on Banking, Finance, and Urban Affairs, House of Representatives, 103rd Congress.* Washington: GPO, 1993.

Harwood, John. "Bush to Propose Aid for Former Soviet Union." *The Wall Street Journal,* March 30, 1992, A3.

"Hearings on HR1804-Goals 2000: Educate America Act." *Hearings before the Subcommittee on Elementary, Secondary, and Vocational Education of the Committee on Education and Labor, House of Representatives, 103rd Congress.* Washington: GPO, 1993.

Hechinger, Fred M. "School Bill's Defeat." *New York Times,* September 4, 1960, IV, 10.

Heclo, Hugh. "The Emerging Regime." Ch. 11 in Richard A. Harris and Sidney M. Milkis, eds. *Remaking American Politics.* Boulder: Westview, 1989.

———. "Issue Networks and the Executive Establishment." Ch. 3 in Anthony King, ed. *The New American Political System.* Washington: American Enterprise Institute, 1978.

Hibbing, John R. *Choosing to Leave.* Washington: University Press of America, 1982.

———. "Contours of the Modern Congressional Career." *American Political Science Review* 85 (June 1991): 405–28.

"Hill Votes More Funds for Thrift Bailout." *The 1993 Congressional Quarterly Almanac,* 1994, 150–57.

Hird, John A. "The Political Economy of Pork: Project Selection in the U.S. Army Corps of Engineers." *American Political Science Review* 85 (June 1991): 429–56.

Hitt, Greg. "Senate Votes to Extend Resolution Trust Another $25 Billion for Thrift Bailout." *Wall Street Journal,* March 27, 1992, A4.

"House Adopts College Aid Conference Report, 258–92." *Congressional Quarterly Weekly Report,* November 8, 1963, 1897–98.

"House Advances Education Reform Bill." *The 1993 Congressional Quarterly Almanac,* 1994, 404–07.

"House Approves Five-Year College Building Program." *Congressional Quarterly Weekly Report,* February 2, 1962, 136–37.

"House Backers of Parochial School Loans, Foes of All Education Aid Stall Kennedy Bill." *Wall Street Journal,* June 12, 1961, 3.

"House Democratic Chiefs Doubt School Aid Bill Can Be Passed in 1962." *Wall Street Journal,* September 1, 1961, 16.

"House of Illusion." *Wall Street Journal,* February 17, 1960, 12.

"House Panel Approves Kennedy's $500 Million Mass Transit Proposal." *Wall Street Journal,* March 29, 1963, 15.

"House Panel Votes $750 Million Reduction in Foreign Aid from Maximum Authorized." *Wall Street Journal*, September 1, 1961, 5.

"House Rules Unit Rejects School Aid Compromise." *Wall Street Journal*, June 23, 1960, 26.

"House Unit Advances School-Aid Measure; Senate Is Likely to Pass Similar Bill Today." *Wall Street Journal*, May 24, 1961, 5.

"House Unit Votes Additional $200 Million for President's Aid-to-Education Program." *Wall Street Journal*, May 9, 1961, 2.

"House Unit Votes $500 Million Aid to Mass Transit." *Wall Street Journal*, May 21, 1964, 8.

"House Votes $18.3 Billion to Fund Resolution Trust." *Wall Street Journal*, September 15, 1993, A8.

"House Votes $3.6 Billion New Foreign Aid Canceling $300 Million of Committee's Cuts." *Wall Street Journal*, September 6, 1961, 4.

"Housing Task Force." *Congressional Quarterly Weekly Report*, January 20, 1961, 73.

Hrebenar, Ronald J., and Ruth K. Scott. *Interest Group Politics in America*. 2d ed. Englewood Cliffs, N.J.: Prentice Hall, 1990.

Hunt, Richard P. "Kennedy Transport Plan." *New York Times*, April 6, 1962, 1, 19.

Hunter, Marjorie. "Kennedy Renews School-Aid Plea." *New York Times*, February 7, 1962, 1, 20.

——. "President Asks Broad Program to Aid Education." *New York Times*, January 30, 1963, 1, 4.

——. "School Aid Plan Split into 4 Bills." *New York Times*, May 23, 1963, 1, 34.

Interviewer's Manual. Revised ed. Ann Arbor: Survey Research Center, University of Michigan, 1976.

Irwin, Lewis G. "Dancing the Foreign Aid Appropriations Dance." *Public Budgeting & Finance* 20 (Summer 2000), 30–48.

"Issues Facing Congress." *Congressional Quarterly Weekly Report*, January 4, 1963, 6.

Jacobson, Gary C. "Deficit-Cutting Politics and Congressional Elections." *Political Science Quarterly* 108 (1993): 375–402.

"Johnson Presses for Transit Help." *New York Times*, January 9, 1964, 18.

Jordan, Mary. "Riley Assails Lack of Progress on Improving U.S. Schools." *Washington Post*, October 1, 1993, A2.

——. "Top Educators Look Back." *Washington Post*, January 12, 1993, A15.

Karr, Albert R. "Conferees Clear Compromise Bill for RTC Funds," *Wall Street Journal*, November 19, 1993, A2.

Katz, Jeffrey L. "School Prayer, Choice Part of Senate 'Goals' Debate." *Congressional Quarterly Weekly Report*, February 5, 1994, 248.

"Kennedy Asks More Foreign Aid Money." *Wall Street Journal*, March 14, 1962, 2.

"Kennedy Legislative Boxscore for 1963." *The 1962 Congressional Quarterly Almanac*, 1963, 102.

"Kennedy Maps Tariff-Cut Bills." *New York Times*, January 13, 1962, 1, 3.

"Kennedy Offers $5.6 Billion, 5-Year Plan for Federal Aid to Education." *Wall Street Journal*, February 21, 1961, 28.

"Kennedy Radically Alters School Aid Plan." *Wall Street Journal*, August 18, 1961, 3.

"Kennedy's Foreign Aid Request Is Slashed Almost $1.5 Billion by House Subcommittee." *Wall Street Journal*, September 18, 1962, 7.

"Kennedy Submits Token Plan to Aid Transit." *Wall Street Journal*, June 20, 1961, 4.

"Kennedy Ties Federal School Aid Bill to Cut in Help for Areas of Big U.S. Installations." *Wall Street Journal*, February 28, 1961, 4.

Kernell, Samuel. *Going Public: New Strategies of Presidential Leadership*. 2d ed. Washington: Congressional Quarterly, 1993.

King, Anthony. *Running Scared*. New York: Free Press, 1997.

King, Gary, Robert O. Keohane, and Sidney Verba. *Designing Social Inquiry*. Princeton, N.J.: Princeton, 1994.

Kingdon, John W. *Agendas, Alternatives, and Public Policies*. 2d ed. New York: Harper, 1995.

———. *Congressmen's Voting Decisions*. 2d ed. New York: Harper, 1981.

Knight, Jerry. "House Approves Funds to Finish Thrift Cleanup." *Washington Post*, November 23, 1993, E1.

———. "House Panel Finds Dollars in a Deadline." *Washington Post*, April 30, 1993, F2.

Knowles, Clayton. "Good Chance Seen for Transit Bill." *New York Times*, June 9, 41.

Kohlmeier, Louis M. "Kennedy's Transit Policy Message Could Goad Revision of Key Laws." *Wall Street Journal*, March 16, 1962, 22.

Legislative Calendar, U.S. House of Representatives' Committee on Banking and Currency. Washington: GPO, 1964, 88th Congress.

Legislative Calendar, U.S. House of Representatives' Committee on Banking, Finance, and Urban Affairs. Washington: GPO, 1994, 103rd Congress.

Legislative Calendar, U.S. House of Representatives' Committee on Education and Labor. Washington: GPO, 1964 and 1994, 88th and 103rd Congresses.

Lewis, Anthony. "Plank-by-Plank Comparison of the Platforms of Democratic and Republican Parties." *New York Times*, July 28, 1960, 15.

Lieberson, Stanley. "Small N's and Big Conclusions." *Social Forces* 70 (December 1991): 307–20.

Loomis, Burdett. *The New American Politician*. New York: Basic, 1988.

MacNeil, Neil. *Forge of Democracy: The House of Representatives*. New York: McCay, 1963.

Manheim, Jarol B., and Richard C. Rich. *Empirical Political Analysis*. 4th ed. Washington: Longman, 1990.

"Mass Transit Aid." *Congressional Quarterly Weekly Report*, April 12, 1963, 557–68.

"Mass Transit Bill Cleared by House, 212–189 Vote." *Wall Street Journal*, June 26, 1964, 3.

"Mass Transit Bill, Losing Favor in Senate." *Wall Street Journal*, March 27, 1963, 3.

"Mass Transportation." *Congressional Quarterly Weekly Report*, July 1, 1960, 1126.

"Mass Transportation." *Congressional Quarterly Weekly Report*, March 31, 1961, 530.

Matthews, Donald R. *U.S. Senators and Their World*. 2d ed. New York: W. W. Norton, 1973.

Mayhew, David R. *Divided We Govern*. New Haven: Yale, 1991.

———. *The Electoral Connection*. New Haven: Yale, 1974.

"Message on Aid." *Congressional Quarterly Weekly Report*, September 9, 1960, 1560–61.

Milkis, Sidney, and Richard A. Harris, eds. *Remaking American Politics*. Boulder: Westview, 1989.

Moe, Terry M. "Interests, Institutions, and Positive Theory: The Politics of the NLRB." *Studies in American Political Development* 2 (1987): 236–99.

Mooney, Richard. "Housing Bill Sent to Senate Floor." *New York Times*, June 15, 1960, 7.

———. "Mayors Ask Congress to Vote 100 Million in Commuter Aid." *New York Times*, May 24, 1960, 1, 59.

———. "Overhaul Asked in U.S. Transport." *New York Times*, March 15, 1960, 1, 77.

Morris, John D. "House Vote Kills School Aid Plan." *New York Times*, August 31, 1961, 1, 17.

———. "Kennedy Will Press School Aid and Wage Bills, Powell Reports." *New York Times*, December 1, 1960, 23.

———. "Senate Approves School-Aid Bill." *New York Times*, May 26, 1961, 1, 16.

———. "2 Key Democrats Stall School Aid." *New York Times*, June 16, 1961, 17.

"Mutual Security Funds." *Congressional Quarterly Weekly Report*, September 2, 1960, 1512.

"The Myth That Won't Die." *Wall Street Journal*, August 4, 1960, 8.

"National Education Goals Set." *The 1994 Congressional Quarterly Almanac*, 1995, 397–99.

"New Bills Appear among Hardy Perennials." *Congressional Quarterly Weekly Report*, January 18, 1963, 44.

New York Times Index. New York: The New York Times Publishing Company, 1960–94.

Novak, Robert D. "White House Seeks to Unite 3 Education Aid Bills in One; Some Democrats Oppose Plan." *Wall Street Journal*, April 28, 1961, 2.

"Omnibus Housing Bills." *Congressional Quarterly Weekly Report*, June 10, 1960, 1025.

"Omnibus School Aid." *Congressional Quarterly Weekly Report*, February 15, 1963, 199–200.

Orfield, Gary. *Congressional Power*. New York: Harcourt Brace, 1975.

Ornstein, Norman J., Thomas E. Mann, and Michael J. Malbin, *Vital Statistics on Congress, 1995–1996*, Washington: Congressional Quarterly, 1996.

Patterson, Samuel C., and Gregory A. Caldeira. "Standing Up for Congress: Variations in Public Esteem since the 1960s." *Legislative Studies Quarterly* 15 (February 1990): 25–47.

Peabody, Robert L., and Nelson W. Polsby, eds. *New Perspectives on the House of Representatives*, 4th ed. Baltimore: Johns Hopkins, 1992.

Peterson, Mark A. *Legislating Together: The White House and Capitol Hill from Eisenhower to Reagan.* Cambridge: Harvard, 1990.

Peterson, Paul E., and Jay P. Greene. "Why Executive-Legislative Conflict in the United States Is Dwindling." *British Journal of Political Science* 24 (1993): 33–55.

Phillips, Cabell. "School-Aid Fight Arouses Lobbies." *New York Times*, April 17, 1961, 1.

Pianin, Eric, and Ruth Marcus. "White House, Hill Democrats Consider Linking Jobs Bill to Russian Aid." *Washington Post*, April 30, 1993, A11.

Polsby, Nelson W., Miriam Gallagher, and Barry Spencer Rundquist. "The Growth of the Seniority System in the U.S. House of Representatives." *American Political Science Review* 63 (1969): 787–807.

Porter, Russell. "President Signs 9 Billion in Bills." *New York Times*, October 1, 1961, A1.

"Powell Chairmanship." *Congressional Quarterly Weekly Report*, January 29, 1960, 169.

"President Asks Congress to Rescue His Education Bill with Parliamentary Devices." *Wall Street Journal*, July 20, 1961, 2.

"President Asks $5 Billion Omnibus Education Program." *Congressional Quarterly Weekly Report*, February 1, 1963, 110–12.

"President Signs Foreign Aid Bill." *New York Times*, May 17, 1960, A1.

"President Signs Foreign Aid Bill." *New York Times*, September 3, 1960, 1.

"President Voices Peace and Optimism." *New York Times*, January 8, 1960, 1, 11.

"President's Transportation Program Heads for Clashes." *Congressional Quarterly Weekly Report*, February 14, 1963, 184.

"Presidential Report." *Congressional Quarterly Weekly Report*, June 23, 1961, 1047.

"The Presidential Report." *Congressional Quarterly Weekly Report*. July 21, 1961, 1294.

Price, David E. *The Congressional Experience.* Boulder: Westview: 1992.

Pullen, Dale. *The U.S. Congress Handbook, 1997.* McLean, Virginia: Pullen, 1997.

Ravitch, Diane. "Clinton's Math: More Gets Less." *New York Times*, May 26, 1993, A21.

Report No. 103–103, Parts I/II. 103rd Congress, House of Representatives. Washington: GPO, 1993.

Report No. 103–125. 103rd Congress, House of Representatives. Washington: GPO, 1993.

Report No. 103–168. 103rd Congress, House of Representatives. Washington: GPO, 1993.

Report No. 103–267. 103rd Congress, House of Representatives. Washington: GPO, 1993.

Report No. 103–380. 103rd Congress, House of Representatives. Washington: GPO, 1993.

Report No. 103–446. 103rd Congress, House of Representatives. Washington: GPO, 1994.

Report No. 204. 88th Congress, House of Representatives. Washington: GPO, 1963.

Report No. 310. 88th Congress, House of Representatives. Washington: GPO, 1963.

Report No. 884. 88th Congress, House of Representatives. Washington: GPO, 1963.

Report No. 2410. 87th Congress, House of Representatives. Washington: GPO, 1962.

Report No. 2540. 87th Congress, House of Representatives. Washington: GPO, 1962.

"Resolution Trust Corporation's Affordable Housing Program." *Hearing before the Subcommittee on Housing and Community Development of the Committee on Banking, Finance, and Urban Affairs, House, 103rd Congress.* Washington: GPO, 1993.

"Ribicoff's Woes." *Wall Street Journal,* September 5, 1961, 14.

Rieselbach, Leroy N. *Congressional Reform: The Changing Modern Congress.* Washington: Congressional Quarterly, 1994.

Robbins, Carla Ann, and Jacob M. Schlesinger. "G-7 Nations Unveil $28.4 Billion Plan to Aid Ex-Soviet Union, Back Yeltsin." *Wall Street Journal,* April 16, 1993, A3.

Robinson, Judith Schiek. *Tapping the Government Grapevine.* New York: Oryx, 1993.

Rogers, David. "House Approves Aid for Russia, Ex-Soviet States." *Wall Street Journal,* June 18, 1993, A14.

Rohde, David W. "Parties and Committees in the House: Member Motivations, Issues, and Institutional Arrangements." *Legislative Studies Quarterly* 19 (August 1994), 341–59.

———. Parties and Leaders in the Postreform House. Chicago: University of Chicago, 1991.

"RTC Expects to Fall Short of Goal for Asset Sales." *Wall Street Journal,* April 16, 1992.

"RTC Gets Ready for Toughest Sell." *Wall Street Journal,* April 1, 1993, A4.

Schattschneider, E. E. *The Semisovereign People.* New York: Holt, Rinehart, and Winston, 1960.

Schmidt, Susan. "Bush Renews Push for $42 Billion to Maintain Funding of S&L Cleanup." *Washington Post,* July 30, 1992, D14.

———. "House Votes against S&L Funding Bill." *Washington Post,* April 2, 1992, A1.

Schneier, Edward V., and Bertram Gross. *Congress Today.* New York: St. Martin's, 1993.

———. *Legislative Strategy: Shaping Public Policy.* New York: St. Martin's, 1993.

"School Aid Bill Badly Received." *New York Times,* February 5, 1963, 8.

Seib, Gerald F. "Foreign-Aid Bill for Former U.S.S.R. Encounters Election-Year Opposition." *Wall Street Journal,* April 30, 1992, A14.

———. "U.S. Foreign Aid, Unpopular at Home, Is Slow to Adjust to a Changing World." *Wall Street Journal*, January 6, 1992, A11.

Seib, Gerald F., and John Harwood. "Bush, Allies Pledge $24 Billion to Russia." *Wall Street Journal*, April 2, 1992, 2.

"Semiannual Appearance of the Thrift Depositor Protection Oversight Board." *Hearing before the Committee on Banking, Finance, and Urban Affairs, House of Representatives, 103rd Congress*. Washington: GPO, 1993.

"Senate Approves Scholarships, Passes College Aid Bill." *Congressional Quarterly Weekly Report*, February 9, 1962, 198.

"Senate Democrats Act to Reverse Defeats on India Aid." *Wall Street Journal*, May 14, 1962, 6.

"Senate Panel Approves Funding for S&L Bailout." *Wall Street Journal*, March 26, 1993, A2.

"Senate Passes College Aid Bill, 60–19." *Congressional Quarterly Weekly Report*, October 25, 1963, 1842–43.

"Senate Sends College Aid Bill to President Johnson." *Congressional Quarterly Weekly Report*, December 13, 1963, 2149.

"Senate Study Backs Vast Transportation Overhaul, Single Agency to Control Field." *Wall Street Journal*, January 5, 1961, 28.

"Senate Unit Votes School Aid above Kennedy Request." *Wall Street Journal*, May 12, 1961, 2.

"Senate Votes Modified Mass-Transit Bill after Supporters Calm Labor's Fears." *Wall Street Journal*, April 5, 1963, 2.

Sharp, Rochelle. "Clinton Package for Schools Has Chance to Pass." *Wall Street Journal*, April 16, 1993, B1, B6.

Sinclair, Barbara. "The Emergence of Strong Leadership in the 1980's House of Representatives." *Journal of Politics* 54 (August 1992): 657–84.

———. *The Transformation of the U.S. Senate*. Baltimore: Johns Hopkins, 1989.

———. *Unorthodox Lawmaking*. Washington: Congressional Quarterly, 1997.

Skowronek, Stephen. *The Politics Presidents Make*. Cambridge: Belknap, 1993.

Smith, Steven S. *Call to Order*. Washington: Brookings, 1989.

Smock, Raymond W. *A Guide to the Research Collections of Former Members of the United States House of Representatives 1789–1987*. Washington: GPO, 1988.

Spivak, Jonathan. "Kennedy's New Education Aid Plan Drops across-the-Board Approach." *Wall Street Journal*, January 28, 1963, 30.

"Status Report of the Resolution Trust Corporation." *Hearing before the Subcommittee on General Oversight Investigations and the Resolution of the Failed Financial Institutions, Committee on Banking, Finance, and Urban Affairs, 103rd Congress*. Washington: GPO, 1993.

"Stopgap Bill Becomes Law after Deadline Threat." *Congressional Quarterly Weekly Report*, April 4, 1992, 890–92.

"Stopgap Spending Bill on Horizon." *Congressional Quarterly Weekly Review*, March 21, 1992, 734.

Stout, Hilary. "Bipartisan Panel on Education Urges National Standards, Voluntary Exams." *Wall Street Journal*, January 27, 1992, B4.

Stout, Hilary, and Alan Murray. "Real Differences on Education between Clinton and Bush Come Down to Commitment, Money." *Wall Street Journal*, August 6, 1992, A14.

Strahan, Randall. *New Ways and Means*. Chapel Hill: University of North Carolina, 1990.

"Strictly on Merit." *Wall Street Journal*, April 8, 1963, 16.

Sullivan, Joseph W. "Johnson Captains Will Press to Clear Bills on Rights, Transit, Federal Pay This Week." *Wall Street Journal*, June 29, 1964, 3.

Sundquist, James L. *The Decline and Resurgence of Congress*. Washington: Brookings, 1981.

———. *Politics and Policy: The Eisenhower, Kennedy, and Johnson Years*. Washington: Brookings, 1968.

Taylor, Andrew. "Bailout Heads to Conference after Squeaker in House." *Congressional Quarterly Weekly Report*, September 18, 1993, 2440.

———. "Bentsen Requests $45 Billion to Finish Thrift Bailout." *Congressional Quarterly Weekly Report*, March 20, 1993, 659–60.

———. "Deal Struck on Thrift Bailout," *Congressional Quarterly Weekly Report*, September 11, 1993, 2378.

———. "Democrats Vow to Return to RTC in September." *Congressional Quarterly Weekly Report*, August 7, 1993, 2147.

———. "Freshmen Shift the Balance on House Banking Panel." *Congressional Quarterly Weekly Report*, January 30, 1993, 209–12.

———. "House Panel Chops $12 Billion from Bailout Request." *Congressional Quarterly Weekly Report*, May 1, 1993, 1070–71.

———. "Judiciary, Banking at Odds over Thrift Bailout Bill." *Congressional Quarterly Weekly Report*, June 12, 1993, 1468.

———. "Minority Contract Provision Stalls Bailout Measure." *Congressional Quarterly Weekly Report*, November 13, 1993, 3110.

———. "Reduced Bailout Bill Headed for First Round in House." *Congressional Quarterly Weekly Report*, April 24, 1993, 1010.

"Text of President Johnson's Economic Report on the Nation." *New York Times*, January 21, 1964, 16–18.

"Text of Republican Planks on Civil Rights, Defense, and Education." *New York Times*, July 27, 1960, 18.

"Texts of the Planks Approved by the Republican Convention." *New York Times*, July 25, 1960, 14–15.

Thomas, Paulette. "Additional Spending for Thrift Bailout is Unexpectedly Rejected in the House." *Wall Street Journal*, April 2, 1992, A16.

"$375 Million Authorized for Urban Transit Grants." *The 1964 Congressional Quarterly Almanac*, 1965, 556–60.

Tiefer, Charles. *Congressional Practice and Procedure*. New York: Greenwood, 1989.

"To Amend and Extend the National Defense Education Act." *Hearings before a Subcommittee of the Committee on Education and Labor, House, 88th Congress*. Washington: GPO, 1964.

"Top Treasury Official Will Serve as Chief of RTC Temporarily." *Wall Street Journal*, March 16, 1993, B10.

"Traffic Jam Costs Placed at 5 Billion." *New York Times*, July 4, 1962, 22.

"Transcript of the President's Address." *New York Times*, January 12, 1962, 12.

"Transit Aid Sought by Jersey Senator." *New York Times*, January 12, 1961.

"Transit Proposals Provoke Bitter Rail-Highway Battle." *Congressional Quarterly Weekly Report*, October 4, 1963, 1727–37.

Truman, David B., ed. *The Congress and America's Future*. Englewood Cliffs: Prentice-Hall, 1965.

Trussel, C.P. "U.S. Transit Bill Asks $500,000,000." *New York Times*, January 10, 1963, 9.

"22 Bills Held Up in House Rules Committee." *Congressional Quarterly Weekly Report*, September 14, 1962, 1528.

"$2.5 Billion Approved for Ex-Soviet States." *The 1993 Congressional Quarterly Almanac*, 1994, 603–17.

United States Statutes at Large. Washington: GPO, 1962–64, and Washington: CIS, 1993–94.

"Urban Aid Wins Senate Test." *New York Times*, June 14, 1962, 35.

"Urban Mass Transit." *Congressional Quarterly Weekly Report*, February 22, 1963, 228.

"Urban Mass Transportation Act of 1963." *Hearings before the Committee on Banking and Currency, House of Representatives, 88th Congress*. Washington: GPO, 1963.

Uslaner, Eric M. *The Decline of Comity in Congress*. Ann Arbor: University of Michigan, 1997.

Vernaci, Richard L. "House Panel Approves 'Final' RTC Funding." *Washington Post*, May 7, 1993, F2.

"Veto Cloud Loomed Large over 1992 Floor Fights." *Congressional Quarterly Weekly Report*, December 19, 1992, 3854–55.

Vogler, David J. *The Third House: Conference Committees in the United States Congress*. Evanston, Ill.: Northwestern, 1971.

Walker, Jack L. "The Origins and Maintenance of Interest Groups in America." *American Political Science Review* 77 (1983): 390–406.

"The Wall Street Journal/NBC News Poll." *Wall Street Journal*, April 23, 1993, A1.

"Washington at Work." *Wall Street Journal*, May 25, 1961, 12.

"Washington at Work." *Wall Street Journal*, May 29, 1961, 9.

Wawro, Gregory. *Legislative Entrepreneurship in the U.S. House of Representatives*. Ann Arbor: University of Michigan, 2000.

Weaver, Jr., Warren. "House Is Reviving Transit Aid Bill." *New York Times*, March 22, 1964, 39.

———. "$375 Million Transit Bill Passed by House." *New York Times*, June 26, 1964, 1.

———. "Urban Transit Aid Is Widely Backed." *New York Times*, April 26, 1962, 35.

"Weaver Asks Expanded Transit and Better Suburban Planning." *New York Times*, January 10, 1964, 40.

Wessel, David, and Carla Anne Robbins. "Clinton Weighs $1 Billion More in Russian Aid," *Wall Street Journal*, March 29, 1993, A8.

White, William S. *Citadel: The Story of the U.S. Senate.* New York: Harper and Brothers, 1957.

Wicker, Tom. "Eisenhower Hits School-Aid Plan." *New York Times*, June 29, 1961,18.

——. "House Approves School-Aid Bill with Ban on Bias." *New York Times*, May
27, 1960, 1, 14.

Wilson, Woodrow. *Congressional Government: A Study in American Politics.* Originally published in 1885. Reprint, 2d ed., New York: Meridian, 1956.

"Youth Corps, Mass Transit." *Congressional Quarterly Weekly Report*, September 21, 1962, 1562.

Zuckman, Jill. "Clinton's School Reform Plan Has High Hopes, Low Funds." *Congressional Quarterly Weekly Report*, April 24, 1993, 1027–28.

——. "New Bill Kills Federal Money for Private School 'Choice.'" *Congressional Quarterly Weekly Report*, February 29, 1992, 471–72.

——. "The Next Education Crisis: Equalizing School Funds." *Congressional Quarterly Weekly Report*, March 27, 1993, 749–54.

——. "Panel Gives Listless Approval to Scorned Reform Bill." *Congressional Quarterly Weekly Report*, May 23, 1992, 1451.

——. "Reform Bill Moves Forward, But Partisanship Recurs." *Congressional Quarterly Weekly Report*, May 8, 1153.

——. "Riley Explains Reform Ideas," *Congressional Quarterly Weekly Report*, February 27, 1993, 466.

——. "School Improvement Bill Snagged by Standards." *Congressional Quarterly Weekly Report*, May 22, 1993, 1297.

——. "School Standards Approved along Party-Line Vote." *Congressional Quarterly Weekly Report*, June 26, 1993, 1663.

——. "Senate Rejects Demonstration of Bush's 'School Choice' Plan." *Congressional Quarterly Weekly Report*, January 25, 1992, 176.

INDEX